EDI DEVELOPMENT STUDIES

Privatization and Control of State-Owned Enterprises

Edited by
Ravi Ramamurti
Raymond Vernon

The World Bank
Washington, D.C.

The Economic Development Institute (EDI) was established by the World Bank in 1955 to train officials concerned with development planning, policymaking, investment analysis, and project implementation in member developing countries. At present the substance of the EDI's work emphasizes macroeconomic and sectoral economic policy analysis. Through a variety of courses, seminars, and workshops, most of which are given overseas in cooperation with local institutions, the EDI seeks to sharpen analytical skills used in policy analysis and to broaden understanding of the experience of individual countries with economic development. Although the EDI's publications are designed to support its training activities, many are of interest to a much broader audience. EDI materials, including any findings, interpretations, and conclusions, are entirely those of the authors and should not be attributed in any manner to the World Bank, to its affiliated organizations, or to members of its Board of Executive Directors or the countries they represent.

Library of Congress Cataloging-in-Publication Data

Privatization and control of state-owned enterprises / edited by Ravi Ramamurti,
    Raymond Vernon.
      p.   cm.—(EDI development studies)
    Includes bibliographical references and index.
    ISBN 0-8213-1863-2
    1. Privatization—Developing countries—Case studies.
  2. Government business enterprises—Developing countries—Case studies.
I. Ramamurti, Ravi. II. Vernon, Raymond, 1913–   .
III. Series.
HD4420.8.P75   1991
338.9'009172'4—dc20   91-21903
                                          CIP

EDI Catalog No. 345/015

CONTENTS

ABOUT THE CONTRIBUTORS

Yair Aharoni is J. Paul Sticht visiting professor of international business at the Fuqua School of Business, Duke University, Durham, N.C. His expertise is in international business and the strategic decisionmaking processes of large organizations, including state-owned enterprises. His books include *State-Owned Enterprise in the Western Economies* (edited with Raymond Vernon) and *The Management and Evolution of State-Owned Enterprises.*

Ivan Bergeron is the president of Econotec, a consulting company based in Montreal, Canada. His areas of expertise include development planning and economics, sectoral studies, investment analysis, and project management. During the past few years he has lived for extended periods of time in several African countries, working in management and technical assistance.

Leroy P. Jones is professor of economics and director of the Program in Economics and Management at Boston University. He is the author of several books and articles on the economics of public enterprise, including *Selling Public Enterprise: A Cost-Benefit Methodology* (with Pankaj Tandon and Ingo Vogelsang). He has also served as a consultant to the United Nations, the World Bank, and several developing countries.

Roger Leeds is executive director of the International Privatization Group, Washington, D.C. Before that, he was the principal corporate finance officer at the International Finance Corporation, where he was responsible for the design and implementation of privatization programs and transactions in various developing countries. As a senior research fellow at the John F. Kennedy School of Government at Harvard University, he taught and directed a research project on privatization.

Klaus Lorch is an economist in the Industry and Energy Operations Division, Asia Region, World Bank. Earlier, he worked in the private sector and studied the question of privatization as a research associate at the Harvard Institute for International Development, Cambridge, Mass.

John Nellis is the principal management specialist in the Public Sector Management and Private Sector Development Division of the World Bank, where he works on reform of state-owned enterprises, privatization, and institutional development. He has written some 30 articles and chapters on these topics and has served on the faculties of the Maxwell School at Syracuse University and Carleton University, Ottawa, Canada.

Ravi Ramamurti is Joseph G. Riesman research professor (1989-91) and associate professor of business administration at Northeastern University, Boston. He was a visiting professor in business, government, and competition at Harvard Business School during 1986-88. He has written extensively on state-owned enterprises and has served as a consultant on the subject to international agencies and the governments of developing countries.

Mary Shirley is chief of the Public Sector Management and Private Sector Development Division of the World Bank. Before that, she was the World Bank's public enterprise adviser. She is the author of several World Bank studies on state-owned enterprises,, including *The Reform of State-Owned Enterprises; Divestiture in Developing Countries* (with Elliot Berg); and *Managing State-Owned Enterprises*. She has held positions in the World Bank's Latin American and Caribbean Programs, the Organization of American States, the University of Bogotá, Colombia, and the Harvard Economic Research Center.

Pankaj Tandon is associate professor of economics and an associate in the Public Enterprise Program at Boston University. His primary research interests are in the fields of public enterprise and the economics of technological change. He has written numerous scholarly articles, and his first book (co-authored with Leroy Jones and Ingo Vogelsang) is on privatization of public enterprise.

Raymond Vernon is Clarence Dillon professor of international relations emeritus at the Center for Business and Government, Kennedy School of Government, Harvard University. He has written several articles on the state-owned enterprise and the multinational corporation and has been a consultant to numerous public and private organizations. His books include *Storm Over the Multinationals; State-Owned Enterprise in the Western Economies* (edited with Yair Aharoni); and *The Promise of Privatization* (editor).

Ingo Vogelsang is professor of economics and an associate in the Public Enterprise Program at Boston University. His research interests include industrial organization, public policy, and public enterprise. He has written numerous articles on these subjects, as well as several books, including *Selling Public Enterprise: A Cost-Benefit Methodology* (with Leroy Jones and Pankaj Tandon).

ABBREVIATIONS

BTMC	Bangladesh Textile Mills Corporation
CCC	Caribbean Cement Company (Jamaica)
CEO	chief executive officer
CP	contract plan
EAC	Experts Advisory Cell (Pakistan)
GDP	gross domestic product
GNP	gross national product
MIS	management information system
MIT	Massachusetts Institute of Technology
NCB	National Commercial Bank (Jamaica)
NIBJ	National Investment Bank of Jamaica
R&D	research and development
SNS	Société Nationale de Sidérurgie (Togo)
SOE	state-owned enterprise
STS	Société Togolaise de Sidérurgie (Togo)
UNIDO	United Nations Industrial Development Organization
USAID	United States Agency for International Development

INTRODUCTION

Ravi Ramamurti
Raymond Vernon

The chapters in this volume contain partial answers to a question that governments of developing countries addressed with renewed interest in the 1980s: what can be done to improve the performance of state-owned enterprises (SOEs) that play a prominent role in the economy and absorb substantial public resources? To be sure, the question is not new, but in the last decade governments came up with more creative answers than perhaps at any time before. By every indication, that creative search for remedies will accelerate in the 1990s.

The chapters that follow offer concepts and case studies involving two types of remedies that proved particularly important in developing countries in the 1980s. The first remedy assumed that the performance of state-owned enterprises could not be improved without the privatization of ownership, while the second sought ways to improve government oversight of state enterprises on the assumption that privatization was either infeasible or undesirable.

A central tenet of this volume is that these two remedies are complementary, not competing or mutually exclusive options. While a great deal has been written on both these approaches, few studies evaluate the results of the measures undertaken. In contrast, several chapters in this volume analyze the consequences of the reforms they describe. Another common feature is the fact that most of the studies were either sponsored by the World Bank or authored by members of its staff. Consequently, they tend to be pragmatic in their approach and address issues of concern to policymakers in developing countries.

The introductory chapter by *Ravi Ramamurti* surveys the experience of developing countries with both types of remedies. He finds that although

1

privatization gained considerable momentum in developing countries, nearly half the transactions up to December 1987 occurred in just eight such countries. He also finds that as governments begin to implement privatization they discover serious conflicts between their desire to privatize quickly, their desire to maximize proceeds from privatization, and their desire to promote efficiency through greater competition. The resulting compromises tend to reduce the gains from privatization. He also notes that the state often retains an important role as part owner or regulator of many "privatized" firms, especially those that are large or dominant in their respective markets. This fact adds importance to the other type of remedy considered in this volume, that is, methods for improving the quality of government oversight of SOEs. These methods were derived from either the "signaling system" or from the French "contract plan" system, although new varieties emerged as countries learned from their own experience and that of others. Ramamurti identifies five dimensions along which these variations differed. He concludes that although neither type of remedy achieved all its stated purposes, each shed new light on the strengths and weaknesses of the public and private sectors, and broadened the options available to policymakers.

Privatization

The first essay in this part, by *Leroy Jones, Pankaj Tandon,* and *Ingo Vogelsang,* presents a model that is intended to answer three key issues in the privatization process: which enterprises should be privatized, at what price should they be sold, and to whom should they be sold. The criterion for responding to all these questions is the net economic yield. The model is designed, therefore, to measure the difference between the net economic yield generated by the enterprise as a state-owned entity and the yield generated by that enterprise as a privatized entity. Two distinct elements are assumed to affect that difference: the transfer of funds from the private sector to the public sector in connection with the purchase of the enterprise, and the transfer of productive facilities from the public sector to the private sector. The model is unique in attempting to take into account the differences in economic yield that are associated with the degree of monopoly power of the private buyer.

The essay by *Raymond Vernon* considers whether the Jones-Tandon-Vogelsang model can be operational in real-life situations and concludes that the maximization criteria and data requirements of the model are likely to limit its application severely. The article explores the criteria for privatization that are implicit in the actions of developing countries, and concludes that such criteria cannot be stated in terms of the maximization of any single variable. Instead, he identifies several different objectives, non-additive in character, that usually must be taken into account if privatization is to occur. These include static and dynamic efficiency considerations, income distribution effects, and consequences for the public fisc. Finally, he suggests some rules of thumb that could guide policymakers in identifying enterprises that satisfy these criteria.

The essay by *Yair Aharoni* addresses the political aspects of privatization. He argues that the "success" of any privatization program can only be measured in terms of the objectives that motivated it, and that those objectives are likely to be different for different actors affected by privatization. Thus, for instance, efficiency gains, which economists commonly regard as the goal of privatization, are sometimes not of special interest to *any* of the real players. Aharoni reviews the diverse objectives that politicians, managers, civil servants, labor leaders, international donors, and other typically bring to privatization, and concludes that consensus among these actors is highly unlikely.

Roger Leeds describes two cases of privatization in Jamaica. "Success" in these cases is measured in terms of whether the government's plan of sale was completed. In these terms, one offering is judged a success, the other a disappointment. The article explores the reasons for the differences in outcome, and concludes that the pricing, timing, and shaping of a public offering are far more matters of subjective judgment than of skilled technical analysis.

The *Klaus Lorch* article addresses the experiences of the Bangladeshi textile industry in the mid-1980s at a time when private mills and state-owned mills were operating side by side. Their relative performance is studied in several dimensions, including static efficiency, dynamic efficiency, impact on income distribution, and impact on public finance. Lorch concludes that, although both sectors suffered from common weaknesses such as inadequate maintenance, the private mills outperformed the state-owned mills by a modest margin in static efficiency terms. One clear disadvantage of the private mills that tended to keep the margin modest was their inability to match the scale economies that the public mills achieved in the purchase of raw materials. In dynamic efficiency terms, neither sector performed well; both seemed mired in unchanging technologies. The income distribution effects of the private operations were distinctly less egalitarian than those of the public mills, and the finances of the public sector seemed not to benefit on balance from the private sector's operations as compared with those of public mills. All told, according to Lorch, neither the private nor the public mills were able to add very much to the country's developmental aims.

Ivan Bergeron analyzes a case in which the government of Togo leased a state-owned steel mill to a foreign-owned private enterprise, an arrangement often regarded as a form of privatization. Valued after the fact, the original form of the lease offered little promise of either static or dynamic efficiencies, and little promise of improving the government's cash position. The principal virtue of the arrangement appeared at the time to be postponing a decision as to how to dispose of a plant whose running costs were burdening the Togo government. The new arrangement, however, developed in unforeseen directions, greatly improving the chances that Togo might in the end gain from the deal.

Improving the Quality of Government Control

In the opening essay in part two, *Leroy Jones* argues that privatization is one way to marry the interests of owners and managers, but that performance evaluation is another. A good system for performance evaluation, he argues, should guide and motivate managers of state enterprises to act in the interests of society as a whole. The introduction of such a system is seen as a precondition for increasing managerial autonomy. Jones addresses systematically a number of conceptual and technical problems involved in designing such a system, including the choice of performance criteria, methods to adjust for noncommercial objectives, corrections for factors beyond the control of managers, and supplementary indicators to capture the longer-term impact of managerial actions. He also discusses how targets might be negotiated annually between government officials and managers.

In a similar vein, *Ravi Ramamurti* argues that the performance of SOEs is unlikely to improve unless countries find a way to improve the quality of government control and reduce the extent of government control over these enterprises. However, governments are likely to find it far more difficult to improve the quality of control than to reduce the extent of control over SOEs, largely because institutional factors create great asymmetry in information and expertise between SOEs and their bosses in government. Ramamurti then presents an outline of a "performance contracting system," combining features of the French contract plan and the signaling system, which offers one way out of the impasse. He describes the basic principles of such a system and the experience of a test in one developing country.

The *Mary Shirley* study analyzes Pakistan's experience with implementing the signaling system between 1983 and 1988. She notes that, contrary to the original intent, the criterion actually employed in Pakistan for performance evaluation and incentives was private rather than public profitability. After analyzing performance data on a sample of firms, she finds that in a third of the cases rewards may have been handed out incorrectly, either to firms registering higher profits but lower efficiency (because of advantageous price movements), or vice versa. She concludes that despite its shortcomings the system may have spurred efficiency improvement, and that it certainly improved the timeliness, quality, and analysis of information by SOEs and the government. Shirley notes that performance may have improved even more if certain other conditions had been met, and that the system could have been exploited further to spur changes in public policy or to identify SOEs that ought to have been liquidated. She concludes her paper with lessons for policymakers in other developing countries.

John Nellis reviews the international experience with contract plans as a tool for guiding and controlling SOEs. After reviewing the mixed record of contract plans in France, where the idea originated, Nellis turns to a detailed analysis of Senegalese experience. Familiar problems of contract plans, such as rapid changes in the environment that make plans obsolete, the difficulty of holding governments to their promises, the shortage of skills in government, and the delays is negotiating contracts, were heightened in the developing country context. With the exception of Morocco, other African countries using the approach, such as Congo, Benin, Côte d'Ivoire, and The Gambia, faced some of the same problems as Senegal. Nellis sees the contract plan as a tool with promise, but beset by a number of practical problems. He concludes that the contract plan system is more likely to succeed if the government agency running it is well-staffed and powerful, and if the SOE in question is already performing quite well.

The experiments in privatization and control launched in several developing countries in the 1980s are likely to be intensified in the 1990s. As the experiments continue, we are likely to learn more about how to reduce imperfections in both the public and private sectors, and about when and how the two sectors can be fruitfully combined in the development process. To carry out these experiments in the most efficient manner, the experiences of individual countries need to be examined carefully and the findings disseminated widely. It is in this spirit that the studies carried in this volume are offered to policymakers in developing countries.

Besides the contributors, whose vital role in the preparation of this volume is self-evident, David Davies and John Didier of the Economic Development Institute deserve special thanks for shepherding the project through the World Bank, as does Sonia Hoehlein for her work in producing the final manuscript. Three anonymous reviewers suggested useful revisions to individual chapters as well as to the organization of the volume. Alice Dowsett of EDI edited the manuscript with great skill. Finally, at Northeastern University, Julia M. Finn and June Remington meticulously maintained revised versions of the manuscript on the computer, while Deans Roger Atherton and David Boyd supported the endeavor at every stage.

1

THE SEARCH FOR REMEDIES

Ravi Ramamurti

In the 1980s, the role of state-owned enterprises (SOEs) underwent close scrutiny in developing countries. Many governments seemed to be concluding that SOEs were not the ideal hybrids they had been made out to be: only rarely did they combine the strengths of the public and private sectors as originally expected, and occasionally they combined the worst of both. SOEs commonly failed to maximize the greater good, or did so at high cost. Fine tuning and marginal reforms had done little over the years to improve their performance, although here and there an enterprise registered remarkable results.[1]

By the late 1970s, the SOE sector had absorbed a large share of governments' budgets in the form of subsidies and capital infusions.[2] As governments ran into severe fiscal problems in the 1980s and loans became increasingly difficult to raise at home and abroad, they were forced to consider relatively radical methods for turning the SOE sector around. Thus, a program of SOE reform emerged in developing countries that in terms of scale and scope had no parallel in the postwar period. Two classes of reform were particularly important. One was privatization, whose novelty is reflected in the fact that the word appeared in standard dictionaries only in the early 1980s (it appeared in *Webster's New Collegiate Dictionary* in 1983 according to Hanke 1988, p. 2). The other

---

1. Widespread disappointment about the performance of SOEs is seen in public reports in various developing countries, including Bangladesh, India, the Republic of Korea, Brazil, and several countries of Sub-Saharan Africa (on the latter, see Nellis 1986).

2. SOEs were estimated to contribute substantially to public sector deficits and to have typically financed less than one-fifth of their investments through internally generated resources (see Nair and Filippides 1988).

important, but less novel, reform was to strengthen the methods by which governments controlled SOEs.

The early adopters of privatization and new forms of government control were working with untested policies rather than sure-fire solutions. The case studies in this volume indicate that neither solution consistently achieved its stated purposes, but at least a creative search for remedies was set in motion in the 1980s, out of which a broader range of policy options than existed before was emerging. Developing countries were discovering new ways to harness the private sector to help achieve national ends, new public-private arrangements that could promote development, and refinements in the methods of government control that could help realize the original promise of SOEs.

Privatization

Privatization gained considerable momentum in the developing world in the 1980s. Table 1.1 indicates that by the end of December 1987, 571 SOEs had been privatized in 57 developing countries. At that time, another five hundred transactions were planned for execution in the future. The table does not include these, nor the several thousand reprivatizations, that is, the return of recently nationalized firms to the private sector. The World Bank labeled the cases included in table 1.1 as "new privatizations." Although countries such as Bangladesh, Chile, and Israel divested some SOEs in the 1970s, privatization gained unprecedented popularity in the developing world in the 1980s.

At the same time, the evidence was not overwhelming that privatization was unstoppable or that the public-private balance was about to be altered dramatically in all developing countries. In only a few developing countries (Chile, Côte d'Ivoire) and developed countries (United Kingdom) did the public-private balance actually change substantially in the 1980s. In many other countries often described as active privatizers, such as Argentina, Bangladesh, or Turkey, few significant cases of new privatization occurred in the 1980s. To be sure, countries such as Brazil, Malaysia, Nigeria, and Turkey were poised to privatize on a large scale, but the slow pace of implementation in the past raised questions about the future pace or scope of privatization in these countries.

Many of the firms privatized in the 1980s were small, specially in the case of private sales, which accounted for nearly half of all the cases (table

Table 1.1 New Privatization Transactions Completed or Underway in Developing Countries, by Region and Type, as of End 1987

Region	No. of countries involved	Public offering No.	Public offering Percentage	Private sale No.	Private sale Percentage	Sale of assets No.	Sale of assets Percentage	Leasing No.	Leasing Percentage	Management contracts No.	Management contracts Percentage	Others[a] No.	Others[a] Percentage	Total No.	Total Percentage
Sub-Saharan Africa	25	6	7.7	98	34.9	41	69.5	22	43.1	48	67.7	19	61.3	234	41.0
Asia	10	27	34.6	31	11.0	2	3.4	8	15.7	15	21.1	10	32.2	93	16.3
Pacific Countries	3	1	1.3	3	1.0	0	0.0	4	7.8	2	2.8	0	0.0	10	1.8
North Africa & Middle East	7	8	10.3	10	3.6	0	0.0	2	3.9	3	4.2	0	0.0	23	4.0
Latin America and the Caribbean	12	36	46.1	139	49.5	16	27.1	15	29.4	3	4.2	2	6.5	211	36.9
Total	57	78	100.0	281	100.0	59	100.0	51	100.0	71	100.0	31	100.0	571	100.0

Note: Excludes reprivatization of recently nationalized companies, liquidations unaccompanied by sale of assets, and planned privatizations.

a. Includes employee buyouts, fragmentation of SOEs, and new private investment in existing SOEs.

Source: Compiled by author from data in Vuylsteke (1988, annex E, table 1, pp. 169-172).

1.1). Privatization was also heavily concentrated in the following eight countries, which accounted for more than half the transactions shown in table 1.1: Côte d'Ivoire, Guinea, Niger, and Togo in Sub-Saharan Africa; Singapore in Asia; and Brazil, Chile, and Jamaica in Latin America and the Caribbean. About half of the 57 privatizing countries had less than five transactions completed or underway by the end of 1987 (Vuylsteke 1988, table 1, pp. 169-172). Indeed, some of the countries recorded as privatizers saw their state-owned sectors expand significantly in the 1980s. Hundreds of companies fell into state ownership in Mexico as the portfolios of major banks came under state control in the course of their nationalization in 1982, and in the Philippines, nonperforming assets worth US$7 billion fell into government control when private firms defaulted on loans to state-owned banks (Haggard 1988, p. 98). The number of companies that fell into state ownership in these two countries roughly equaled the new privatizations in all other developing countries through December 1987.

Yet in both Mexico and the Philippines, most of the assets that were taken over were quickly earmarked for reprivatization. At another time, they may well have remained in state hands for years. More significant, in developing countries in the 1980s, few new SOEs were created as a matter of deliberate, premeditated public policy. Thus, even though state ownership did not shrink dramatically in the 1980s, one did see almost a complete halt in the launching of new SOEs and the beginning of a potentially major reversal of ownership. Recent developments, such as the willingness of countries like Argentina and Mexico to privatize their telephone companies and airlines, indicate that even large, monopolistic SOEs might be swept up by the privatization tide.

As shown in table 1.1, privatization took many different forms. A single term has come to be used for heterogeneous policies and a mixed bag of ideas. Some definitions of privatization are broader than the one used in the World Bank survey; the term sometimes includes any policy change that enlarges the scope for private enterprise to compete with SOEs, or even ones that might cause SOEs to behave more like private firms. As the definition of privatization gets broader, finding a unifying theme for the variations it encompasses becomes more and more difficult.

One cannot even say that all forms of privatization expand the role of the private sector and shrink that of the state. Even though the term privatization sounds like the opposite of state ownership—and hence attracts some followers—the actual record in developing countries reveals a more complex picture. For instance, when a government sells a minority position in an SOE to thousands of passive investors, the state gains access to private resources without losing control over the firm. Public offerings, which accounted for 13.7 percent of all new privatizations (table 1.1) commonly fit this description, especially when large SOEs or natural monopolies are involved. Similarly, leases and management contracts, which accounted for 21.3 percent of all transactions, entailed no transfer of ownership. Thus, in more than a third of all transactions—and, quite likely, in a much higher share of the assets involved—privatization altered the state's role without clearly diminishing it. The organizational arrangements that resulted in these cases were hybrids, like SOEs, that combined elements of the public and private sectors. Partial privatization mixed private and state ownership; management contracts and leases mixed private management with state ownership and control; other arrangements mixed private ownership with state regulation.

Besides taking different forms, many different goals motivated privatization. Country studies show that these goals included improving a government's cash flow, enhancing the efficiency of the SOE sector, promoting "popular capitalism," curbing the power of labor unions in the public sector, redistributing incomes and rents within society, and satisfying foreign donors who would like to see the government's role in the economy reduced (see for instance, Ramamurti forthcoming). Occasionally, privatization was consistent with some or all of these goals; more commonly it was not (see chapters 2, 3, and 4).

One common conflict was between the desire to privatize quickly and extensively and the desire to maximize proceeds from privatization. Country studies suggest that if a government sells a sufficient volume of state assets, it can rake in a tidy sum of money in the short run: the United Kingdom raised £17 billion through privatization between 1979 and 1988 (Aharoni 1988, table 1, pp. 25-26), while Chile raised US$850 million between 1975 and 1980 (Nankani 1988, p. 19). Yet, observers believe that in both countries the government realized less than it could have if privatization had been implemented more slowly and carefully (on the United Kingdom see Vickers and Yarrow 1988; on Chile see Yotopoulos 1989).

Governments that prospective buyers saw as strongly committed to privatization sometimes weakened their hand at the bargaining table, especially in developing countries, where the number of bidders for SOEs was usually small. In Bangladesh, as Lorch notes in his case study (chapter 6), the government returned textile enterprises to their former owners at prices equal to those at which the firms had been nationalized a decade earlier, even though the government had invested large sums in the mills in the interim.

In public offerings, SOE shares were often underpriced, especially if wide share ownership or a quick and "successful" sale was desired. In the United Kingdom, according to one study (Seth 1989), SOE shares were underpriced by about 51 percent on average in fixed-price public offerings, compared to 3 percent in similar private sector offerings (the 51 percent figure excludes the privatization of British Petroleum; the 3 percent figure for private sector initial offerings is the average for 1983-85). In addition, employees (and occasionally customers) received free or matching shares as well as subsidized credit to pay for those shares (see chapter 5). In one case in Sri Lanka (Noorani Tiles), a large part of the proceeds the government received went toward severance pay for laid off workers (Nankani 1988, p. 118). In other cases, the government made generous concessions to the new owners by converting the SOEs' loans to equity, writing off large chunks of debt, or injecting cash into the firm before privatization.

When buyers were given credit to pay for an SOE—sometimes at subsidized rates—the government's short run proceeds fell even further. In one case, for instance, the buyer was given 15 years to pay 90 percent of the price even though the original advertisement called for full payment within 90 days (Nankani 1988, p. 118). In Bangladesh, where 22 textile mills were reprivatized in ten months, the new owners and the government haggled for years after the deals were consummated about who was responsible for what portion of the mills' debts. In the interim, the private owners refused to service the disputed debt, and the threat of renationalization was hardly credible, since that would have embarrassed the government and played into the hands of those who had opposed privatization in the first place.

Several other factors could also lower a government's cash realization from privatization. Sometimes workers have to be assured that no one will be fired after privatization (Bangladesh). In one case in Malaysia, the government promised that employee compensation and benefits would be maintained after privatization for at least five years for all those who chose not to accept a generous severance package prior to the sale (Leeds 1989). Bids received by government are bound to reflect these constraints on future cost reduction. Similarly, the decisions of governments not to sell SOEs to foreigners or certain types of local buyers (Chinese in Malaysia, Asians in the countries of black Africa, or "cronies" of former president Ferdinand Marcos in the Philippines) could not fail to lower realizations from privatization.

To be sure, some of these losses may be avoided as countries gain experience with privatization, but others may be inescapable if a government wishes to seize a political window of opportunity for privatization and move swiftly. Conversely, a government that takes all the time and care in the world to maximize proceeds from privatization may give opponents of the policy too much time to organize their resistance. Countries like Nigeria and Turkey took several years to draw up master plans for privatization, introduce legislation to permit divestiture, prepare SOEs for sale, and create organizational arrangements in government for carrying out the transactions, thereby increasing the opportunities for the opposition to mobilize (Leeds 1988, especially pp. 156-169).

To offset revenue losses from the above factors, there is a real danger that governments will compromise on another common goal of privatization: raising an SOE's economic efficiency. To be sure, not all governments seem to be as concerned with efficiency as economists who write about privatization, but even those that are commonly mistake privatization for competition. Empirical evidence suggests that reforms designed to promote competition—or even the threat of competition—may well improve efficiency. Yet a firm facing little or no competition will usually sell for more—and possibly sell faster—than one facing high competition, all else being the same. When several large SOEs were privatized in the United Kingdom, various opportunities to sharpen competitive conditions were passed up, perhaps because the firms would have sold for less if the opportunities had been seized (Vickers and Yarrow 1988, pp. 426-429). Competition may be compromised during privatization for another reason as well: governments may prefer buyers from the same industry as the SOE because they may regard them as more likely to be able to turn around the firm. One study of private sale transactions from six developing countries found that in 60 percent of the cases the private buyer operated in the same industry as the SOE[3] (Seth 1989, table 12, p. 37); in these cases, privatization may have weakened competition rather than strengthened it. Governments may have sold SOEs to such buyers because their bids were among the highest, but as Jones, Tandon, and Vogelsang argue (chapter 2), the highest bidder is not always the "best" bidder, that is, the one who maximizes the social value of a firm after privatization.

What if competition is infeasible and undesirable, as in the case of natural monopolies? In these cases, efficiency depends at least as much on the quality of government regulation as on the ownership of the equity. Thus, privatization may have to be accompanied by liberalization in some instances and better regulation in others if efficiency is to be improved (see, for instance, Vickers and Yarrow 1988, p. 3, who assert that "the degree of product market competition and the effectiveness of regulatory policy typically have rather larger effects on performance than ownership *per se.*") Yet, these conditions are not easily achieved in developing countries. As a rule, markets are small and governments are weak. In such cases, debates on the relative merits of state versus private ownership may distract policymakers from the more important and difficult tasks of remedying market failures or regulatory failures.

Thus, when one wrestles with privatization in the concrete rather than the abstract, its implications often appear to be complex and uncertain. This may be one reason why progress on executing privatization programs is usually so slow. Yet despite such problems, certain kinds of enterprises are obvious candidates for privatization in developing countries that are not driven by ideological objectives or external pressures. Examples include small SOEs operating in competitive markets, especially if they were once in private hands. Almost every developing country has at least a few such firms. Sometimes, the nationalization of a large firm may have brought some small subsidiaries into state ownership. At other times a state-owned bank's decision to take over the assets of a defaulting private firm may have been the triggering event. In still other cases, an industry that used to

---

3. The corresponding figure for a sample of transactions in developed countries was 74.2 percent.

be dominated by an SOE may have evolved to include several private competitors. Sometimes, SOEs can be returned to their former owners, thus shortening one of the steps involved in divestiture. Not surprisingly, many of the privatizations that occurred in developing countries in the 1980s involved reprivatization or the divestiture of small SOEs. In both Brazil (Kapstein 1988) and Mexico, for instance, privatization seems more extensive when measured by the number of firms sold than the magnitude or proportion of state assets divested.

However, the largest part of the state sector in most developing countries is made up of SOEs that monopolize or dominate markets and that are very large by national standards. In the typical developing country, the 10 or 12 largest SOEs account for 70 to 80 percent of the SOE sector's total assets. In these cases, privatization has been hard to evaluate and even harder to implement, and, as table 1.1 shows, hybrid arrangements of various kinds have been common.[4] In Latin America, where many countries had relatively well-developed capital markets, governments commonly sold a part of the equity to the public. By contrast, in Africa, where capital markets were underdeveloped or nonexistent, governments used management contracts and leases to privatize SOEs that were large or dominated their markets. The performance implications of these hybrids are far from clear. For instance, we do not know whether a mixed enterprise with minority private shareholders behaves like an enterprise wholly owned by the state, like a private enterprise, or like an enterprise distinguishable from the other categories.

Several studies have noted that privatization tends to get bogged down at the implementation stage (see, for instance, Austin and others 1986). Workers, managers, civil servants, and politicians are known to resist the policy because the costs of privatization are often concentrated in these groups while the benefits are thinly dispersed across customers, investment bankers, and prospective buyers. Nevertheless, several case studies, including those in this volume (see chapters 5, 6, and 7), show that the obstacles to privatization are not insurmountable. In most countries, the government can garner workers support, overcome or

---

4. Although the World Bank survey did not distinguish between public offerings in which the government sold all its equity and those in which it sold only a portion, a review of individual cases in the report's appendix indicates that partial divestiture was by far the most common case, especially when large SOEs were concerned.

bypass civil service resistance, induce managers to support the policy, and find buyers to privatize at least a few SOEs, including some large ones. Commitment at the highest political level appears to be a necessary, though insufficient, condition for seeing privatization through. Where commitment at the top is not genuine, the government may undertake "token privatization" to satisfy foreign aid donors, for instance, while studies and committee deliberations delay major moves (according to Calaghy and Wilson 1988, this may have been the case in some African countries). Given commitment at the top, policymakers have to choose how quickly and how openly they would like privatization to proceed. The biggest reason for privatizing quickly and secretively is that opponents are likely to be taken off guard, but the downside, as we have seen, is that several mistakes are likely to be made in the course of implementation.

In the final analysis, the indirect impact of privatization may be at least as important as the direct consequences. The privatization movement is forcing countries to reexamine the rationale for state ownership of firms, is leading them to think more carefully before creating new SOEs, and is inducing them to search for better ways to manage SOEs. Some evidence suggests that even the performance of state-owned firms that have not been privatized improves, at least in the short run, when a program of privatization is launched in a country (Yarrow 1986). Besides, although privatization and competition are independent factors, privatization may make it easier for a government to promote competition. For example, franchising, which is one possible solution to the natural monopoly problem, may be infeasible if the incumbent firm is an SOE with high exit barriers. Similarly, "yardstick competition" may be more effective if the regional monopolies belong to different owners than if they all belong to the same government.[5]

In the long run, privatization is also likely to strengthen the institutions necessary to make markets work, whether through the establishment of stock exchanges, the tightening of managers' accountability to

---

5. Franchising refers to the strategy of auctioning the right to provide a (natural) monopoly service. Franchising creates competition *for* the market when competition *in* the market is infeasible or undesirable. Yardstick competition is a method for promoting competition between several regulated, regional monopolies, such as regional electricity companies. For a succinct review of these concepts, see Vickers and Yarrow 1988, pp. 110-119.

shareholders, the establishment of bankruptcy laws, or the strengthening of regulatory institutions.

Improving the Quality of Government Control

In the 1980s, governments also recognized that the methods by which SOEs were controlled required overhauling. Problems of control were of concern to all countries, as none of them intended to privatize all SOEs. In the typical developing country, natural monopolies, public utilities, and firms in extractive industries accounted for two-thirds or more of the assets of all SOEs, and typically governments had great reservations about pursuing widespread programs of privatization in these "strategic" sectors. Besides, even countries with ambitious plans for privatization could not be certain of achieving their goals, and, as we have seen before, some forms of privatization, such as partial divestiture or the sale of firms with high market power, left the state responsible for supervising and regulating the "privatized" enterprises. Thus, governments stood to benefit from an improvement in their ability to control SOEs. In the long run, such improvement could permit the eventual privatization of firms that were not slated for sale right away because the government lacked the sophistication to regulate them effectively.

Programs to improve controls over SOEs have a longer history than privatization programs. Indeed, privatization gained momentum in the 1980s partly because previous attempts at reforming government control had produced less than impressive results. In the early efforts of governments to improve their control over SOEs, they had usually been content to add a new layer of management as in a holding company, to create a new coordinating agency for SOEs, to shuffle SOEs from one ministry to another, or to increase the volume of information flowing from SOEs to government ministries. However, in the 1980s, governments were taking bolder and more innovative steps to strengthen their control policies. The objective of these new approaches was to increase simultaneously the autonomy and accountability of SOE managers. According to conventional wisdom, there was a tradeoff between these two elements. The typical objective, therefore, was to improve the quality of the controls that were being exercised while reducing their scope.

Of these two measures, the first was decidedly more difficult to achieve than the second. In theory, governments could lower the quantity of control overnight by giving managers the freedom to set prices, fix wages, invest resources, or borrow funds without government approval; but to raise the quality of control, governments had to learn how to hold managers accountable for results. That, in turn, required new skills, manpower, and organizational systems in government, all of which took time to build. Yet the quantity of control could not be reduced until a system was in place to hold managers accountable for results. The essays by Jones and Ramamurti (chapters 8 and 9) discuss the technical and organizational problems inherent in controlling SOEs by results. The case studies from Pakistan and Africa (chapters 10 and 11) illustrate the practical difficulties in improving the quality of government control. Like privatization, reforms in government control showed promise but were far from being a panacea for the ills of the SOE sector.

In 1988, 25 developing countries had World Bank-assisted programs to reform government oversight of SOEs (Shirley 1989, appendix). Nellis (chapter 11) notes that among those 25 countries were 14 African countries that had 93 "contract plans" under execution between governments and SOEs, while at least an equal number were under consideration in these and other developing countries. In addition, countries like Argentina, India, the Republic of Korea, and Mexico initiated reforms in this area on their own in the 1980s.

Although each country took a distinctive approach to improving the quality of government control, the many variants were usually derived either from the "signaling system" (chapter 8) or from the French contract plan system (chapter 11). Yet, as each country learned from its own experience and that of others, new varieties emerged. The resulting variations differed along five key dimensions.

First, they differed in the *scope* of issues brought into the new control system. Some countries limited reforms to the methods by which SOEs were evaluated (Pakistan, Korea). Decisions on other aspects of the SOE-government relationship, such as pricing, budgeting, investment, financing, and subsidies were allowed to continue as before. Other countries attempted to integrate several issues surrounding an SOE into an annual planning and contracting exercise (Senegal).

Second, countries differed on the *time horizon* for the target setting exercise. Some countries drew up targets for only the following year (Pakistan, Korea), while others (Senegal) drew up goals and targets for 36 months or longer. In the latter case, targets for the later years were revised on a rolling basis.

Third, countries differed on the extent to which they were concerned with the system's *fairness* to managers, on the one hand, and the country, on the other.[6] Changes in prices, demand conditions, the availability of inputs, general economic conditions, and so on were often outside managers' control, but could swamp their contribution to an SOE's performance. From the managers' point of view, the better a system was at separating their contribution to performance from other uncontrollable factors, the fairer it was likely to be. One set of uncontrollable factors of special interest to managers had to do with government itself. Promises by government to clear arrears in payment, permit price increases, or approve investments and borrowings on time had significant impacts on the performance of many SOEs. However, adjusting for uncontrollable factors added a great deal of technical complexity to the control system and created political problems if the government itself was partly to blame for missed targets. Here again, countries differed in the extent to which they adjusted for such factors. Contract plans typically specified the obligations of both SOEs and the government, while the systems in Pakistan and Korea specified goals only for the SOE.

From the country's point of view, fairness demanded that the SOE maximize national welfare rather than goals such as market share or profits. Again, governments could be as sophisticated as they wished in aligning the goals and targets of SOEs with national welfare. At one extreme, governments could evaluate all operational issues (for example, production decisions) and strategic issues (for example, investment decisions) using shadow prices and could even tie managerial rewards to the firm's "social" performance, that is, its contribution to the country's economic and social objectives. (No country actually applied this approach.) At the other extreme, governments could evaluate SOEs by their profits as conventionally measured at current or constant market prices (Pakistan). In between were approaches that adjusted an SOE's accounting profits for price distortions or the cost of achieving noncommercial objectives.

---

6. The notion of fairness that follows builds on Leroy Jones' work on performance evaluation (see chapter 8).

Fourth, countries differed in the nature of the link between an SOE's performance, as assessed by government, and the *incentives* offered to managers and workers. In some countries, including those using variants of the contract plan system, there was commonly no formal link at all. In others, a link was evident. For example, in Korea both managers and workers received a bonus of three to six months' salary depending on their SOE's performance. In between were countries like Pakistan, where managers received bonuses based on the government's evaluation of their performance, while workers received bonuses based on the company's profits. For senior management, the publicity surrounding their firm's performance was itself an important nonpecuniary motivator, particularly in Korea, where the annual ranking of SOEs by performance was widely publicized.

Finally, countries differed on the extent to which they increased the *formal autonomy* of managers in exchange for the strengthened accountability created by the new control system. The boldest reform seems to have been made in South Korea, where a clear break from the past was made in matters such as budgeting, personnel management, procurement, and auditing. For instance, after the new control system was put in place, operating budgets and appointments below the level of director, which once required the supervising ministry's approval, were placed entirely within the purview of the SOE's board of directors. Likewise, the authority for purchasing was decentralized and the number of audits was reduced from as many as eight per year in some cases to just one per year (Song 1988, pp. 16-18). Both the new control system and the new levels of managerial autonomy were legislated through a special law on SOEs (Government of Korea 1984). However, in several African countries, autonomy was increased on a case-by-case basis in individual contract plans rather than through sweeping changes in the law, but the autonomy promised in these plans did not always materialize in practice.

Thus, countries differed in the boldness with which the SOE-government relationship was redefined, especially with respect to managerial autonomy, and in the sophistication of the control system employed. Systems that focused on short-term targets, operational issues, and did not address the issue of fairness made minimal demands on the government's scarce expertise and resources. Those that addressed longer-term effects and fairness issues typically strained the government's administrative abilities.

Oddly enough, contract plans, which typically had multi-year targets and were ambitious in scope, were popular in countries in which the government's administrative capability was relatively weak. Perhaps the most attractive feature of the contract plan was that it highlighted the government's obligations, which in many African countries were an important determinant of SOE performance. Even though, as Nellis notes (chapter 11), governments typically failed to keep their end of the bargain, contract plans laid bare those lapses. It would appear the contract plans were adopted in Africa more to discipline governments than SOEs!

Indeed, one of the benefits of these newer forms of control—even those that did not explicitly identify a government's obligations—was their ability to draw attention to weaknesses in government policy or administration. When managers had to defend their performance or explain why targets proposed by government were too high, they drew attention to external constraints, including those that government action might lift. At the same time, in varying degrees, the new systems seem to have increased managerial autonomy and the pressure on SOEs to be more efficient. Nellis notes the difficulty of measuring the impact of contract plans on the performance of SOEs, but concludes that the most important benefits may have been intangible in nature, including a better understanding between governments and SOEs about each others' concerns and constraints. Shirley (chapter 10) concurs with this view from her study in Pakistan, but after analyzing the performance trends of a sample of SOEs, she concludes that the reforms probably promoted efficiency, although macroeconomic conditions and other changes in government policy also played a part.

Reforms in government control were relatively easy to introduce provided they had support at the highest levels of government. The chief source of resistance was often within the government itself: civil servants and ministers in supervising ministries feared they would lose power if SOEs truly gained operational autonomy. With the exception of Pakistan, such fears were justified, as any increase in the operational autonomy of managers was usually at the expense of officials in supervising ministries, while the agency that gained power as a result of the reforms was usually some central ministry, such as the president's office, the planning agency, or the finance ministry.[7] Managers of SOEs, by and large, supported the reforms. Although some feared that government control might be expanded further in the name of reform, most seemed willing to risk that outcome for the possibility of gaining autonomy, obtaining greater clarity about government policy, and operating under a more rational system of performance evaluation. Employees and unions tended to get involved if the government seemed likely to tamper with existing incentives. Other stakeholders, such as suppliers, customers, and banks, typically paid little attention to reforms in this area, presumably because they did not expect to be affected by the changes. Thus, the primary source of resistance to reforms in this area came from within the government, and the support of the country's prime minister or president was often sufficient to overcome that resistance. In that respect, reforms in government control were easier to implement than privatization.

However, overcoming some fundamental institutional obstacles to improving the quality of government control of SOEs was not easy. One such obstacle was the tremendous asymmetry in expertise and information that existed between SOEs and their controllers in government. Countries overcame this problem to some extent by obtaining help from foreign experts as in Senegal, or by creating new centers of expertise in quasi-governmental agencies as in Pakistan. In Korea, a rather creative approach was used: local experts from universities, research organizations, and the private sector were drawn into task forces that helped the government set targets and evaluate performance at the end of the year. The task forces complemented the government's resources and expertise for control, lent credibility to the evaluation process, and made minimal demands on scarce government resources. Although the task forces were supposed to be temporary when first used in 1984, they were still in use in 1990 and promised to continue indefinitely. Building on this innovation, India in 1991 was using similar task forces, with slightly different compositions, to set targets and evaluate its largest SOEs.

---

7. In Pakistan, most manufacturing SOEs were under one ministry, whereas in other countries manufacturing SOEs were commonly supervised by several different ministries.

The Elusive Hybrid

Neither the chapters in this volume nor the exploding literature on SOEs are sufficient to serve the needs of policymakers who must act in the face of incomplete understanding and information, and must develop solutions that reflect the unique circumstances in individual countries or industries. However, many new management practices in the private sector evolved through a similar process of trial and error, as innovative managers experimented with creative solutions to new problems, discarding those that failed and perfecting others that worked (see Chandler 1962).

Unfortunately, most governments stumbled into their role of owners of enterprises without much prior thought or experiment. They found themselves having to take up many commercial or quasi-commercial activities that for one reason or another were not being performed in the private sector. In pursuing those activities, governments did not wish to sacrifice the advantages that were perceived as being available to the autonomous firm. Therefore, they tried to create a hybrid institution that would combine the strengths of the public and private sectors. With minor variations from country to country, the state-owned enterprise was seen as such an institution. Yet when the SOE concept failed to work as well as expected, most governments displayed limited imagination in perfecting the concept until the fiscal pressures of the 1980s forced them to make up for lost time.

Thus, we are in the midst of intense experimentation with respect to SOEs. To be sure, policymakers may not look on their reform programs as experiments, but at the present stage that is what they really are. Out of those experiments may come a better understanding of how elements of the public and private sectors can be fruitfully combined. We may learn in the end that the ideal hybrid varies with the size or strategic significance of a firm, the structure of its market, the depth and capabilities of the private sector, and the quality of government regulation. International sharing of the lessons of such experiments will help to speed the process of learning. It is in this spirit that the studies in this volume are offered to policymakers in developing countries.

References

Aharoni, Yair. 1988. "The United Kingdom: Transforming Attitudes." In Raymond Vernon, ed., *The Promise of Privatization: A Challenge for American Foreign Policy.* New York: The Council on Foreign Relations.

Austin, James E., Lawrence H. Wortzel, and John F. Coburn. 1986. "Privatizing State-Owned Enterprises: Hopes and Realities." *Columbia Journal of World Business* 21(3):51-60.

Calaghy, Thomas M., and Ernest James Wilson III. 1988. "Africa: Policy, Reality, or Ritual?" In Raymond Vernon, ed., *The Promise of Privatization: A Challenge for American Foreign Policy*, pp. 179-230. New York: The Council on Foreign Relations.

Chandler, Alfred D. 1962. *Strategy and Structure: Chapters in the History of the American Industrial Enterprise.* Cambridge, Massachusetts: MIT Press.

Government of Korea, Economic Planning Board. 1984. *Introduction to the Government-Invested Enterprise Management Act.* Seoul.

Haggard, Stephen. 1988. "The Philippines: Picking up After Marcos." In Raymond Vernon, ed., *The Promise of Privatization: A Challenge for American Foreign Policy.* New York: The Council on Foreign Relations.

Hanke, Steve H., ed. 1988. *Prospects for Privatization.* New York: American Political Science Academy Press.

Kapstein, Ethan B. 1988. "Brazil: Continued State Dominance." In Raymond Vernon, ed., *The Promise of Privatization: A Challenge for American Foreign Policy*, pp. 128-148. New York: The Council on Foreign Relations.

Leeds. Roger. 1989. "Malaysia: Genesis of a Privatization Transaction." *World Development* 17(5):741-56.

_____. 1988. "Turkey: Rhetoric and Reality." In Raymond Vernon, ed., *The Promise of Privatization: A Challenge for American Foreign Policy*, pp. 149-178. New York: The Council on Foreign Relations.

Nair, Govindan, and Anastasios Filippides. 1988. *How Much Do State-Owned Enterprises Contribute to Public Sector Deficits in Developing Countries—and Why?* Policy, Planning, and Research Working Papers WPS 45. Washington, D.C.: World Bank.

Nankani, Helen. 1988. *Techniques of Privatization of State-Owned Enterprises*, Vol. II, *Selected Case Studies*. Technical Paper No. 89. Washington, D.C.: World Bank.

Nellis, John. 1986. *Public Enterprise in Sub-Saharan Africa*. Discussion Paper No. 1. Washington, D.C.: World Bank.

Ramamurti, Ravi. Forthcoming. "Why Are Developing Countries Privatizing?" *Journal of International Business Studies* (under review).

Seth, Rama. 1989. "Distributional Issues in Privatization." *Federal Reserve Bank of New York Quarterly Review* (Summer):34.

Shirley, Mary. 1991. *Reform of State-Owned Enterprises: Lessons from Bank Lending*. Washington, D.C.: World Bank.

Shirley, Mary, and John Nellis. 1991. *Public Enterprise Reform—The Lessons of Experience*. EDI Development Studies. Economic Development Institute. Washington, D.C.: World Bank.

Song, Dae-Hee. 1988. *New Korean Public Enterprise Policy and Efficiency Improvement*. Working Paper No. 811. Seoul: Korea Development Institute.

Vickers, John, and George Yarrow. 1988. *Privatization: An Economic Analysis*. Cambridge, Massachusetts: MIT Press.

Vuylsteke, Charles. 1988. *Techniques of Privatization of State-Owned Enterprises*, Vol. I, *Methods and Implementation*. Technical Paper No. 88. Washington, D.C.: World Bank.

Yarrow, George. 1986. "Privatization in Theory and Practice." *Economic Policy* 2:324-77.

Yotopoulos, Pan A. 1989. "The (Rip) Tide of Privatization: Lesson from Chile." *World Development* 17(5):683-702.

Part I

Privatization

2

SELLING STATE-OWNED ENTERPRISES: A COST-BENEFIT APPROACH

Leroy P. Jones
Pankaj Tandon
Ingo Vogelsang

Public divestiture is the sale of government-owned enterprises to the private sector. Such public *dis*investment increasingly dominates *in*vestment as the focus of public policy debates in the world's mixed economies. Actual divestitures have, however, been only a fraction of those announced, let alone of those debated. If reality has thus lagged rhetoric by a considerable margin, analysis has lagged reality by an even greater margin, since only recently has the economic literature begun to treat the issue systematically, with virtually nothing in a cost-benefit framework (see, however, Beesley and Littlechild 1983; Domberger and Pigott 1986). This chapter tries to make a start on redressing this imbalance by doing for the divestiture decision what the project evaluation literature has done for the investment decision, that is, introduce a systematic element of analytically based empiricism to an otherwise subjective process.

The chapter addresses three fundamental questions:

1. Should the state-owned enterprise be sold?
2. To whom should it be sold?
3. At what price should it be sold?

This chapter is based on *Selling Public Enterprises: A Cost Benefit Methodology* (Cambridge: MIT Press, 1990). We would like to thank Jack Mintz, Geri Sicat, and the editors for helpful comments on an earlier draft.

To answer these questions, we focus on the various values of the firm. The basic variables are first introduced, and then incorporated into decision rules. In both steps, the differences between public and private divestiture are stressed and the respective values are identified at the most general level. Subsequent sections specify the determinants of the various values as functions of increasingly complex market conditions. Finally, the concepts are made concrete by suggesting their applicability to selected policy issues.

Decision Variables

As is common in public enterprise work, a helpful start is to specify the private relationships and then add the modifications necessary for public analysis.

Public Versus Private Divestiture

Private exchange of assets occurs only when the buyer values them more highly than the seller, thus creating a positive-sum game. The strike price allocates the proceeds of the game within limits set by the minimum supply price and maximum demand price. Private/private exchange is thus rooted in two values and three prices.

Two additional elements must be added in public divestitures. First, the private sector might value the firm more highly because it planned to exploit a monopoly sector. The public seller might care about this, meaning that the seller must take into account a third value of the firm, namely, the value to society after privatization. Second, the government must consider not only the impact of the transfer of physical assets, but also the fiscal trade of a future stream of earnings for a current payment. If the sale is financed by reducing private investment elsewhere but the proceeds are used to reduce taxes, is society better off, worse off, or unchanged? Answers to this question are summarized in the difference between the private and government revenue multipliers.

Public/private exchange is thus rooted in three values, three prices, and the difference between two parameters:

V_{pp} : private value under private operation,

V_{sp} : social value under private operation,

V_{sg} : social value under continued government operation,

λ_g : premium on government revenue (a multiplier),

λ_p : premium on private revenue (a multiplier),

Z_g : the minimum price acceptable to the government,

Z_p : the maximum price acceptable to the private buyer,

Z : the actual price at which the sale is executed.

Private Value Under Public Operation (V_{pp})

The private value of the company is simply the present discounted value of the stream of expected net benefits accruing to the new owners. By definition, this gives us the maximum willingness to pay of the private buyer:

$$V_{pp} \equiv Z_p \tag{1}$$

Two variants of V_{pp} are particularly important, namely:

V_{ppa} : the private value as a stand-alone operation;

V_{ppc} : the private value to a larger corporate group.

A corporate group might be willing to pay more than the stand-alone value of the firm for a number of reasons, including the following:

1. economies of scope associated with spreading some overhead over a larger base;
2. reductions in transaction costs and risk associated with traditional horizontal or vertical integration;
3. ability to use otherwise unmarketable assets of the firm, such as accrued or expected tax liabilities;
4. higher risk-adjusted return through portfolio diversification;
5. exercise of newly created monopoly, oligopoly, or monopsony power.

While some of these private synergies are also socially desirable (for example, 1 and 2), others are only transfers (for example, 3), and still others are clearly undesirable (for example, 5).

An understanding of the determinants of V_{ppa} and V_{ppc} is thus useful for the government for a number of reasons. First, merely knowing what the private sector is willing to pay is insufficient; the government should have some idea why it is willing to pay this amount. Second, the sale should not necessarily go to the highest bidder. For example, in the United

States, Norfolk Southern might have been willing to pay more for Conrail simply because of the resulting change in its competitive position. Third, even where noncompetitive practices are precluded, existing private companies will often be willing to pay more than independent individuals or groups of individuals or fiduciaries, and this may conflict with the social goal of diversified ownership. Fourth, understanding private motivations helps structure terms and conditions to facilitate sale. Fifth, as part of the bargaining strategy, for the government negotiator to have some independent idea of the private sector's demand price or the maximum amount it is willing to pay is useful. Finally, this understanding is a precondition to establishing the social value under private operation, which in turn is a precondition to establishing the government's supply price or the minimum it is willing to accept.

Social Value Under Private Operation (V_{sp})

The social value under private operation is the present value of expected net benefits accruing to society as a whole from the private operation of the enterprise. It differs from V_{pp} because social goals differ from private goals, resulting in:

1. Different classifications of flows: some private costs, for example, taxes, are not social costs; some private benefits, for example, sales gained through predatory pricing or other noncompetitive behavior, are not social benefits; and so on.

2. Different pricing of flows: the private benefits from increasing output or reducing inputs is evaluated at controlled or protected domestic prices, which may differ from the corresponding benefits to society evaluated at shadow prices.

In sum, the private valuation is concerned with returns to the equity shareholder, evaluated at market prices, while the social valuation is concerned with returns to all economic actors evaluated at shadow prices.

Social Value Under Continued Government Operation (V_{sg})

The value to society under public operation is the present value of expected net benefits accruing to society as a whole from the continued public operation of the enterprise. It differs from V_{sp} for two quite distinct sets of reasons:

1. For a given economic environment, private behavior will differ from public behavior, ideally in terms of both static efficiency and dynamic entrepreneurship;
2. As part of the terms and conditions of sale, the economic environment will change (for example, tax rates, tariff protection/exemption, output pricing policies, financial structure, and credit availability).

The first set of factors is critical because it constitutes the single most important, though by no means the only, economic motivation for divestiture in the first place. The second set is critical analytically because ignoring it obscures the true benefits of divestiture. For example, in one developing country divestiture, a losing public enterprise was turned into a profitable private enterprise, in part because of increased efficiency, but in part because of a five-year grant of effective prohibition of competing imports. Accordingly, distinguishing between two alternative values under continued public operation is useful:

V_{sga} : value under continued operation "as is,"

V_{sgr} : value under restructuring under conditions paralleling those of divestiture as closely as possible.

Premium on Government Revenue (λ_g)

Society may value a dollar of benefits or costs differently depending on which segment of society is affected. The most obvious reason is equity, but efficiency enters in as well. To see the latter point, compare the value of a dollar of private consumption with a dollar of government revenue. If the government raises a dollar via taxation, private consumers would be willing to pay more than a dollar to avoid the tax, because the associated deadweight welfare loss imposes an excess burden. If we use private consumption as the numeraire in our accounting system, then the parameter λ_g summarizes our answer to the question: "By what multiple is a dollar in government hands worth more than, less than, or the same as a dollar of consumption?" Alternatively and equivalently, this means that a dollar increase in government revenue yields the same increase in social welfare as λ_g dollars of private consumption.

How big is λg? This is ultimately an empirical matter that must be settled on a country-by-country and period-by-period basis, but a few general remarks are in order. First, consider three stereotypical knee-jerk reactions:

Conservative: government funds worth less ($\lambda_g < 1$)

Liberal: government funds worth more ($\lambda_g > 1$)

Neutral neoclassicist: neither, just a transfer ($\lambda_g = 1$)

While there is clearly room for debate on the magnitude of λ_g, we would argue that it is unrelated to any such simple philosophical position as to the correct size of government. Instead, it depends on the counterfactual use of the funds. For example, assume that additional revenue of $100 (for example, from sale of the enterprise) allows the government to reduce taxes on consumption by $100, thereby eliminating the distortion created by that taxation, and hence restoring benefits of more than $100. If the benefits so restored are worth $125 to society, then each dollar of government receipts should be multiplied by a factor of 1.25. In this case, even a Ronald Reagan might agree than $\lambda_g > 1$. Alternatively, if consumption were debited and government funds expended on torturers, then liberals might agree that $\lambda_g < 0$.

The point is not that determining λ_g is simple, but only that it is not a philosophical question, but a technical one, to be addressed in the context of a particular place and time. In conducting this analysis, help is available from the standard project evaluation and public finance literature (for example, see Browning 1987; Newbery and Stern 1987; and for more in-depth discussion see chapter 4 of the book on which this chapter is based). In any event, what is needed is not λ_g alone, but its differential with λ_p.

Premium on Private Revenue (λ_p)

Divestiture advocates often neglect one of the more important costs of the process, namely, the opportunity cost of the bundle of private investment and entrepreneurship now devoted to the privatized firm. Even if some hotshot entrepreneur dramatically improves the performance of the divested enterprise, it does not necessarily follow that the country is better off. What if that entrepreneurial bundle would otherwise have been applied to some other private activity where the gain to the nation would have been even greater?

To incorporate such a possibility into the analysis, we introduce the private revenue multiplier (λ_p),which gives the consumption equivalent of a dollar of after-tax corporate profits. In a perfectly competitive neoclassical world, $\lambda_p = 1$. However, in an interesting world this need not hold. For example, if the level of investment is suboptimal, then λ_p might be greater than one because a dollar of corporate profits creates investment, which in turn creates a stream of consumption whose present value is greater than a dollar. This possibility is particularly likely in a developing country context.

The value of λ_p is a function of how the project is financed. At one extreme, consider sale to a foreign buyer in a macroeconomic context where the entire purchase price ultimately results in an additional foreign exchange inflow of the same magnitude, and profits are entirely repatriated with an equivalent foreign exchange outflow. Then, λ_p is zero, since the initial investment has no opportunity cost in terms of domestic consumption or investment. The profits are similarly valued at zero, since they do not benefit domestic actors.

In sum, the relative magnitudes of λ_p and λ_g are important in the analysis of divestiture. Divestiture has both a behavioral impact (reflected in the $V_{sp} - V_{sg}$ differential), and a fiscal impact (reflected in the $\lambda_g - \lambda_p$ differential).

Decision Rules

We now have the tools which allow us to answer the basic questions, the first of which is whether or not to sell.

Should the Enterprise be Sold?

An asset should be sold only if the seller is better off after the sale, that is, if the change in welfare (ΔW) is positive. If the government behaved as a private seller, then this would simply require that the sale price exceed the value of the future earnings stream foregone, or:

$$\text{sell if } \Delta W = Z - V_{sg} > 0 \tag{2}$$

However, if the government is to exercise its fiduciary responsibility as custodian of all national resources, it must also care about the impact on other segments of the national society. That is, it must also consider the firm's performance after sale (V_{sp}) and the impact of transferring funds from private to public hands ($\lambda_g - \lambda_p$), as follows:

$$\text{sell if } \Delta W = V_{sp} - V_{sg} + (\lambda_g - \lambda_p)Z > 0 \tag{3}$$

Interpretation of equation (3) is straightforward. The first term gives welfare after sale, the second term gives welfare before sale, and the last term gives the welfare effect of the sale transaction itself[1]

Rearranging yields:

$$\text{sell if } V_{sp} + (\lambda_g - \lambda_p)Z > V_{sg} \tag{4}$$

This simply says that the government should sell if welfare under public ownership is less than that under private ownership plus any sale premium.

If $\lambda_g > \lambda_p$[2], the sell rule can be rewritten as:

$$\text{sell if } Z > \frac{V_{sg} - V_{sp}}{\lambda_g - \lambda_p} \tag{5}$$

The right-hand side of this expression represents the government's supply price (Z_g) or the minimum that it should accept for the enterprise:

$$Z_g = \frac{V_{sg} - V_{sp}}{\lambda_g - \lambda_p} \tag{6}$$

Note that whenever social welfare is higher under private operation than under public operation ($V_{sg} < V_{sp}$), and $\lambda_g > \lambda_p$, this price will be negative, meaning that the government should be willing to pay the private sector to take over the enterprise. This might happen, say, if the enterprise

---

1 . A complete description of the welfare effect of the transaction requires inclusion of the transaction cost of executing the sale. We treat this as a second-order effect, and for the sake of simplicity omit it here.

2.   If not, see equation (7).

is loss-making under government operation, but becomes viable under private operation without large deleterious welfare effects on consumers or workers. If the government is neutral between funds in public and private hands ($\lambda_g = \lambda_p$), then it should be willing to pay the private sector any arbitrarily large amount to take over the enterprise. If λ_g exceeds λ_p, the amount the government should be willing to pay becomes finite, but it should still be willing to pay the amount indicated by equation (6).

This rather strong result may seem surprising at first, but it is really quite intuitive. If the nation is economically better off with the enterprise in private hands, then the government should be willing to pay something to accomplish this improvement. If, in addition, the government is neutral between funds in private and public hands, then it should be willing to pay anything, since the payment is in this case only a transfer and is welfare neutral. This extreme result may be politically infeasible, but the weaker result of a negative supply price may help to explain (or justify) the observed "underpricing" of public issues.

Now consider the possibility that $\lambda_g < \lambda_p$. If so, then the higher the value of Z, the lower the change in welfare. Accordingly, the direction of the inequality in equation (5) is reversed[3] and the sell rule would now be:

$$\text{sell if} \quad Z < \frac{V_{sg} - V_{sp}}{\lambda_g - \lambda_p} \tag{7}$$

The government now has no minimum supply price, only a maximum supply price. They should not accept a price higher than that given by (7) since any larger transfer of private funds to the government would make society worse off from the transaction as a whole (this assumes that $V_{sp} > V_{sg}$, otherwise the expression would give the minimum price the government should pay to have the burden taken off its hands). That is, society is better off under private operation ($V_{sp} > V_{sg}$), and funds are also more productive in private hands ($\lambda_p > \lambda_g$), meaning that too high a Z can have a negative welfare effect more than offsetting the gain from the change in enterprise operations.

---

3. Algebraically, this follows from the fact that when dividing or multiplying both sides of an inequality by a negative number, the inequality sign is reversed.

The main results of this section are equations (6) and (7), which give us the boundaries of the government's supply price. For example, if $\lambda_g > \lambda_p$, (6) gives us a formula to determine the minimum price at which government should be willing to sell. The supply price is, of course, not the price at which the sale should actually be executed, a topic to which we now turn.

At What Price Should the Enterprise Be Sold?

What price (Z) should be chosen if the government wishes to maximize ΔW, other things being equal? Equation (3) gave the net welfare effect of divestiture, for any given buyer. Inspection of this expression reveals that the sale price (Z) affects social welfare only through the factor $(\lambda_g - \lambda_p)$. Formally:

$$\partial \Delta W / \partial Z = (\lambda_g - \lambda_p) \tag{8}$$

This says that as Z rises, welfare rises at the rate $(\lambda_g - \lambda_p)$.

There are now three cases. If $\lambda_g = \lambda_p$ (that is, there is no premium on government revenues), then $\partial \Delta W / \partial Z = 0$, and the gain in welfare is unaffected by the sale price. This is the usual neoclassical result where the price paid is a pure transfer between the purchaser and the government, of no social significance whatsoever. In other words, the sale price does not matter and any price, positive or negative, is just as good as any other. Thus, anyone who believes that $\lambda_g = \lambda_p$ has a very simple answer to the basic question of what price to charge: just flip a coin.

The second case is where $\lambda_g < \lambda_p$. In this case, equation (8) would be negative, indicating that the government would want to minimize the sale price. In principle, this means that the government should pay the private sector an arbitrarily large amount to take over the enterprise. In fact, an assumption that $\lambda_g < \lambda_p$ implies that it would be optimal at the margin for the government to simply transfer funds to private firms.

The third case is the one we regard as the most reasonable, namely, $\lambda_g > \lambda_p$. In this case, equation (8) shows that $\partial \Delta W / \Delta Z > 0$, and therefore that the government should attempt to obtain the highest possible sale price for the enterprise from any given buyer. This, however, is simply the maximum the private buyer would be willing to pay, so that:

$$Z^* = Z_p = V_{pp},$$

(9)

where the asterisk denotes the optimal value of the variable. It follows that the maximum welfare increment (ΔW^*) is:

$$\Delta W^* = V_{sp} - V_{sg} + (\lambda_g - \lambda_p) V_{pp}$$

(10)

It is, of course, exceedingly unlikely that this price will actually be obtained. Recall that Z_p reflects the price at which the buyer is indifferent between buying the enterprise and retaining the existing portfolio; the buyer would simply be trading one asset for another of equal value. The situation is obviously symmetrical, with Z_g representing the price at which society neither wins nor loses from the transaction. One asymmetry that does arise, however, is that while this transaction has only one seller (the government), more than one buyer may exist. Competition between buyers could force the eventual buyer to pay close to his or her maximum willingness to pay. In most developing countries, this may be less likely because of the small overall size of the private sector.

In any case, the point is that Z_g and Z_p provide only boundaries for the actual sale price. If the former exceeds the latter, then no transaction can take place, but given the likelihood of a negative supply price, a considerable economic range for bargaining is likely. Within this range, where will the price be set? For a given set of terms and conditions of sale, the answer is indeterminate in a small-number bargaining environment, and depends upon the skill of the two bargaining parties.

In practice, of course, the terms and conditions of sale are anything but predetermined and are the focus of negotiations. If anything, a case can be made that the bargaining sequence be reversed, with the price first determined arbitrarily and the terms and conditions then negotiated so as to make this price acceptable to both parties. This is, while a negative price will generally be economically acceptable it will seldom be politically acceptable. Under such circumstances, a minimally acceptable political price becomes the starting point and negotiations focus on terms and conditions that make this mutually acceptable.

Note that all the expressions for ΔW and for its rate of change are derived with respect to a particular buyer. Thus, we have demonstrated that for any given buyer, the government should seek to maximize the sale price. This is not the same as saying government should choose the buyer with the highest bid, because the high bid may be associated with a low social valuation.

To Whom Should The Enterprise Be Sold?

To repeat, the previous section does not say: "sell to the highest bidder." The Conrail example given earlier makes clear why this is nonsensical. Rather, it says extract the highest possible sale price from the "best" bidder (or given a number of identical bidders, choose the one with the highest bid). How then is the best bidder to be determined?

Once again, the fundamental equation (3) gives the starting point for an answer. Rank bidders according to their ΔWs and focus on the highest. Unfortunately, this will often only provide a starting point for the selection, because Z will remain subject to negotiation, and if some bidders can be induced to raise their final bids (or adjust the conditions of sale more favorably), then the rankings may change. Exactly how this process will work itself out depends on the bargaining/negotiating structure employed. However, equation (3) provides the basis for the iterative calculation. Further, as one step in the screening procedure, calculation of ΔW^* (equation 10) allows identification of the bidders with the highest potential for striking the best deal for the country. Note also that in the developing country context, having a plethora of qualified bidders should be considered a luxury for which some iterative indeterminancy is a small price to pay. Finally, note that the concept of ranking bidders by their ΔWs to choose between them is valid regardless of the relative magnitudes of λ_g and λ_p.

The Difference Principle

In answering the basic questions, we have nowhere needed to know V_{sp} or V_{sg} individually, but only their difference $(V_{sp} - V_{sg})$. This turns out to be immensely fortuitous, because otherwise this exercise would be of purely theoretical interest with no practical import whatsoever. Except under the most egregiously simplistic assumptions (for example, competitive equilibrium), the individual values are simply unknowable. We believe, however, that analytic tools are available that allow reasonable approximations to the difference. This point will be elaborated upon in concrete terms as we proceed. For the present, note only that this difference principle simplifies our task considerably and constitutes our final basic concept.

Conclusion

This section has shown how the basic divestiture questions can all be answered if we can agree on the difference between two parameters, λ_g and λ_p, and can estimate one value, V_{pp}, and one difference in values, $(V_{sp} - V_{sg})$. Accordingly, subsequent sections focus on methodologies for quantifying these values in increasingly complex environments.

Valuation, Firm Behavior, and Policy

To set a simple standard, we first discuss the case where privatization would result in no efficiency change conventionally measured.

A Trivial Case ($\lambda_g = \lambda_p$)

If there is no premium of government revenue over private funds, we have a trivial case, because if public behavior is the same as private behavior and all prices are the same, privatization cannot change the wealth of society, but only its distribution. However, if $\lambda_g = \lambda_p$, then distribution does not matter either, so the government should be completely indifferent as to whether the enterprise is in public or private hands (that is, $V_{sg} = V_{sp}$). Further, given no change in wealth and distributional neutrality, the government would be happy to accept Z_p (whatever that might be) for the enterprise. However, it would be equally happy to accept any other price for the enterprise, or indeed, to pay the private sector any amount of subsidy to take the enterprise. The intuition is obvious and algebra confirms the result:

$$Z_g = \frac{V_{sg} - V_{sp}}{\lambda_g - \lambda_p} = \frac{0}{0} = \text{undefined} \tag{11}$$

In summary, if conduct does not change and government revenue does not matter, then nothing matters, and we need not bother calculating V_{sg}, V_{sp}, or anything else.

Revenue Motive ($\lambda_g > \lambda_p$)

In reality, government revenue does matter, and one of the major motives for privatization is to relax a fiscal constraint. We therefore introduce a revenue concern by assuming public goods exist, lump sum taxes are not feasible, and therefore $\lambda_g > \lambda_p$.

Now a bit more calculation is required. We establish the general result under two assumptions: first, that only an operating capital good is being sold (that is, there are no debts, working capital, or nonoperating assets); and second, that the capital good yields a stable stream of profits (quasi-rents, or π) in perpetuity. These assumptions are only made to simplify the exposition, and both can be relaxed with no loss of generality.

Under these assumptions the private calculation is simply:

$$Z_g = V_{pp} = \frac{\pi - X^d}{r} \tag{12}$$

where X^d is the direct tax paid and r is the discount rate (assumed the same for buyer and seller and constant over time).[4]

The value to society of this outcome differs only in the positive value attached to X^d.

$$V_{sp} = \frac{\lambda_p \pi + (\lambda_g - \lambda_p) X^d}{r} \tag{13}$$

In the event of continued public operation, the government revenue premium applies to the entire stream of quasi-rents:

$$V_{sg} = \frac{\lambda_g \pi}{r} \tag{14}$$

Now, from equation (6):

$$Z_g = \frac{V_{sg} - V_{sp}}{\lambda_g - \lambda_p}$$

---

4.   We use $\pi - X^d$ rather than $\pi(1 - x^d)$ because the applicable corporate tax rate 'x^d' is not charged on quasi-rents, but on π less interest, depreciation, and a host of other accounting charges. Also note that π is defined as a quasi-rent.

Substituting:

$$Z_g = \frac{\dfrac{\lambda_g \pi}{r} - \dfrac{\lambda_p \pi + (\lambda_g - \lambda_p) X^d}{r}}{\lambda_g - \lambda_p} \tag{15}$$

Rearranging:

$$Z_g = \frac{\pi - X^d}{r} \tag{16}$$

which is precisely V_{pp}. The general result is, therefore, that in the absence of behavioral changes or price distortions:

$$Z_g = Z_p = V_{pp} \tag{17}$$

That is, the minimum price at which the government is willing to sell is just equal to the maximum that the private sector is willing to pay.

Intuitively, this result may be explained as follows. The government is relinquishing a portion (not all, because of taxes) of its claim on future earnings. To make itself whole, it must receive at least the present value of that claim today. Note that the value of λ_g does not matter (so long as it is not unity) because it enters symmetrically on both the future and present value sides. Stripped of λ_g, which is the only difference between public and private valuations, the resulting public calculation is precisely the same as the private calculation except that benefits and costs are reversed (the buyer gives up cash now for a future claim). The public minimum thus becomes the private maximum.

Under these conditions, no sale is likely to occur. If there are any transaction costs (for example, the cost of typing up a contract and walking across the street to sign it), then Z_p will fall and Z_g will rise, leaving no mutually acceptable Z.

Allocative Versus Cost Efficiency: The Fundamental Tradeoff

A positive-sum game is created once private behavior differs from public. Typically, policymakers hope that divestiture will increase efficiency, but fear that it will also lead to exploitation of consumers. In this section, the methodology is extended to deal with this fundamental tradeoff.

The change in welfare depends upon the change in consumer surplus, the change in pretax profits, and the difference between the buyer's willingness to pay and what the buyer actually pays, as follows:

$$\Delta W = \sum_{t=0}^{\infty} \left[1/(1+r)^t \right] \left[\Delta S(t) + \lambda_g \Delta \pi(t) \right] - \left(\lambda_g - \lambda_p \right) \left(Z_p - Z \right) \tag{18}$$

where t indicates the time period, $[1/(1+r)^t]$ is the discount factor, $\Delta S(t)$ is the change in consumer surplus, and $\Delta \pi(t)$ is the change in pretax profits. Note that the first term is negative when market power is exercised, the second term is positive when efficiency is increased, and the last term drops out when the strike price is the maximum willingness to pay. Equation (18) becomes very simple if the government manages to achieve a selling price equal to the private willingness to pay (that is, if $Z_p = Z$). Then the change in welfare due to privatization simplifies to the change in consumer surplus plus the change in profits weighted by λ_g. This remarkable result holds because the government is able to capture the full discounted profit after divestiture in the form of the selling price Z. As the government cannot expect to receive more in selling price than Z_p, any fundraising argument for privatization will have to rest on an increase in expected profit due to privatization (or a lower discount rate of the private buyers compared to the public sellers). Maximizing profits may be a good strategy for a public enterprise prior to privatization, because the resulting profit will be taken as an indicator for the profit potential after privatization. This will decrease the risk for private buyers that a particular profit level can be achieved and it will tend to move Z toward Z_p. For example, British Airways had remarkable profit increases after privatization was announced but before it was implemented. The question remains to be answered why such a strategy of increasing profit should be possible only for a public enterprise scheduled to be privatized.

In equation (18) we can use the difference principle alluded to above. Clearly, consumer surplus is hard to estimate because it depends on the exact demand curve over a whole range of prices and quantities. The change in consumer surplus, however, only depends on the range of prices and quantities before and after privatization. If there is no nonprice rationing, then a simple approximation and lower (upper) bound for the increase (decrease) in consumer surplus is given by multiplying the change in price with the initial quantity. Thus, we only have to estimate the change in price to get the most pessimistic estimate for the change in consumer surplus.

Equation (18) captures the basic Williamsonian tradeoff that can be expected due to privatization: pressure to reduce cost and increase prices. However, this equation does not fully capture a host of subtle issues, including shadow pricing of inputs and outputs, direct and indirect taxes, and synergies. Many of these cannot be explicitly treated in this chapter. However, as Jones and others (1990) show, all of these can be accommodated in a straightforward manner.

Consider the case of synergies. Synergies are most relevant for monopolistic and oligopolistic industries. We accommodate synergies in our framework by viewing the public enterprise before and after divestiture in a multiproduct context. Synergies are present if for two firms 'A' and 'B' and the merged firm 'A + B' the value $V('A + B') > V('A') + V('B')$. Assume a public enterprise 'A' that has synergies with a public enterprise 'B' and is bought by a private firm 'C'. Then the value $V_{sg}('A + B') + V_{sp}('C')$ before public enterprise divestiture has to be compared to the value $V_{sg}('B') + V_{sp}('A + C')$ after divestiture.

Synergies have been the most discussed issue in the recent privatization of Conrail in the United States. This cargo railroad company would have had quite a different value if sold to its (partial) competitor Norfolk Southern than if sold to the general public. Three types of synergies can be illustrated in this example. First, there are synergies that operate through the cost of production, predominantly economies of scale and economies of scope. In the case of Conrail/Norfolk Southern such synergies could have been realized through shutting down parallel lines or through better utilization of railroad cars. Second, there are synergies that operate through a change in market power. In the case of Conrail/Norfolk Southern these could also have resulted from shutting down parallel lines that would have changed duopoly situations to monopolistic supply. Third, there are financial synergies that directly affect only the distribution of (unweighted) social surplus. In the case of Conrail/Norfolk Southern these would have resulted from tax savings that Norfolk Southern could have realized through the purchase of Conrail. While all three types of synergies are privately profitable, the social judgment is quite mixed. Synergies of the first type tend to increase welfare, whereas synergies of the second and third type tend to have the opposite effect. In terms of measurement, synergies of the third type are most easily evaluated while the other two can be quite elusive. The government may therefore want to safeguard against increases in market power by regulating the enterprise after privatization. However, this may water down other desired privatization effects, such as vigorous cost containment and productivity improvements. The regulators must therefore keep these tradeoffs in mind. The price-cap formula RPI-X used by British Telecom may be an example of how this could be achieved.

Lifting Constraints on Public Enterprise Behavior

Determinants of the various values of the firm are, of course, subject to government action, and an active divestiture policy means manipulating V_{sp}, V_{sg}, and Z to maximize the benefits of divestiture. V_{sg} is influenced by the counterfactual policies taken instead of divestiture (for example, increasing autonomy or financial restructuring); V_{sp} is influenced by the policies affecting the period after divestiture (for example, tariff protection or price regulation); and Z is influenced by both of the above plus sale-related policies for the time before divestiture (for example, assuming part of corporate debt or pension funding).

An important question for any government considering privatization concerns the evaluation of alternatives. Such alternatives often appear difficult to implement because the government faces certain political constraints. Here we assume that some of these constraints on public enterprise behavior have been lifted. We have already distinguished between two alternative values under continued public operation:

V_{sga} : value under continued operation "as is";

V_{sgr} : value following restructuring under conditions paralleling those of divestiture.

Such restructuring should be undertaken instead of divestiture if $V_{sgr} >$ V_{sga} and if $Z_{gr} > Z$, where Z_{gr} is the minimum acceptable sale price after restructuring. This restructuring could be internal or external to the firm. First, let us consider an example of internal restructuring.

EFFECT OF A CHANGE IN HIRING POLICY ON V_{sg}. Many people believe that cost inefficiency is the major problem of public enterprises. Constraints on input prices and input quantities, in particular for labor, may well be responsible for this cost inefficiency. Without the threat of privatization, these constraints tend to be politically entrenched. In many countries, public enterprise employees cannot be fired, and their pay, especially in lower ranks, is above that in comparable private industry jobs. Under the threat of privatization, employees may accede to some reduction in pay and job security. How would this affect V_{sg}? Assuming that workers in the reference situation (denoted by superscript ('0') were paid above their social opportunity wage, we have $w_s < w^0_g$. Now, in the counterfactual scenario their wage is reduced. In this new situation (denoted by superscript '1') $w^1_g < w^0_g$. At the same time the work force is reduced. Assuming that the alternative wage for laid off workers is $\underline{w}$, the resulting change in ΔW^*, assuming that output price and quantity does not change, can be expressed as:[5]

$$\Delta W^* = -\Delta V_{sg} = \left(1 - \lambda_g\right)\left(W^0_g L^0_g - w^1_g L^1_g\right) + \underline{w}\left(L^0_g - L^1_g\right)$$
$$= \lambda_g \Delta \Pi + \Delta M \tag{19}$$

Here M is the factor rent workers received. Equation (19) then says the following: the change in the public enterprise wage bill is a saving to the treasury weighted by λ_g and a loss to the workers weighted by one. The loss to workers, however, is reduced because those laid off receive the alternative wage $\underline{w}$.

How does this counterfactual policy compare to the divestiture option? Clearly, if divestiture would only result in the same layoff as the public enterprise is now considering, and if no behavioral changes occur, then $Z_{gr} = Z_p$. Therefore, if the cost saving achieved through the layoff were not fully reflected in Z, then $\Delta W < 0$ as a result of the layoff policy.

---

5. Note that the use of δW^* instead of δW assumes that the government receives the buyer's reservation price, that is, $Z = V_{pp}$.

Next, consider the example of an external policy change: a change in the regulated price of the output of the public enterprise.

EFFECT OF A CHANGE IN P ON V_{sg}. We had assumed earlier that after privatization the monopoly firm would raise the price for the output. What is the firm under continued government operation were allowed to do the same? Assume the simple one-period case without discounting and without adjustment for shadow prices. In this case, the effect of a price change for the public enterprise can be expressed as the derivative:

$$\partial V_{sg} / \partial p = -\partial \Delta W * / \partial p_g = \partial \lambda_g \Pi_g / \partial p + \partial S / \partial p$$
$$= (\lambda_g - 1)q + \lambda_g (\partial q / \partial p)(p - \partial C / \partial q) \qquad (20)$$

Equation (20) is quite familiar from the literature on optimal public enterprise pricing. In the case of $\lambda_g = 1$, it would simply say that the effect of a price change on V_{sg} is proportional to the difference between price and marginal cost. This would lead to marginal cost pricing as the optimal government policy. With $\lambda_g > 1$ the optimal price is above marginal cost.

Improving the Net Benefit of Divestiture

Finally, we consider two issues that affect the net benefits of divestiture: price regulation after divestiture and the sale of state-owned enterprises to foreign buyers.

THE EFFECTS OF PRICE REGULATION AFTER DIVESTITURE. The monopoly case is the obvious one where the government would not want the firm after divestiture to choose the unconstrained profit maximizing price. The question then arises, what is the effect on the privatization decision of regulating the price after divestiture? For the moment, let us assume that price regulation has no effect on the X-efficiency of the firm. While the American literature on rate of return regulation suggests that price regulation increases costs relative to unregulated firms (see, for example, Weiss and Klass 1981), the opposite effect may also occur due to additional pressure on the firm to survive. Also, less distorting forms of price regulation than experienced in the United States may exist. One such example could prove to be the RPI-X formula developed by Littlechild for the privatization of British Telecom (Littlechild 1983).

For the one-period case with a proportional corporate income tax, we find that a marginal change in p results in:

$$\partial V_{sp} / \partial p = \lambda_p \partial \pi_p / \partial p + \left(\lambda_g - \lambda_p \right) \partial X^d / \partial p + \partial S / \partial p =$$
$$\left[q + \left(\partial q / \partial p \right) \left(p - \partial C / \partial q \right) \right] \left[\lambda_p + \left(\lambda_g - \lambda_p \right) x^d \right] - q \tag{21}$$

$$\partial V_{pp} / \partial p = \partial \pi_p / dp - \partial X^d / \partial p =$$
$$\left[q + \left(\partial q / \partial p \right) \left(p - \partial C / \partial q \right) \right] \left[1 - x^d \right] \tag{22}$$

We know that $\partial \Delta W / \partial p = \partial W / \partial p = \partial V_{sp} / \partial p + \left(\lambda_g - \lambda_p \right) \left(\partial Z / \partial p \right)$. Assuming that $Z = V_{pp}$, we then get

$$\partial W^* / \partial p = \left(\lambda_g - 1 \right) q + \lambda_g \left(\partial q / \partial p \right) \left(p - \partial C / \partial q \right) \tag{23}$$

Thus, a price change after divestiture has the opposite effect of a price change under continued public operation (equation 20). A welfare enhancing price change under continued public operation makes divestiture less attractive, while the same type of price change for the privatized firm would make divestiture more attractive.

THE EFFECTS OF A FOREIGN BUYER FOR THE PUBLIC ENTERPRISE. Should the public enterprise be sold to a foreign buyer or not? If a foreign buyer acquires the public enterprise, then profits no longer accrue to the domestic economy. This could change our calculations. Thus, knowing the effects of buyer nationality is important to assess whether the government should establish a policy of favoring domestic acquirers.

The main effect of foreignness is that the social value of the firm after divestiture no longer includes profits going to the foreign owner. Thus, in the one-period framework without discounting

$$V_{pp} = \pi_p - X^d$$

$$V_{sp} = S_p + \lambda_g X^d$$

Thus, under foreign ownership, denoted by subscript F,

$$\Delta W_F = V_{sp} - V_{sg} + \lambda_g Z \qquad (24)$$

This differs from our previous formula, because the sale price Z is not paid by domestic agents; thus, Z gets the full weight λ_g because for this case $\lambda_p = 0$. Despite this, for the case of $Z = V_{pp}$ the net result remains unchanged:

$$\Delta W_F^* = V_{sp} - V_{sg} + \lambda_g V_{pp} = \lambda_g \Delta \pi + \Delta S \qquad (25)$$

The difference arises only if the government cannot capture all the rents of the purchaser in the sales price. Thus, if the government can only capture a fraction θ, $0 \le \theta \le 1$ of the firm's rent, V_{pp}, in the purchasing price, then

$$\Delta W_F = \Delta S + \lambda_g (1 - x^d)(\theta \pi_p - \pi_g) + \lambda_g x^d \Delta \pi \qquad (26)$$

Compared to this the welfare change from selling to a domestic buyer would be

$$\begin{aligned} \Delta W &= \Delta S + (1 - x^d)[(\theta \pi_p - \pi_g)\lambda_g + (1- \theta)\pi_p] + \lambda_g x^d \Delta \pi \\ &= \Delta W_F + (1 - x^d)(1 - \theta)\pi_p \end{aligned} \qquad (27)$$

Without synergies and with the shadow price of foreign currency being the exchange rate, the government would therefore always do worse by selling to a foreigner, as long as the price is the same and assuming the efficiency and behavioral effects are also the same. The difference in net benefit from selling to a foreigner is directly proportional to the selling price for the firm. At the same sale price, only if foreign ownership would result in more substantial cost savings can a case begin to be made for selling to foreign buyers. The consequence of this is not: do not sell to foreign buyers, but rather: bargain more aggressively with a foreign buyer than with a domestic buyer.

Furthermore, the question may arise, is a foreign capital inflow a net addition to domestic resources? For example, it has been argued in Pakistan that privatization will attract repatriation of capital by expatriate nationals operating in the Gulf states. Does this not enhance the gains from privatization? The answer is "not necessarily." Total foreign inflows may ultimately be limited by foreign exchange constraints that restrict the ability to service debt and repatriate capital. Accordingly, even "untied" inflows can ultimately crowd out marginal inflows as the national macro-managers impose or strengthen exchange controls or as foreign sources become reluctant to lend. For reasons such as these, the standard project evaluation assumption is that foreign project funding ultimately crowds out domestic investment at the margin. However, under the reasonable assumption that the project is small relative to international capital markets, then the addition of the new investment opportunity will not alter the attractiveness of other domestic opportunities and they will not be crowded out, but total inflows and investment will increase.

Note that this result can obtain even if the initial source of investment is domestic. With a small project and open capital markets, the government creates a new investment opportunity yielding more than the world rate. If a domestic investor takes advantage of this in the first round, the marginal project will not be crowded out, but financed by an inflow of foreign funds, since it still lies above the preexisting world cutoff rate of return. This possibility—open capital markets—probably constitutes the strongest case for a low value of λ_p.

Conclusions

In the last few years, privatization has become the dominant theme of the public enterprise literature, just as deregulation has become the main subject in the literature on government regulation. What deregulation has been for the United States, privatization has been for the United Kingdom: an indicator of political shifts towards the free market and a hope for major improvements in productivity and pricing. From 1979 to 1987, the contribution of public enterprises to GDP in the United Kingdom fell from 11.5 percent to 7.5 percent (Vickers and Yarrow 1988). Deregulation and privatization have stirred a wide international debate about copying the American and British examples, but less has happened in less developed countries (with notable exceptions such as Chile and Mexico). One reason for the reluctance to divest public enterprises may be a misconception in society about the value of public enterprises. Government hesitate to sell public enterprises that make money, while private buyers shy away from the public enterprises that lose money. The normative question addressed in this paper then is: under what circumstances should the government sell a public enterprise to private economic agents and at what price? This question has been answered in a cost-benefit framework.

The same basic framework can be applied to *ex-post* evaluation. Here we shift from the prescriptive task of suggesting what should be done in future privatizations, to the descriptive task of ascertaining what actually happened in past privatizations. At present, divestiture can only be supported or opposed on the basis of ideology, theory, or politics, since there is only the most limited empirical support for either position. Instead, what one finds is little more than elaboration on the following anecdote. Visit a country and be taken to see a "success story" of privatization, where profits have risen dramatically thanks to both lower costs (attributed to more efficient use of all inputs) and higher sales (attributed to improved product quality and marketing). Then visit the opposition and be informed that: "Of course sales rose, because as a side-condition of the sale, a high tariff was imposed on competing imports; and of course, costs fell, because the sale contract included the government's taking over some debt and refinancing the balance at a lower rate." There is presumably some truth to both sides of the story, but how much? We suggest that the analytic framework developed in this chapter can be used to answer this question systematically. The goal is to improve future privatization decisions by an understanding of past decisions, thus further reducing the gap between rhetoric and reality.

References

Beesley, M., and S. Littlechild. 1983. "Privatization: Principles, Problems and Priorities." *Lloyd's Bank Review* (149):1-20.

Browning, E. K. 1987. "On the Marginal Welfare Cost of Taxation." *American Economic Review* 77(1): 11-23.

Domberger, Simon, and John Pigott. 1986. "Privatization Policies and Public Enterprise: A Survey." *The Economic Record* 62(June): 145-162.

Jones, Leroy P., Pankaj Tandon, and Ingo Vogelsang. 1990. *Selling Public Enterprises: A Cost-Benefit Methodology*. Cambridge, Massachusetts: MIT Press.

Littlechild, S.C. 1983. *Regulation and British Telecommunications' Profitability*. Report to the Secretary of State. London: Department of Industry.

Newbery, D., and N. Stern, eds. 1987. *The Theory of Taxation for Developing Countries*. New York: Oxford University Press.

Vickers, J., and G. Yarrow. 1988. *Privatization: An Economic Analysis*. Cambridge, Massachusetts: MIT Press.

Weiss, L., and M. Klass, eds. 1981. *Case Studies in Regulation*. Boston: Little, Brown.

3

A TECHNICAL APPROACH TO PRIVATIZATION ISSUES: COUPLING PROJECT ANALYSIS WITH RULES OF THUMB

Raymond Vernon

Any comprehensive guide to privatization policy must consider many problems, broad and narrow. Some of these were considered in Vernon (1987). Various papers prepared by World Bank staff members have addressed others (see particularly Shirley 1987).

This paper focuses on a comparatively narrow set of issues, namely, those that arise when choosing state-owned enterprises (SOEs) for sale to the public. Specifically, the paper addresses three pivotal questions that arise in connection with such choices: Should the enterprise be sold? To whom should it be sold? At what price should it be sold?

Applying Project Analysis

In the previous chapter three economists describe an approach that allows policymakers systematically to identify many of the key variables involved in addressing these questions (these ideas are presented in detail in Jones and others 1990). One cannot do justice to the scope and subtlety of their presentation in only a few pages, but its overall characteristics are clear. It draws heavily on the familiar concepts and assumptions of standard project analysis; at the same time, it shows marked sensitivity to the behavioral patterns of participants in imperfectly competitive markets.

State-owned enterprises, according to the authors' argument, can be valued in various ways. Two values in particular are critical when attempting to answer the three pivotal questions mentioned earlier.

The social value of the enterprise under continued government operation is one such critical value. The version of social value chosen by the authors is familiar enough to economists. In shorthand, it represents the discounted present value of the firm's real net output over time. This is not a figure that will actually have to be calculated; but it is a concept on which some critical figures that are calculated will depend.

The social value of the enterprise under private operation is a second key value. Once again, this figure need not be actually calculated, even though the concept itself may be critical. The value of the firm under private operation is likely to be different from that under government operation for various reasons. The firm's static efficiency in private hands—as measured by the output it extracts from any given level of inputs—may prove to be higher than if the firm remained in state hands. And the capacity of private management for "dynamic entrepreneurship"— a catch-all term that picks up all the positive features of private ownership that static efficiency does not—could well add to the social yield. Moreover, the private buyers may conceivably extract some changes in the regulatory economic environment from the government that would add further to the real net output of the national economy, such as "getting the prices right," lowering trade barriers, and increasing credit availability.

The difference between these two values, according to the authors, will go a long way toward determining if an enterprise should be privatized. Indeed, if the social value of the firm in private hands would exceed its social value in government hands, the government might be rational if it gave the enterprise away to the private sector, perhaps even paying the private sector to take the enterprise over.

Some governments have already adopted that idea or something like it. The Canadian province of British Columbia, for instance, has given away to its citizens some of the shares representing interests in a commingled pool of its state-owned enterprises. Similarly, various governments have sold state-owned enterprises at prices that obviously grossly understated their value, thus offering a windfall to buyers.

The authors, however, see one more important parameter as essential in determining the difference between the social value of the enterprise in government hands and the social value of the enterprise in private hands, namely, the consequences that flow from the private buyers' paying money to the government in connection with the purchase of the enterprise.

Some extraordinarily complex economic phenomena are associated with the private sector's passing over its funds to the public sector. For one thing, determining the amount of such funds may be complex in itself, inasmuch as buyers are sometimes helped to make their stock purchases through deferred payments or loans by public agencies. For another, the effects may be quite different and their consequences difficult to determine, depending on whether a given transaction is considered in isolation or as part of a larger program of divestiture. As part of a program, the stock purchases may generate some "crowding out" of other capital needs in the country, creating a dearth of funds available to the private sector itself. That, indeed, was a major problem in some of Chile's privatization efforts, which led to the bankruptcy of many of the very enterprises that had been sold to the private sector. (The government may, however, use its windfall income to retire some of its own debt, thereby releasing new funds to the private sector that could offset the crowding out effect.) Moreover, some funds may be drawn in from foreign sources, representing capital previously shipped abroad; and as these funds pass across the exchanges, they may alter exchange rates, interest rates, and money supply. Accordingly, instead of having to wrestle with a crowding out problem, the government may find itself threatened by an expanding monetary base, with uncertain repercussions.

In a giant intuitive leap, the authors venture the guess that the consequences of the transfer will be positive, that is, that the added funds in government hands will generate higher social value than if those funds had remained in private hands. Their case on that point is undocumented and unpersuasive; but no one can doubt that the transfer of funds will have some effect, whether positive or negative, and that the effect should be taken into account when calculating the difference between the two critical social values.

Once the analyst makes guesses as to the direction and size of the transfer effect, it becomes possible to determine the lowest sale price that would make the social value of the enterprise in private hands higher than that in public hands. (Note that theoretically the answer could even be zero or negative, indicating that the best alternative may be to give the enterprise away.)

Before offering the equity of a state-owned enterprise for sale, however, the analyst must estimate another price, namely, *the highest price that a private buyer would pay for the enterprise.* If a sale is to be consummated, the state's offer price cannot exceed that figure; if it does, no transaction will take place.

In calculating their highest acceptable price, private buyers will be concerned with the firm's private value rather than social value. The enterprise's private value is determined by its capacity to earn a profit for the owners as measured by nominal prices, that is, the prices actually prevailing in the economy. That figure departs from the enterprise's social value in two basic respects. Social value measures the value of the net output of the enterprise in so-called "real" terms, that is, by its opportunity cost or by world prices. It measures such value from the viewpoint of society as a whole, irrespective of whether the surplus is captured by the owners, the tax collectors, the labor force, subsidized consumers, or bribe-taking officials.

Because nominal profits determine the value of the enterprise to private buyers, different buyers will place different values on the enterprise. For instance, private firms that had been in competition with the state-owned enterprise would have an incentive to buy the enterprise to acquire a monopoly position, whereas other private buyers would be unable to count on adding to their monopolistic rents. In the same vein, private firms with taxable profits would place some value on the right to offset those profits with the losses of the state-owned enterprise, thereby reducing their tax liabilities. Similarly, private buyers who think they will be able to increase the enterprise's efficiency—say, by sharply reducing the workforce—will be willing to pay more than the private buyers who have no intention of taking on that challenge.

The authors make the important point that any government, if guided by the criteria that the authors have developed, would not necessarily sell to the highest bidder. This is so because the different private buyers will not only place a different private value on the enterprise, but will also pursue different firm policies, thus generating a different social value for the firm. The monopolist will charge different prices than the competing firm. The private owner who is in a position to reduce the tax burden through the acquisition of the state-owned enterprise will transfer a different amount of funds to the state than the private owner who is not in such a position. And the private owner who is prepared to reduce the labor force of the acquired firm will generate a different level of efficiency, a different wage bill, and a different stream of tax payments than the private owner who is not so prepared. All these differences would figure not only in the price that the buyer would be willing to pay, but also in the social value of the enterprise in private hands. Accordingly, the highest bid might not be the best bid from the government's viewpoint.

This brief summary barely does justice to the authors' detailed presentation of their case, which deals with many other issues, including oligopoly (a far more complex and more typical case than monopoly), vertical and horizontal integration, problems of shadow pricing, of job rationing and product rationing, and various other issues that are endemic to the markets of developing countries. Acutely sensitive to the costs and difficulties of making the necessary computations in individual cases, they strive for shortcuts and simplifications, looking always to shed the factors that are unimportant in determining the outcome.

The results that the authors get in applying their method to an actual case are not surprising, and are therefore reassuring about the general good sense of the underlying approach. In the selected case, sensitivity tests identify the main factors that principally influence the size of the social gains from privatization. The factor that is most sensitive in increasing such gains is the size of the increase in productivity that the authors associate with private ownership, and the factor that is most sensitive in reducing such gains is the prospective growth in demand for the enterprise's product.

The Gap Between Theory and Application

The foregoing concepts are likely to prove useful for policymakers who are addressing the three questions formulated at the beginning of this paper. However, before they can make the approach operational, they must take some added factors into account.

Transaction Costs

The first factor is the cost of application of the concepts. If the costs refer only to computational costs, the problem might not be too formidable. The authors' ideas, combined with some uninhibited guesses, might generate a stripped-down, standardized set of calculations that in many cases policymakers could apply to the available data.

The more forbidding problem of costs, however, stems from the fact that when governments execute privatization policies on a case-by-case basis, the kinds of judgments required demand the time and attention of two sorts of people whose availability cannot be assured and whose time is scarce—highly skilled analysts and busy ministers. Any privatization exercise based on rational criteria that proceeds on a case-by-case basis demands analysts whose knowledge of the public and private sectors (including in the latter both domestic and foreign possibilities) is sufficient to make informed judgments on the alternatives available and on the value of the critical parameters. Remember that these parameters include such slippery estimates as the private value of the enterprise to the prospective private buyer, the likely efficiency consequences of private ownership, the likely demand consequences, and so on—estimates that imply knowledge and judgment of a sort not ordinarily available.

That problem may be less important than the ineluctable fact that a program of case-by-case privatization is invariably a highly politicized process that demands the time and attention of ministers. Some privatization transactions require statutory amendments. Some require the government to override the opposition of important stakeholders in the existing operation, such as labor unions worried about job tenure, consumers concerned about losing a subsidy, and suppliers fearful of losing a market. Moreover, an exploration of alternatives involves possibilities that are inescapably political, such as the possibility of liquidating the enterprise, relieving it of some of its debt, assuming some of its pension obligations, modifying some of the regulatory requirements that affect it, and so on.

Because such cases demand political attention over sustained periods, and because politicians' time, if available at all, is tightly rationed, privatization cases have to be limited to a handful, and that handful really must matter in terms of the objectives sought.

Governments are not insensitive to this critical point. Those that have been serious about privatization have as a rule limited their attention to just a few enterprises. One or two exceptions exist to be sure: Chile and Bangladesh have privatized a considerable number of enterprises, for example. In the Chilean case, the broadside approach produced a chain of unintended adverse consequences, such as the creation of many new monopolies and the development of a string of bankruptcies (Marshall and

Montt n.d.). In the case of Bangladesh, the program consisted of reprivatizations for the most part—a return of nationalized enterprises to previous owners. The programs have been based on faith rather than reason; faith in the idea that the country's social welfare would be well served by the return. Based on the criteria outlined earlier, some of those reprivatized enterprises will probably rise in their social value as a result of privatization, while others' social value might be reduced. Candidates for the latter category, for instance, would be cases that reestablished private monopolies and cases that provided a large windfall profit to the restored private owner. Where governmental programs proceed based on faith, the analyst's contribution is bound to be of secondary importance.

The issue of transaction costs does not greatly reduce the value of the analytical approach described earlier. It does mean, however, that governments will have to target the approach to a relatively small group of promising cases at best, and that they will have to develop some rule-of-thumb, easy-to-apply criteria to identify what that group may be.

The Rational Unitary State

Another problem that analysts must confront is the danger of assuming that the state employs a single set of criteria by which it evaluates an enterprise's social value. That assumption is very weak. Indeed, the internal differences within governments about what constitutes social value may represent the crux of the problem in privatization decisions.

One dimension of that problem is the income distribution effects of any proposed privatization. The income effects might be viewed by some as enhancing the enterprise's social value and viewed by others as reducing its social value.

Without addressing particular cases, generalizing about the income distribution effects of the operations of state-owned enterprises is dangerous. In some instances, those enterprises follow policies that favor the urban rich at the expense of the rural poor, and that favor well-to-do industrial workers at the expense of the taxpaying public. Nevertheless, at times, people see privatization projects as a threat to the poor, because they presage increased prices for buses, food, or electric power.

The methodology described earlier does not cover the issue of income distribution effects as they bear on an enterprise's social value. To bring such effects into the calculation in terms consistent with the methodology would require the development of some kind of formal trade-off function, such that a given shift in the distribution of income would be construed to affect aggregate social value in some specified way. But trade-off functions of that sort are usually so arbitrary, so mechanistic, and so unsubtle as to capture very little of the social value implications as seen by the disputants.

A second respect in which the rational unitary state assumption proves unsatisfying is in calculating the added value to society of the funds shifted from the private sector to the state. In most states, the use of the added funds transferred from the private sector is determined by a struggle among groups that have noncommensurate values, or that have different perceptions of the likely future consequences of any given course of action, or both. In cases of partial divestiture, for instance, some government ministers may be entertaining a totally different concept of the likely future steps in the process than other ministers. Some ministers may see the undertaking as the first step in a process that will eventually place control in the hands of the private sector. But other ministers will see the partial divestiture as nothing more than a way to provide the state-owned enterprise with added funds to replace the capital that the enterprise had previously drawn on, namely, capital provided by the government budget, the domestic financial intermediaries, and the foreign banks. For the latter group of decisionmakers, the divestiture will represent a measure aimed at preserving or extending the role of the state-owned sector, not a measure for curtailing it. Indeed, such an interpretation would not be wholly inconsistent with the visible facts, inasmuch as the first step would entail a shift in resources from the private to the public sector.

Unresolved differences about the ultimate purpose of the privatization exercise need not represent a challenge to the validity of the proposed measures described in the first section of this paper. But they do pose a challenge to analysts attempting to assess the future implications of a partial divestiture operation—an assessment that is required in any application of the proposed methodology. The odds are that the two different perceptions of goals, sitting side-by-side and unresolved in the government, would produce widely different expectations of future outcomes.

As it turns out, a high proportion of proposed privatization undertakings for large enterprises consist of partial divestitures; and many of these contemplate no significant shifts in management personnel, management practices, or government regulation. In such cases, partial divestitures could conceivably increase productivity through three possible routes: by providing the state-owned enterprises with added resources whose marginal yield is relatively high, such as working capital to finance the purchase of spare parts; by creating a group of shareholders whose demands would stir management to a higher level of performance; and by creating a political force that could help to persuade the government to relieve the enterprise of onerous, efficiency-destroying regulations. But in the circumstances encountered in most developing countries, none of these routes to increased efficiency offers much promise. The idea that public stockholders might stimulate managers' performance seems especially implausible.

The more general difficulty that these partial divestitures create for the analysts is that they confuse the otherwise clear dichotomy between the public and the private sectors. As a first approximation, analysts can assume that privately-owned enterprises are seeking to maximize their profits at some chosen level of risk; they can plausibly assume—although many people are likely to challenge the assumption—that a state-owned enterprise is trying to maximize some objective function of the state. But what objective function can a mixed enterprise have? Neither the profit-maximizing private enterprise nor the enterprise owned by the rational unitary state offers much of a model for formulating behavioral assumptions. This is virtually unexplored territory for economic analysts, a fact that threatens the utility of the approach described earlier, at least in its present form.

The Time Factor

Time plays a heavy role in the decisions of most governments engaged in privatization exercises, a role not adequately recognized in the approach described above.

Governments badly strapped for cash are likely to place a very heavy discount on future benefits, discounts unrelated in size to any economist's estimates of a justifiable time-discounting factor. The reason is obvious. Governments often see an acute shortage of cash as a threat to continued political control, a threat to be overcome at all odds. "Outside" analysts may be entitled to disregard that fact; but "inside" analysts may have to be responsive to it. Perhaps outside analysts need do no more in this case than be aware that the objective function they have assumed for the government often does not reflect the government's values, and would probably be rejected if it were made explicit.

Time plays another important role in governmental choices. Once the public is aware that its government has targeted a particular state-owned enterprise for divestiture, the government acquires a new and compelling objective: to ensure that the divestiture will "succeed," that is, to ensure that the shares offered for sale will in fact be bought. This compelling need can be explained in two rather different ways: that an uncompleted sale will be interpreted as a "failure" of government, a sign of poor planning and poor management; or that the success of the privatization program over the long term depends on providing a windfall to buyers in the early offerings. My own view is that the first of these propositions is usually the principal motivation for underpricing.

In any event, the result has been that governments have systematically offered shares at prices that were substantially lower than the public was prepared to pay, and have found ways of rationing those shares to lucky buyers. One ironic aspect of this tendency is that it has sometimes overridden and defeated the government's original purpose in undertaking a privatization exercise, namely, that of staunching or reversing an adverse cash flow. The tendency has had other consequences as well. It has, for instance, affected the social value of the enterprise as a private undertaking as well as the sale's income redistributing effects.

This is not to imply that sales of the equity of state-owned enterprises at depressed prices are always worse than no sale at all. The contrary may well be closer to the truth, and the decision rules suggested by the methodology described earlier may well have indicated as much. Nevertheless, any realistic program of state divestiture must take into account the compelling power of the government's urge to "succeed."

The Foreign Buyer

A bid by a foreign buyer to purchase the shares of a state-owned enterprise entails added considerations not encountered when the bid is from domestic sources. Some of these differences are political, created by government policies, and some are economic, generated by the characteristics of foreign exchange markets and product markets typical of developing countries. For example, when foreigners earn supernormal profits as a result of monopoly or of the government's protectionist policies, that condition will affect the size of the servicing outflow that will subsequently occur. Whereas supernormal profits may simply represent an internal transfer of funds when they accrue to domestic investors, they will represent a real drain when earned by foreigners. If, in addition, the government maintains an overvalued exchange rate, the problem of foreigners' remissions will be exacerbated even further. (Of course, domestic investors who enjoy a monopoly rent may also be responsible for an enlarged subsequent outflow if they systematically diversify their savings portfolios into foreign currencies.)

In any event, most countries' plans allow for some buying by foreigners—a possibility somewhat enlarged by the various debt-equity swap schemes that several Latin American countries are promoting. Accordingly, a workable divestiture plan should offer some guidelines on the second-best policies that may be required to deal with such issues.

Exercises in policy choice, irrespective of the degree of their sophistication, always entail some implicit or explicit assumptions about the counterfactual case, that is, assumptions about what would happen if the proposed action were not adopted. The difference between what would happen with the proposed measure and what would happen without it determines whether the proposed action is worth taking. In some situations, one can make a plausible pass at describing the difference between the proposed action and the counterfactual case; but in others, the difference almost defies formal description.

So it is with the effects of foreign direct investment in many developing countries. Such investment can conceivably be the key to securing proprietary technology or gaining access to foreign markets; but it can also dampen such efforts on the part of nationals. Such investment can also significantly alter the money supply, interest rates and exchange rates, as can the subsequent servicing of such investment. Chile's recurrent worries about the effects of its swap deals on the domestic money supply are a case in point. Because of the complexity and uncertainty of the consequences of foreign direct investment, any formal counterfactual assumptions built into the model in this instance would probably be thinly justified and intuitively unpersuasive. This is a case, therefore, in which a shrewd guess is likely to serve at least as well as a formal model.

Guesses, Shrewd and Otherwise

What analysts and politicians need most of all is a crude scanning device, readily implemented, that will permit them to concentrate on the cases that offer promise of the largest salutary change. For that purpose, a single ranking measure, such as the difference between social value in private hands and social value in public hands, is likely to prove inferior to rankings on a number of different dimensions, rankings they can scan and weigh even in the absence of explicit additivity rules. The list that I find useful for this purpose reflects a multivalent approach to the choice of projects; one that acknowledges not only the relevance of expanding output through static efficiency increases and dynamic developments, but also the relevance of income distribution effects and cash generating effects.

The Static Efficiency Criterion

The object is to identify those cases in which static efficiency changes can produce the largest increase in the firm's output. Obviously any ranking of cases is bound to be highly subjective, because it depends on so many idiosyncratic factors. However, large firms are likely to produce more significant changes than small firms; and firms with internal processes that require difficult coordination, such as steel mills, are more likely to produce such results than firms with tightly packaged processes, such as hydroelectric power plants. Beyond such obvious criteria, the following illustrations, which are based on soft evidence from many different sources, may begin to provide a calibrating mechanism:

1. Some prospective privatization undertakings envisage no changes in management policies, in the structure of national markets, or in government regulations affecting those markets, as when the government proposes merely to sell off a minority interest in a natural monopoly such as a public utility. In that case, one possible source of increased efficiency may be the added capital provided by the private sector, assuming that the capital is in fact allocated to the plant and would not otherwise be available. If, for instance, a lack of working capital or inadequate plant size had been handicaps to achieving a high level of efficiency, such added capital could conceivably raise efficiency. On the whole, however, projects of this sort are not promising candidates for large efficiency increases.

2. Some privatization undertakings envisage a change in the enterprise's management from public to private managers, while leaving the enterprise's monopoly position in local markets unaffected. This will occur, for instance, in the case of large enterprises that dominate the import-substituting industries of a developing country. In that case, efficiency increases will likely depend principally on the strength of the private managers' incentives for cutting costs. These in turn will depend on two factors: the nature of the market that the private firm confronts, and the nature of the regulatory pressures to which the firm is exposed. For instance, the incentive to cut costs will not be very strong if price changes can easily be passed on to buyers, as in the case of intermediate products. Nor will it be strong if the firm can easily influence the regulatory authority. In such cases, the expectation of efficiency increase may still be stronger than in the first group of cases, but not substantially so.

3. In some instances, the privatization project contemplates not only a change in management, but concurrently, the end of a monopoly position for the state-owned enterprise and a shift to private competitive markets. Such cases usually offer greater promise of efficiency increases than cases 1 and 2.

4. The final case is that of the state-owned enterprise that has been operating in competitive markets, whether domestic or international. If the enterprise has been performing about as well as the domestic enterprises against which it has been pitted, the possibility of efficiency increases is presumptively not very high. If, however, the enterprise has been performing less well, the opportunity for efficiency increases may be as attractive as the cases mentioned in 3 above.

Obviously, the cases cited above do not represent all the available possibilities and are intended simply to illustrate the principal factors that are likely to provide a basis for an ordinal ranking. The underlying factors that have produced the relative rankings (changes in scale, shifts in management, changes in the structure of markets, and changes in government regulation), will be present in different combinations and will carry different weights. But a crude ordinal ranking for a limited number of large enterprises is likely to be possible.

Augmenting the Stock of Productive Resources

The productive resources that policymakers wish to augment, of course, are capital and human resources, notably management. Once again, a precise ranking of enterprises in terms of their likely contributions is infeasible, yet some guides to such a ranking are available.

Where domestic capital is concerned, augmentation will occur through either of two channels: through the importation or repatriation of capital from abroad, or through an increase in domestic savings at the expense of consumption or of capital exports. Not all equity offerings will appeal to the same type of buyer or require the same methods of distribution. Some may attract foreign buyers, some will not. Some may be distributed widely to relatively small purchasers, some to a single buyer. In the short run, these differences are likely to have different implications for domestic saving and for capital imports.

The longer-term effects of any given sale of equity in a state-owned enterprise upon the growth of capital will be harder to track. The problem arises because each sale is likely to have unique effects on efficiency and on income distribution, but the effects will be very complex. Where increases in efficiency are likely, increases in saving and investment are also likely; and where the income to investors can be expected to increase at the expense of households and labor, as through the exercise of monopoly power, a similar shift in saving and investment is likely to take place. But those savings may not remain in the country. Foreign owners may take their earnings home, while domestic owners may diversify their savings by shipping them abroad. In any case, the causal sequences associated with such shifts can be quite attenuated, producing uncertain outcomes. Still, analysts should not give up on the possibility that some crude rankings might be justifiable on this dimension as well.

Whether a given privatization project increases the supply of management in any country depends on the particular circumstances. In most developing countries, a market for managerial talent does not exist. Nevertheless, privatization can augment the national supply of management in at least two ways. When foreigners are allowed to acquire equity in state-owned enterprises, they may bring added management skills and management systems into the country. And when private domestic buyers take over the management of former state-owned enterprises, that step may enlarge the supply of management by ending a mismatch between the country's distribution of physical capital and the distribution of managerial capabilities.

The possibility of ending a mismatch is especially likely in developing countries in which the indigenous private sector has already been gaining strength. As long as the private sector was weak, governments have typically created state-owned enterprises to launch large-scale industrial projects. Over the years, the private business sector in some countries has grown in financial strength and managerial capabilities, reaching the stage in some cases at which its members may be ready to acquire and manage the state-owned enterprises involved (Aylen 1987 stresses this point).

The possibility exists, of course, that the private sector's acquisition of a public enterprise may do no more than divert the available managerial resources from one set of enterprises to another. The increase in managerial opportunities and compensation, however, should enhance the supply where a market for managers has begun to appear. Besides, the private managerial groups that have established themselves in developing countries such as Brazil, Korea, India, and Mexico frequently operate with some slack and with some capability to expand their managerial activities.

Here again, analysts will have an opportunity for a crude classification of privatization projects based on their analysis of the enlargement of the supply of management.

Income Distribution Effects

Different privatization projects are likely to affect the distribution of income in quite different ways, in terms of both magnitude and direction State-owned enterprises that were buying their inputs and selling their outputs in competitive markets and were making an adequate profit will presumably continue to do so, thus their privatization will have little effect on the distribution of income. As a rule, however, the transition from state ownership to private ownership will be accompanied by some implicit or explicit changes in the conditions under which the firm acquires its inputs or sells its outputs, as well as changes associated with some relaxation of governmental policies relating to the firm's behavior. Once privatized, for instance, firms may be permitted to reduce their labor force, hold down wages, and increase prices.

Changes in governmental policies such as these may well be salutary, contributing to objectives already mentioned, such as an increase in static efficiency and an increase in productive resources; and in principle, analysts will already have taken such salutary consequences into account in the process of rating each project under each of those objectives. But the same changes will also affect the distribution of income, which presumably the country will wish to consider separately.

In some cases, the rankings generated by considering the relative income effects from privatizing given state-owned enterprises may point the decisionmaker in the same direction as the rankings generated by the efficiency factor and the resource augmentation factor. However, the various measures relating to a given state-owned enterprise under consideration for privatization could provide conflicting signals to decisionmakers, requiring tradeoffs of one factor against another. I have no advice to offer on how that tradeoff function should be constructed. It is likely to prove highly sensitive, in any case, to the conditions prevailing in each country at a given time. But an explicit effort to marshall such ratings for a limited number of large firms should provide rich insights into the likely consequences of any given choice.

Short-Term Effects on Cash Flows to Government

When choosing enterprises for privatization, the short-run cash-flow effects may be thought of either as an objective or as a constraint. From the viewpoint of governments, they are likely to be seen as an objective; from the viewpoint of others, as a constraint. Note that those short-term cash flow effects can have consequences for both the efficiency objective and the resource augmentation objective, inasmuch as they represent the extent to which the government will have captured savings from the private domestic sector and drawn in the savings of foreigners in the process of selling the equity of a given state-owned enterprise. These same data will in any event have some considerable value in estimating whether the privatization process is likely to create some short-term monetary problems that require managing, such as the crowding out of the private sector or the expansion of the monetary base.

Technically, the challenge is to estimate the short-term cash flow effects of each possible transaction, net of the flows that would have occurred if the equity or assets of the enterprise had remained in the public sector. Elements in the calculation include the sale price of the equity or assets, less the cash costs of preparing the enterprise or assets for sale, less the transaction costs, less the consideration received in forms other than cash (such as loans by the government to purchasers).

Remember that these same transactions will have medium-term and long-term effects as well, effects that result from changes in efficiency, in resource augmentation, and in income distribution. Eventually, those effects may prove more important for the government's cash flow position than the short-run effects. However, they are likely to be so complex and uncertain in size and direction, and so remote from the considerations of government officials, that for analysts to devote much time to their analysis will prove unprofitable.

Conclusions

The available data on state-owned enterprises do not conclusively demonstrate the validity of any sweeping generalizations about such enterprises, whether in terms of efficiency, resource augmentation, or income distribution. As a class, state-owned enterprises tend to be associated with negative cash flows to the public sector, at least as compared with private enterprises in similar fields. But these negative cash flows are due in part to policies on inputs and outputs that are the economic equivalent of transfer payments, such as the hiring of excess labor. Although in some cases, such negative cash flows may also be due to a lower level of efficiency than that of private enterprises performing the same business functions in the economy, the character and extent of those differences are not well documented. The income redistributing effects of the transfer payments are also not subject to easy generalization. Sometimes they appear to be egalitarian in direction; but at times they may penalize a poor agricultural sector in favor of an urban middle or upper class.

Accordingly, the economic basis for widespread programs of privatization, which ordinarily rests heavily on assumptions about efficiency, is not yet firmly developed. The transfer payment policies that many developing countries pursue through state-owned enterprises are probably quite uneconomic in many instances; but that issue could be addressed independently of the ownership issues.

If there is no solid basis for pressing for an unselective program of privatization, neither is there a basis for resisting such a program where governments are convinced that it is desirable. One danger in instituting such a program is the threat of high transaction costs, particularly costs in the form of the attention that such programs can demand from high-level policymakers and analysts. But there are ways to minimize those costs.

One approach is to refuse to address the three questions with which this paper began. Governments that are prepared to base their privatization programs on general conviction, for instance, could refuse to choose selectively among enterprises, could give away the shares by lottery or by per capita distribution rather than sell them, and could rely on the chance nature of the distribution or on various screening devices (supplemented perhaps by antitrust legislation) to avoid the risk that private monopolies might acquire an unwanted dominant position as a result of the distribution of the shares. Such policies would not transfer cash to the government sector, but a government that was sufficiently convinced of the superiority of private ownership to accept a nonselective program of privatization would presumably not see any great merit in capturing large dollops of the private sector's savings.

For governments that were unprepared to take such a broadside approach and eager to weed out selectively the state-owned enterprises whose privatization would serve their goals, some of the candidates for privatization might prove so obvious as to require no analysis. Some governments are so incapable of providing for the efficient management of their enterprises, and some enterprises are so notorious for their inefficiency, that almost any alternative to state ownership would be superior. Given the costs of analysis and the limits of its results, overintellectualizing the process of choice could be unwise.

Beyond such obvious cases, if a process of case-by-case selection is inescapable, the main drive should be to narrow the range of cases for analysis as rapidly and inexpensively as possible. In that case, the categories that are likely to be least promising are monopolistic enterprises that sell their products or services on domestic markets, and that use technologies that make few demands on management. Those that are likely to emerge at the top of the priority list are relatively large state-owned enterprises that are operating poorly in competitive markets when compared with private firms in the same markets. Such enterprises may merit the detailed level of scrutiny suggested in this discussion.

References

Aylen, Jonathan. 1987. "Privatization in Developing Countries." *Lloyd's Bank Review* 163 (January):15-30.

Jones, Leroy P., Pankaj Tandon, and Ingo Vogelsang. 1990. *Selling Public Enterprises: A Cost-Benefit Methodology.* Cambridge, Massachusetts: MIT Press.

Marshall, Jorge, and Felipe Montt. n.d. "Privatization in Chile." Draft.

Shirley, Mary M. 1987. "Bank Lending for State-Owned Enterprises." Washington, D.C.: World Bank. Draft.

Vernon, Raymond. 1987. *Economic Criteria for Privatization.* Washington, D.C.: Economic Development Institute of the World Bank.

4

ON MEASURING THE SUCCESS
OF PRIVATIZATION

Yair Aharoni

This chapter examines possible yardsticks for measuring the success of privatization in mixed economies with democratic political systems. Much of the work economists have done on privatization assumes that the goal of privatization is improved efficiency (for example, Bos 1987) or social welfare (Jones and others 1990). The main point of this chapter, however, is that the success of any privatization program can only be measured in terms of the objectives that motivated it, and that those objectives are likely to be different for different actors affected by privatization. Therefore, judging the success of any privatization program is likely to be difficult unless there happens to be a consensus in society about the goals prompting that program, which is highly unlikely, or unless one imposes one's own criteria for evaluation, as economists frequently tend to do. Thus, privatization has been and is likely to remain a controversial policy issue whose merits policymakers cannot easily evaluate.

Nevertheless, policymakers can benefit from an improved understanding of how different actors are likely to see the issues surrounding privatization. In any given situation, the relative power of these actors is likely to determine which objectives will in fact be paramount, and which will merely receive lip service or be overlooked altogether. That, in turn, is likely to affect the manner in which privatization will be implemented.

Governments of at least 50 countries from all points along the political spectrum have announced programs to sell their state-owned enterprises (SOEs) to private citizens (Commander and Killick 1988). Rolling back the boundaries of the public sector has become very popular politically. The World Bank and IMF have also encouraged announcements of privatization (see, for instance, Hemming and Mansoor 1988; Nellis 1986).

An optimal policy of privatization must consider several issues. Which types of SOEs should be privatized? When should they be privatized? How should the privatization program be carried out, for example, to whom should SOEs be sold and at what price? The answers to questions of this sort depend on the objectives of the divestiture. To say that the success of privatization can be judged by the extent to which it improves the performance of an SOE begs the question, what does "good performance" mean? Any attempt to define performance takes us back to a discussion of the underlying objectives of privatization (Aharoni 1988b).

Objectives as Seen by Different Actors

We noted earlier that different actors are likely to view the objectives of privatization differently. We focus below on how economists, politicians, civil servants, SOE managers, and a few others tend to view privatization.

Economists

Economists have influenced the debate on privatization both through their writings on the subject and their participation in international agencies that advise developing countries. The economist's case for privatization usually rests on the expectation that it will enhance efficiency in the supply of a product or service. Privatized firms are expected to be more efficient than state-owned ones (see, for example, Savas 1987).

Gains or losses of efficiency stemming from privatization can be the result of changes in technical efficiency, that is, the minimization of costs for a given level of output; or they can stem from changes in allocative efficiency, evidenced by a closer alignment of prices to long-run marginal costs. Presumably, both kinds of efficiency will improve with privatization. However, an improvement in efficiency is more likely to be the result of a strengthening of the influence of market forces than of a change in ownership as such. Competition can be introduced without privatization, and in many cases privatization does not result in increased competition.

Privatization alone, without the introduction of competition, may simply transform a public monopoly into a private monopoly. The privatized firm may pursue profits more vigorously, but that pursuit, if it took the form of increased prices, could worsen allocative efficiency. Moreover, private monopolies may be more formidable defenders of their market power than SOEs. For example, if a developing country privatizes inefficient import substitutors without first reducing the level of protection from import competition, it might find itself unable to lower protection later on. In Chile's case, the government sharply reduced tariffs at the time of the first privatization program, but several privatized firms went bankrupt and the public sector had to reabsorb others. In short, a change of ownership without a change in market structure may not improve efficiency (see Aharoni 1986; Domberger and Piggott 1986; Millward 1988; Pryke 1981; Yarrow 1986).

Some economists see other benefits ensuing from privatization. Among them is the opportunity that privatization offers to depoliticize economic decisionmaking. Many assert that the depoliticization of decisionmaking and the improved efficiency resulting from privatization will enable governments to reduce public outlays, cut taxes, reduce budget deficits, and shrink public sector borrowing. In addition, they expect privatization to increase government receipts through the sale of assets. Finally, they see the removal of a certain enterprise or service from government responsibilities as a way to reduce the monopoly power of unions, which tend to be especially strong in state-owned enterprises.

However, the objective evidence on the comparative performance of the public and private sectors presents no clear picture in support of such expectations. On the contrary, as asserted earlier, the strength of competitive forces seems to be a more important determinant of efficiency than ownership. Thus, if the success of privatization is judged by its effect on efficiency, the critical consideration may be the extent to which the privatization exercise changes market structure.

The inclination of many economists to believe that the private sector is more efficient than the public may stem from the assumption of "economic man" that underlies mainstream economic theory. According to this view, self-interest dominates in each individual whenever that interest is at variance with the interest of a group to which the individual belongs. Given this assumption, it follows that SOE managers are likely to maximize their own interests rather than those of the government. Thus, unless they are constrained, SOE managers may maximize output and growth rather than efficiency and profits to increase their bureaucratic rewards, or may maximize side payments to themselves (see, for example, 1981). Furthermore, governments are poorly equipped to prevent managers from exercising this kind of managerial discretion because their access to the relevant information is characteristically limited. Nor can the owners (that is, the public at large) exercise effective control. The usual limitations on the effectiveness of owners are exacerbated by the fact that the public does not actually hold shares in SOEs and cannot register disapproval by selling them. Thus, the costs of contracting, negotiating, and enforcing property rights are high and the firm becomes inefficient because the principal-agent relationships are particularly difficult to structure (see Rees 1984, 1989).

While this line of reasoning has some merit, it fails to address how a change of ownership would make managers more accountable to their owners. One might argue that the presence of private shareholders would alter managers' incentives, but where the enterprise is a monopoly, the problem of asymmetrical access to information is likely to persist, irrespective of ownership. Moreover, the threat that a government minister can exercise against a public monopoly, weak though it may be, is likely to be stronger than the threat of stockholders in a private monopoly. Nor need the managers of private monopolies worry about takeover bids. The capital market in most developing countries is in its infancy and takeover bids are not carried out easily. Thus, when SOEs have high market power, it is not evident that privatization will achieve the goal of improved efficiency.

Politicians

From the economist's viewpoint, political factors represent a constraint that must be overcome to achieve economic efficiency. For the politician, the prospective political gains are the objectives, not the constraints, of a privatization exercise.

From a politician's standpoint, the success of privatization may be measured by which political groups gained and which lost. Privatization, it has been observed, is "substantially driven by attempts to capture and preserve rents, not by a concern for the abstract concept of efficiency" (Chamberlain and Jackson 1987, p. 589). Active debates on privatization will be concentrated "where there is the largest potential for creating, dissipating, or redistributing rents" (Chamberlain and Jackson, 1987, p. 590). Rent may be pecuniary in form, but it may also take the form of power and prestige. It might also be measured by the ability to change an entrenched class structure or to develop a new business class that is beholden to the regime in power. Marxists sometimes explain in these terms the widespread privatization of state enterprises in 19th century Japan that led to the creation of the zaibatsu. Further, privatization may make political sense if the reasons that led to nationalization no longer appear valid. Holter (1982, p. 370) talks of nationalization as a tool to "revive a faltering capitalist economy" in which "the state functions both as a crisis solver and as a regulator between capitalist interests." When conditions in the private sector change and the underlying crisis has been solved, privatization may appear to be the appropriate course. In any event, the politician's motives in promoting and evaluating privatization prove to be profoundly different from those of the economist.

In the current wave of privatization, politicians have generally emphasized two different objectives: first, the promotion of popular capitalism through a wider ownership of shares; and second, a diminution of the power of trade unions in the public sector. In countries like the United Kingdom, both of these objectives were designed to strengthen the Conservative Party at the expense of Labor and the Social Democrats (Aharoni 1988a). In the case of Chile, however, some observers attributed the extensive privatizations of the 1970s to the government's desire to reward those groups—largely groups from the middle and upper classes—that helped bring it to power.

Politicians also think that minimizing the negative political repercussions of privatization is important. The British government would have liked to privatize the electricity industry without abandoning its commitment to nuclear energy and without imposing severe burdens on British Coal, which was selling its coal to the state-owned electric utility at prices well above world levels. To achieve these two secondary objectives, the government proposes to limit competition in coal and electricity even after these are privatized. For an economist, such a result is suboptimal. For the politician, it is what makes privatization feasible. Selling shares of SOEs to foreign citizens is another example of a situation that economists may welcome if it facilitates privatization, but that politicians may frown upon.

Partially as a result of citizens' growing resistance to increased tax burdens, privatization has become a politically attractive way to reduce budget deficits. Committed socialists have finally learned that to protect the public interest the state does not have to own all the shares of an SOE. Therefore, they have not resisted the idea of selling minority interests in SOEs to the private sector.

Another method for retaining control without 100 percent ownership has been to require that a designated number of directors be nominated by the government irrespective of the size of the government's equity. That was the technique the U.S. administration used when it caused the formation of Communications Satellite Corporation (COMSAT). A third method is to retain a "golden share" in the privatized firm as the U.K. government has done.

Civil Servants

On the one hand, civil servants may resist privatization because it threatens to shrink their power base by reducing the resources under their command. On the other hand, they may welcome it for several reasons. For one thing, privatization may make cutting subsidies or raising prices for products such as electricity, water, or telephone services easier, thereby freeing fiscal resources for other purposes. Civil servants may also welcome the fact that managerial discretion will be more tightly curbed under private ownership than under government ownership; among other things, the firm's financial discipline may improve after privatization. Civil servants may also weigh the benefits stemming from a reduction in the time spent monitoring the performance of SOEs and in the budgetary costs allocated to cover their losses. In some countries the overloading of the monitoring capacity is a convincing argument for selling small SOEs, even at substantial losses.

Management theorists point out that from the viewpoint of the public, the degree of transparency of the relations between the government and the enterprise is likely to increase dramatically following privatization. Governments often compel SOEs to cross-subsidize services, to be employers of last resort, or to hold price increases in check. When enterprises are publicly owned, such decisions may be made within the bureaucratic network, removed from public scrutiny. Once private shareholders own the firm, decisions such as these may become more exposed. However, such assumptions are highly vulnerable, and depend on the regulatory style of the government concerned.

SOE Managers

Managers are likely to be concerned with a different set of issues associated with privatization. One issue of special interest to them is the likely impact of privatization on their autonomy (Aharoni and Lachman 1982). Managers may feel that operating under the watchful eyes of a ministry constrains them more than managing a firm owned by many shareholders. Managers may also believe that the remuneration paid to them under public ownership is lower than what they would receive under private ownership. Managers are also sometimes presumed to be looking for what Hicks (1935) called the "quiet life," and therefore to be opposed to competition. If that is their objective, they may judge privatization by whether it will change their ability to block the entry of new foreign and domestic competitors. In the British privatization program, for instance, there were signs that the managers of some SOEs tried hard to protect the dominant market positions of their firms as they went through the privatization process.

An alternative view of the value system of managers in the public sector is that they are ideologically committed to public ownership and are motivated by a desire for public service. Although the notion of a public-spirited manager is greeted skeptically in Western economic thinking, the idea has had wide currency at times in the past. Only empirical work, which is scarce at present, can tell us conclusively what motivates public managers. In the interim, a likely safe assumption is that motivations are highly diverse, yet not random. Thus, managers in a defense-related industry operating in a time of crisis may respond more readily to public values than those that produce and sell standard consumer products.

Others

Most privatization projects also affect the interests of other groups in the economy. On the one hand, consumers who are subsidized by the government through the SOE and who expect to lose those subsidies after privatization will see themselves as worse off. On the other hand, privatization may bring lower costs and better service, particularly if it is accompanied by an increase in competition, and in such cases, consumers could benefit.

Labor usually sees itself as especially likely to be affected by privatization. SOEs often pay higher wages and maintain larger work forces than the private sector. Not surprisingly, therefore, the employees of SOEs and their trade unions often oppose privatization.

In addition, suppliers of SOEs frequently see themselves as endangered by privatization. Suppliers often assume that managers of SOEs, preferring the quiet life or being more open to side payments, are less diligent in searching out the cheapest and best sources of supplies than managers of private enterprises.

Another group that may feel imperiled by a proposed privatization is the professional politician. Some political leaders have used SOEs as a source of patronage, wealth, and power. "The role of the state," reports Ghai, "has therefore been to enable groups which have acquired control over the state apparatus to establish an economic base for themselves" (1983, p.182). However, privatization may also be used to confer largesse on those able to buy SOEs at throw-away prices or able to extract policy concessions from the government that generate rents for the enterprise.

Privatization may also be assessed by its impact on the budget. The proceeds of the sale to the private sector improve the government's budget in the short run, unless the government finds itself obliged to invest even more in the SOE before it can arrange a sale. Over the longer term, however, the impact on the budget may be indeterminate or clearly negative. The assets that the government gives up may command a price that is lower than the enterprise's long-term contribution to the budget. By contrast, the transfer of the enterprise to private hands could so increase its efficiency as to enhance its contribution to the government's fiscal resources.

Obviously, disentangling all the impacts of divestiture on public finance is not easy. In addition to these relatively direct effects, one also has to take into account such indirect effects as an increase in the national interest rate resulting from a major privatization program, as well as the impact exercised through changes in savings, investment, and the exchange rate.

The Problem of Aggregating Preferences

The above discussion shows that stakeholders will reach conflicting conclusions about how to evaluate the success of privatization. Estimates based on short-run effects will vary, while those that take the long-term impacts into account will vary even more.

One lesson we can draw from actual cases of large-scale privatization to date—whether in Meiji Japan, in Chile in the 1970s and 1980s, or in the United Kingdom under Prime Minister Thatcher—is that large-scale programs were seldom motivated by a single-minded concern for national economic goals (on the United Kingdom, for instance, see Kay and Thompson 1986; Kay and others 1986). Other goals were also critical, such as a desire to change the social fabric of society, to weaken powerful unions, to protect the economic interests of certain groups, or to develop a professional management class. In each of these cases, improving allocative efficiency was not a major factor. Indeed, in Japan and Chile, privatization created (or restored) a high level of ownership concentration and interconnected family control of enterprises, and did little to promote competition.

Implications for Implementation

The methods chosen to implement a privatization program are also likely to vary according to the objectives motivating the adoption of the program. Thus, if the objective is wide distribution of ownership, the method employed could be a public offering through the facilities of a stock exchange, or possibly off the exchange at a concessional price. In pursuit of widespread distribution, there could be limitations on the number of shares each individual is allowed to acquire, and payments for shares through salary deductions or subsidized credit. If the object of the privatization is to support and encourage an incipient business class, the government may not place any limitation on the number of shares bought by any individual or group, and may sell shares through *ad hoc* negotiations with a small group of prospective buyers.

The government's policies with respect to foreign purchases may also be affected by its objectives. Governments commonly limit the ownership of large enterprises by foreigners, citing such reasons as military security or the protection of national culture. If, however, the government is interested in access to export markets or to foreign technology, it is likely to allow equity ownership by foreign firms.

Governments are often willing to sell noncontrolling interests in key enterprises to the public, while retaining some power to direct the enterprise in public hands. In such cases, the usual objective of selling the shares is to direct private savings to the public domain. Such sales of minority interests in state-owned enterprises usually do not arouse a great deal of opposition. If the government uses these new funds to invest further in SOEs, to reduce the public sector's borrowing requirements, or to reduce income taxes, as has sometimes been the case, it may realize high political gains with very little political costs. At the same time, such undertakings can have some substantial effects on the operations of state-owned enterprises over the longer term. In the case of the United Kingdom, for instance, the steps that state-owned enterprises took in preparation for the public sale of some of their shares produced significant gains in efficiency. Those gains, according to some studies, were of greater importance than the gains following privatization (Yarrow 1986).

Conclusion

Large generalizations about how to evaluate the effects of privatization are likely to prove of only limited value because different stakeholders are likely to be looking for different results from privatization. Thus, any attempt to reach a national consensus on what should constitute a successful privatization in the abstract is likely to fail. The economist's characteristic assumption that the goal of privatization is to improve efficiency is rarely shared by the major stakeholders, and sometimes may not be shared by any of the real players.

Under the circumstances, searching for some degree of consensus at the level of individual SOEs is more useful than searching for general rules applicable to all cases. Therefore, governments are well advised to approach the merits of privatization on a case-by-case basis. For instance, some firms will be seen as gaining from foreign ownership more than others, some may offer greater potential for efficiency improvement than others, and so on. Likewise, some measures of privatization may garner stakeholder support more readily than others. The sale of minority interests in SOEs that enjoy a monopoly position, for instance, is likely to be more acceptable than the sale of controlling interests in such enterprises.

In the end, the largest impact of privatization may come in subtle and indirect ways. For instance, where privatization is widely believed to make a difference, it may prove a self-fulfilling prophecy. The expectations of government agencies, the public, the labor force, and the managers themselves may be altered by the changes in ownership of the enterprises concerned. Those changes in expectations may prove more important in the long run than the measurable economic consequences.

References

Aharoni, Yair. 1986. *The Management and Evolution of State-Owned Enterprises.* Cambridge, Massachusetts: Ballinger.

_____. 1988a. "The United Kingdom: Transforming Attitudes." In Raymond Vernon, ed., *The Promise of Privatization: A Challenge for American Foreign Policy*, pp. 23-56. New York: The Council on Foreign Relations.

_____. 1988b. "Why Do Governments Privatize?" *Technovation* 8(1):7-23.

Aharoni, Yair, and Ran Lachman. 1982. "Can the Manager's Mind be Nationalized?" *Organization Studies* 3(1):33-46.

Bos, Dieter. 1987 "Privatization of Public Enterprises." *European Economic Review* 31(1-2)(Feb.-Mar.):352-360.

Chamberlain, John R., and John E. Jackson. 1987. "Privatization as Institutional Choice." *Journal of Policy Analysis and Management.* 6(4):586-604.

Commander, Simon, and Tony Killick. 1988. "Privatization in Developing Countries: A Survey of the Issues." In Paul Cook and Colin Kirkpatrick, eds., *Privatization in Less Developed Countries*, pp. 91-118. New York: St Martin's Press.

Davies, David G. 1981. "Property Rights and Economic Behavior in Private and Government Enterprises: The Case of Australia's Banking System." *Research in Law and Economics* 3:111-142.

Domberger, Simon, and John Piggott. 1986. "Privatization Policies and Public Enterprise: A Survey." *The Economic Review* 62(117):145-162.

Ghai, Y. P. 1983. "Executive Control Over Public Enterprise in Africa." In R. G. Reddy, ed., *Government and Public Enterprise*, pp. 181-219. London: Frank Cass.

Heald, D. A., and Thomas D. 1986. "Privatization as Theology." *Public Policy and Administration* 1(1):49-66.

Hemming, Richard, and Ali M. Mansoor. 1988. *Privatization and Public Enterprise*. Occasional Paper No. 56. Washington, D.C.: IMF.

Hicks, J. R. 1935. "The Theory of Monopoly," Reprinted in 1983 in *Classics and Moderns*. Cambridge, Massachusetts: Harvard University Press.

Holter, Darryl. 1982. "Mineworkers and Nationalization in France: Insights into the Concept of State Theory." *Politics and Society* 11(1):29-49.

Jones, Leroy P., Pankaj Tandon, and Ingo Vogelsang. 1990. *Selling Public Enterprises: A Cost Benefit Methodology*. Cambridge, Massachusetts: MIT Press.

Kay, J. A., and D. J. Thompson. 1986. "Privatization—A Policy in Search of a Rationale." *Economic Journal* 96(March):18-32.

Kay, John, Colin Mayer, and David Thompson. 1986. *Privatization and Regulation: The U.K. Experience*. Oxford, U.K.: Clarendon Press.

Millward, Robert. 1988. "Measured Sources of Inefficiency in the Performance of Public and Private Enterprises in LDCs." In Paul Cook and Colin Kirkpatrick, eds., *Privatization in Less Developed Countries*. New York: St. Martin's Press.

Nellis, John R. 1986. *Public Enterprises in Sub-Saharan Africa*. Discussion Paper No. 1. Washington, D.C.: World Bank.

Pryke, Richard. 1981. *The Nationalized Industries: Policies and Performance Since 1968*. Oxford, U.K.: Martin Robertson.

Redwood, J., and J. Hatch. 1982. *Controlling Public Industries*. Oxford: Basil Blackwell.

Rees, R. 1984. "A Positive Theory of Public Enterprise." In M. Marchand, D. Pestieau, and H. Tulkens, eds., *The Performance of Public Enterprise.* Amsterdam: North-Holland.

_____. 1989. "Modelling Public Enterprise Performance." In D. R. Helm, J.A. Kay, and D. J. Thompson, eds., *The Market for Energy.* Oxford, U.K.: Oxford University Press.

Savas, E. S. 1987. *Privatization: The Key to Better Government.* Chatham, New Jersey: Chatham House.

Yarrow, G. 1986. "Privatization in Theory and Practice." *Economic Policy* 1(2):322-377.

5

PRIVATIZATION THROUGH PUBLIC OFFERINGS: LESSONS FROM TWO JAMAICAN CASES

Roger Leeds

In December 1986, the Jamaican government privatized 51 percent of the National Commercial Bank (NCB), the country's largest bank. The J$90.6 million (US$16.5 million) public offering, by far the largest of its kind in the nation's history, was 170 percent oversubscribed and attracted more than 30,000 individual applications from Jamaican citizens and institutional investors, including 98 percent of the Bank's own employees.[1] On the first day the stock traded on the Jamaican Stock Exchange, it rose to a 67 percent premium. Prime Minister Edward Seaga described the offering as "a spectacular success [that] marks a milestone in the government's privatization program."[2]

Six months later, the government sold a second state-owned enterprise by public offering, the Caribbean Cement Company (CCC). The CCC divestiture was a far larger transaction, raising almost J$200 million, partly because 100 percent of the company's equity was sold, compared to only 51 percent in the case of NCB. Also, this sale involved a foreign investor. Another significant difference was the result: the offering was undersubscribed, and when the shares opened for trading, the price dropped well below what it had been on the offering date.

The author wishes to acknowledge the support of the United Nations Development Programme, which financed a portion of the research costs of this chapter.

1. US$1.00 = J$5.5 (March 1986), J$5.3 (October 1987).
2. *The Daily Gleaner*, December 6, 1986.

Despite contrasting outcomes, the similarities between the two transactions are more notable than the differences. Moreover, a number of useful lessons emerge for other developing nations that envisage privatization as an important component of their development strategies. Contrary to conventional wisdom, a developing country with a relatively low level of per capita GNP (US$940) had been able to mobilize domestic savings from a broad spectrum of the populace, channel those funds through a small, undeveloped stock market, and shift control of two major state-owned enterprises (SOEs) to the shareholding public. The offerings were politically popular and even enjoyed the support of the two companies' management and staff, who benefited from generous employee purchase schemes.

Given the paucity of successful privatizations in developing countries, empirical evidence on what works and what does not is invaluable to decisionmakers. This case analysis is written with the following questions in mind:

- How are the two cases relevant to other developing country governments contemplating privatization?

- What do the cases suggest for donor agencies, such as the United Nations Development Programme, World Bank, and the U.S. Agency for International Development (USAID), that are recommending privatization as part of a broader structural adjustment program?

- How can developing country governments effectively employ foreign, private advisers to implement privatization schemes?

A caveat about what this chapter is not. The point of departure for the study is after the Jamaican government had decided to privatize particular SOEs. Thus, the chapter does not address the extremely important question of when privatization of an SOE is desirable from an economic, financial, and sociopolitical point of view. Rather, the focus is on implementation, that is, the mechanics and tactics governments use to steer the divestiture process past the many obstacles that commonly render this strategy unworkable.

Background

By the late 1970s, Jamaica had more than 200 state-owned enterprises, not counting an even larger number of statutory bodies and government agencies.[3] Their activities spanned a broad spectrum, ranging from financial services and commodity trading to the production of meat, vegetables, garments, shoes, and furniture. The World Bank (1985) estimated that these enterprises accounted for more than 20 percent of GDP, and by the end of the decade the fiscal deficit had increased to almost 18 percent of GDP, compared to 4 percent in 1971.

Edward Seaga, campaigning against incumbent Prime Minister Michael Manley in 1980, promised to reduce the government's role in the economy and privatize some of the state-owned enterprises. He spoke about creating "a new foundation for Jamaica's economic growth," and reversing what he perceived as the socialist trends of the Manley regime (Cowan 1983, p. 22). Like Prime Minister Margaret Thatcher, he hoped to gain considerable political mileage with privatization by heightening public awareness of the benefits to be derived from creating "a new breed of owners" in the country.

The Government's Approach to Privatization

During the early years of his administration, Seaga experimented with a variety of approaches and employed an array of local and foreign advisers. For example, the government successfully negotiated management contracts that effectively transferred operating control of several major hotels to the private sector, sold about 80,000 acres of government-owned agricultural lands to private holders, leased 59 of the 69 rural agricultural marketing boards to the private sector, contracted street cleaning and garbage collection services for Kingston to private companies, and earmarked some 30 SOEs ranging in size from Air Jamaica to a small spice company for sale or lease. A report presented to the cabinet by Prime Minister Seaga in 1986 listed the following objectives of the privatization program:

---

3. A government study completed in 1982 identified more than 200 public enterprises, about 230 statutory boards, and various other public agencies.

- to improve the efficiency of the economy by placing more productive capacity under private control;
- to develop the local capital market and stimulate "the involvement of a large number of citizens in the free market system";
- to encourage more private investment and reduce the crowding out effects of state ownership;
- to reduce the fiscal deficit;
- to raise foreign exchange in those privatization cases where foreign investors would be permitted to participate.

One close aide to Seaga, reviewing the privatization record of Canada and the United Kingdom, concluded that "the raising of money was not the highest priority." The prime minister's 1986 cabinet submission reflected this sentiment.

By contrast, Seaga's privatization strategy diverged from the approach taken by most other developing countries in one important respect. "It is my firm belief," he explained, "that endless studies and long-term privatization plans dealing in specifics are counterproductive. So far as I am concerned, you must take the best enterprises you have and just do the deed if you want to accomplish objectives such as ours" (speech before the International Democratic Union, Germany, September 24, 1987). The approach to privatization in Jamaica, therefore, would be based on a case-by-case selection of enterprises considered to have a reasonably good chance of attracting buyers from the private sector, rather than an elaborate blueprint that established long-term targets. In the prime minister's view, this latter approach was simply unrealistic.

The Role of External Assistance

The prime minister's objectives were also influenced by the principal development institutions that were active in Jamaica: the International Monetary Fund (IMF), the World Bank, and the U.S. Agency for International Development. All were providing financial assistance to Jamaica and, as a consequence, they hoped that the government would heed their recommendations for policy adjustments.

The preferred approach of the development institutions and the government did not diverge widely. As the World Bank acknowledged: "Since coming to power in October 1980, the present government has been endeavoring to change the policy environment...with the stated aim of reducing the role of the public sector, and creating a framework in which the private sector will develop rapidly." Rather than reluctant participants in an externally orchestrated campaign, the key players were firm believers in free markets and private enterprise.

Nevertheless, the donor agencies were concerned with the pace of change. The staff of the development institutions felt that efforts to reduce the fiscal drain caused by government expenditures on SOEs were progressing too slowly, even though the budget deficit as a percentage of GDP had declined markedly from 16.5 percent in fiscal year 1984 to some 7.8 percent in 1985. As one World Bank official explained: "We were trying to reverse 20 years of ill-advised policies; one component of our new approach was to push privatization." Thus, loan disbursements from the aid agencies became contingent to one extent or another upon the government's progress to reduce the fiscal deficit and implement policies that would stimulate private investment.

USAID also pushed hard for policy adjustments and divestments, but unlike the World Bank, USAID became more directly involved in the effort to privatize SOEs, and insisted that covenants in loan agreements stipulate in detail the steps that the government should take as conditions for disbursement.

Prime Minister Seaga's privatization agenda was similar to USAID's in substance, but more sensitive to the country's political realities. He was particularly concerned that his privatization strategy be able to withstand a barrage of attacks from the political opposition, including the predictable charge that the prime minister was a pawn who was being manipulated by his foreign benefactors. No politician could survive such charges in a country known for deepseated resentment that government policy was too heavily influenced by people and events in Washington, D.C. Therefore, although the prime minister may have agreed with the thrust of USAID's policy prescriptions, he was careful to maintain some distance from the agency.

The Privatization Team

USAID did, however, play a major role in moving the government toward its first privatization by the public offering route. In a decisive turn of events, the local USAID mission in Kingston invited one of the prime minister's key advisors, Richard Downer, to attend a USAID-sponsored conference on privatization in Washington in February 1986. One of the speakers at the conference—John Redwood—was a former member of Prime Minister Margaret Thatcher's privatization team who had recently moved to N.M. Rothschild, a London merchant bank. Downer was so impressed by Redwood that he immediately arranged to meet in London with the public servant turned private banker to discuss whether Rothschild would help the Jamaican government conduct its first public stock offering of an SOE.

The personal chemistry that developed between these two individuals resulted in the formation of the nucleus of a privatization team that became responsible for privatizing NCB and CCC. Ironically, although the assets being sold were government owned, all the key players were from the private sector: the attorneys, the accountants, the investment bankers, and the government's principal advisor. Moreover, all of them had hands on experience in the implementation of other transactions with similar characteristics (for example, actual privatizations, mergers, and acquisitions).

Downer had the personal qualities and professional expertise required to undertake the politically sensitive and technically complicated tasks inherent in implementing major privatization transactions. He was a Jamaican citizen and a senior partner in one of the largest international accounting firms; he had unquestioned professional judgment and skill; by all accounts, his integrity was beyond dispute; during an earlier stint working for the prime minister, he became politically astute and learned to operate quietly behind the scenes; and most important, he enjoyed the complete confidence of the most important actor in the process, the prime minister. This combination of technical competence, political savvy, and integrity were essential for effective leadership of the privatization program.

Joining Downer on the privatization team were the merchant bankers from N.M. Rothschild. Redwood had been Thatcher's principal adviser on privatization, and had been heavily involved in the design and implementation of Britain's privatization strategy since the early 1980s. A second member of the Rothschild team, Oliver Letwin, had also recently joined the merchant bank after serving for a number of years as Redwood's deputy in the Thatcher government.

Thus, the Rothschild team was familiar with the intricacies of preparing documents, orchestrating a major marketing campaign, attending to pertinent legal issues, and determining an appropriate price for a new issue of this type. Their role was to transfer and adapt this vast reservoir of practical and technical knowledge they had acquired from their privatization experience in the United Kingdom. As one member of the Rothschild team explained: "Our role was to take the transaction from theory to practice. We tried to determine what they wanted to achieve, identify the obstacles, and get the deal done."

While Downer provided overall leadership to the effort and served as the public spokesman, the Rothschild team played an indispensable behind-the-scenes role, attending to the myriad technical details associated with bringing an issue to market. As Downer reflected after the NCB privatization: "It makes a big difference to bring in advisers from out-of-town who have the credibility, organizational skills, and technical know-how. Another benefit is that when they are here, they devote full-time to the project, unlike locals who have many other day-to-day commitments."

The other essential individuals on the privatization team were local counsel who represented the SOE being privatized and the government. Supported by the technical guidance of the Rothschild team, they were responsible for drafting all the legal documents, including the prospectus, the employees' share purchase scheme, new articles of agreement (incorporation), and the papers required to transfer legally the ownership of the SOEs from the government to private shareholders. Other important participants included the companies' management and the team from the Jamaica Information Service that was responsible for the marketing campaign. The technical competence of this team of advisers as well as its internal chemistry proved to be important factors contributing to the success of the privatization effort.

The NCB Public Offering

NCB was established in Kingston in 1837 as the Colonial Bank of London. In 1925, the bank was acquired by Barclays Bank of London, which retained control for more than 50 years. In August 1977, during the administration of Prime Minister Michael Manley, the bank was nationalized along with numerous other enterprises, and its name was changed. At that time, the bank was the second largest commercial bank in

Jamaica, with total assets of J$236 million. During the next ten years, the bank continued to grow, maintained a record of moderate profitability, and eventually became the nation's largest commercial bank. NCB's profits reached their highest level in 1985, before declining somewhat in 1986. By November 1986, at the time of privatization, NCB's total assets had grown to J$2.7 billion (US$490 million), after-tax profits were about J$17.6 million (US$3.2 million), and the company's shareholders received a 16.6 percent return on equity.

During the ten years of government ownership, the bank was not subjected to a high degree of political interference in its day-to-day operations, although the board of directors was comprised of political appointees. The managing director, Donald Banks, acknowledged that throughout the period of state ownership "we fought tooth and nail to retain our independence." Banks was a life-long employee of NCB who had been trained as a Barclays employee, moved up through the ranks of management to the top post, ran the bank throughout the years of government ownership, and remained firmly in control as chief executive officer in 1986. Most other key members of management had equally long tenure.

NCB operated in a relatively competitive domestic banking environment (in 1987 Jamaica had ten commercial banks) and received no special treatment or protection due to its status as a government institution. Yet the bank never created a financial burden on the public treasury and continued to pay corporate taxes at the same rate as its competitors. Thus, privatization was unlikely to have a significant impact on the government's fiscal position, other than the one-time receipt of proceeds from the actual sale.

In June 1986, the government took the first concrete steps to privatize NCB when the prime minister decreed that the shares be transferred from the office of the accountant general, the government's trustee, to the National Investment Bank of Jamaica (NIBJ), which would be responsible for executing the transaction. At about the same time, NIBJ injected J$20 million of new capital to strengthen NCB's balance sheet in exchange for an equal number of NCB shares (the J$20 million was needed because NCB had a particularly low capital/assets ratio compared to other commercial banks in the private sector). With these moves NCB was financially and juridically ready for sale.

The Government's Motive

Although NCB was not the Seaga Administration's first privatization, it was by far the largest—projected to raise J$90 to J$100 million—and the first to involve a public share offering on the Jamaican stock exchange. As this was the first privatization by public offering, the prime minister and the implementation team wanted to ensure that the NCB transaction set the standard for future public sales of government assets. In addition to this broad goal, their sights were set on a number of specific objectives.

Ownership: The prime minister and his close aides hoped that privatization would democratize the ownership of major Jamaican enterprises. As one internal government memorandum explained: "What the government wants to achieve in Jamaica [is] thousands of ordinary people directly owning a share in their own future. The sale of NCB is just the first step."

Capital market development: The government also anticipated that the NCB transaction would increase the size of the Jamaican stock exchange by about 10 percent and introduce an entirely new class of prospective investors to the stock market.

Demonstration effect: The government's privatization program was ambitious and long term. The program's success would hinge on the public's perception that the NCB transaction was a success.

A more efficient NCB: The government believed that the privatization of NCB would result in efficiency gains, especially with a new and independent board of directors. It also hoped that with additional capital from private sources, the bank would have the resources to expand internationally.

A reduced government role: The Seaga administration believed that government should not be involved in the business of commercial banking; that it was a waste of government time and resources. Moreover, even though NCB had been a profitable SOE, there was concern that the government would always be the ultimate guarantor of the bank's liabilities, which was unnecessary and inappropriate. Another argument, albeit speculative, was that a more efficient NCB would result in higher earnings and more government tax revenues.

Politics: If the privatization of NCB succeeded in spreading ownership among thousands of new, small shareholders, former Prime Minister Michael Manley and his People's National Party would be hard pressed to criticize the transaction. It would be a political coup for Prime Minister Seaga if he could achieve privatization and simultaneously attract new voters to his party.

Preparing for the Offering

Preparations for the public offering began in earnest in August, when one of the Rothschild advisers arrived in Kingston. The offering would be more than twice as large as any previous public stock sale in Jamaica's history, and there was no way to gauge how the public would respond. In the following three months, the key actors worked full-time to prepare NCB for sale. By November 1986, when 170,000 copies of the prospectus were distributed throughout the country, all the details were in place, and 30.6 million shares of NCB stock were ready to go on sale to the public at a price of J$2.95 per share, which would raise just over J$90 million. A number of distinctive features that marked the offering are described below.

THE MARKETING CAMPAIGN. According to one of the marketing strategists: "Prior to the NCB offering, most people believed you could not explain what a share is to people in a developing country." As one participant explained: "We had to demystify the stock market." The marketing group included Downer as the overall coordinator, the merchant bankers from Rothschild, who relied heavily on their experience with marketing British Telecom, British Gas, and other U.K. privatization candidates, a local advertising agency that represented NCB, and senior officials from the Jamaican Information Service, a government agency modeled after the British Information Service. During the four-month period prior to the public offering, the group launched a coordinated publicity campaign that included television, radio, press conferences, special video productions, and confidential briefings for key interest groups. Their stated purpose was "to give NCB high public visibility" and "to get prospective shareholders to develop confidence in a Jamaican-run enterprise."

The task was complicated by two major obstacles. First, as in most countries, the issue of privatization was politically controversial. Former

Prime Minister Michael Manley was an outspoken critic of the government's privatization policy, declaring in a speech that the NCB privatization was "an act of ideological aggression," and he threatened that the government would buy back all privatized shares as soon as his party was reelected to power. Second, the publicists had to address the question of how to introduce an unknowing public to the advantages of investing in the stock market without participating in an imprudent oversell that would obscure the risks associated with stock market investments.

The widespread publicity succeeded in diffusing much of the public's skepticism. The task was facilitated by the nature of the enterprise, which was well known to the public due to its national branch network, and because it had a history of profitability. It also had a management team that was recognized for its competence and political neutrality. These assets became central themes in the advertising campaign.

As the bulwark of support for Michael Manley's People's National Party was organized labor, the network of union leaders became a prime target. A series of special briefings and meetings were arranged with both the leadership and rank and file of each of the major union organizations. Much of the criticism and skepticism was deflected by emphasizing that the shares would be widely distributed among the public, and that preference would be given to small shareholders and the bank's employees. Every effort was made to reassure the public that NCB would not fall prey to a handful of large, wealthy, institutional shareholders.

Other major interest groups were also targeted, and the public endorsements were recorded in the local press:

- The president of the Jamaican Agricultural Society commented that the upcoming NCB privatization "was a good opportunity for farmers," and "an obvious area in which to encourage farmers to invest their money" (*The Daily Gleaner* Dec. 1986).

- The president of the Jamaican Employers Federation supported the NCB divestment and commented: "I am pleased to see the effort to make the ownership of the bank as broad-based as possible" (*The Daily Gleaner* Dec. 1986).

- The chairman of the executive committee of the All-Island Jamaican Cane Farmers Association told the press: "I believe all [of the

Association members] should invest in NCB because I believe it is a worthwhile investment " *(The Daily Gleaner* Dec. 1986).

- The president of the Private Sector Organization of Jamaica (PSOJ) put the weight of his entire membership behind the Seaga privatization program: "The PSOJ welcomes the government's speed-up of the divestment process, which carries benefit for the public treasury as well as for greater economic efficiency" *(The Daily Gleaner* Dec. 1986).

Prospective buyers could obtain copies of the prospectus for more detailed information about NCB and the offering. An application form was conveniently placed inside each prospectus. The prospectus was distributed by the four registered stockbrokers in Kingston, all post offices, several supermarkets, and local branches of the major banks. The week before the offering, the entire prospectus was also reprinted in the national newspaper.

In addition to the prospectus, a special four-page leaflet, "Questions and Answers About the Share Offering," was available. Beginning with "What Is a Share?" the document posed and then answered 20 of the most common questions about the stock market. It explained in clear terms the function of the prospectus, how to apply and pay for NCB shares, and how the Jamaican stock exchange functioned. Reprinted in *The Daily Gleaner* and distributed individually to almost 200,000 individuals, well over 10 percent of the entire Jamaican population probably read this document.

As the date of the offering drew closer, the media blitz intensified, with full-page newspaper advertisements that warned of "an opportunity not to be missed." Finally, in the days immediately preceding the sale, the newspaper-reading public was bombarded with banner headlines such as "Get Ready, the Shares Are Coming."

LIMITED OWNERSHIP. The prime minister had diffused much of the political opposition to the NCB sale at the outset, when he publicly announced that "nobody will be allowed to own more than 7-1/2 percent of the issued capital of the NCB Group." He went on to explain that "the broad ownership of the bank will also make it virtually impossible for any government to renationalize the bank." Many complained that the 7-1/2 percent limitation was too low, arguing that it would hinder the bank's future growth by undermining its ability to attract institutional sources of capital. However, the prime minister insisted on this provision, even though he agreed that it might seriously limit the bank's future growth.

ALLOCATION OF SHARES. In a further effort to ensure that the primary beneficiaries of the sale would be small shareholders, an allocation scheme gave preference to individuals who purchased a small amount of shares in the event of excess demand for the offering. If the shares had been allocated on a straight *pro rata* basis, each applicant would have been allotted 35.5 percent of the amount applied for. In the event, however, large subscribers requesting 100,000 or more shares were allocated only 8.5 percent of the requested amount, while those applying for fewer than 1,000 shares received all of them. A graduated scale was used to allocate shares to those falling within this range.

DISTRIBUTION NETWORK. The postal service was judged too unreliable for the collection of share applications and the distribution of stock certificates. Thus, a system was devised that relied on the local branches of the post office and the branches of eligible banks as the physical collection and distribution points. On an island with only 2.2 million inhabitants, 400 retail outlets were created to ensure that interested applicants would have easy access to the distribution system.

GOVERNMENT OWNERSHIP. Although the offering was only for 51 percent of the outstanding common shares of NCB, the government was effectively eliminated as a factor in the operational or financial control of the bank. The 49 percent of the stock that remained in government hands was declared nonvoting and, according to the prospectus, the government was legally committed to gradually sell its holdings "as the circumstances of NCB Group Limited and market conditions permit."[4] The government also rescinded its right to appoint members to the board of directors. Thus, the government effectively achieved a total withdrawal from NCB.

EMPLOYEE SHARE SCHEME. The largest single group of shareholders in the privatized NCB became the bank's own employees, who controlled about

---

4. It remains a point of contention whether the government should be forced to sell all of its 49 percent within a two-year period, as originally mandated, or should be given more time to ensure that the price of the public's shares are not depreciated by a sudden influx of new shares.

12.8 percent of the voting shares after the public offering. Approximately 98 percent of the bank's management and staff opted to participate in a special employee share scheme that permitted qualified employees, regardless of seniority or years of service, to purchase shares at preferential prices. According to the scheme, employees could receive one free share for every share purchased at the offer price, up to a maximum of 350 shares. An additional 850 shares could be purchased at a 40 percent discount, followed by a further 850 shares that would be allotted on a priority basis at the offer price. Employees also received 20 free shares if they bought shares under scheme. An employee participating in the scheme to the fullest extent possible would pay an average price of J\$2.50 per share for 2,070 shares compared to the offer price of J\$2.95.[5]

FINANCING EMPLOYEE SHARE PURCHASES. NCB established a J\$10 million special loan fund that enabled employees to obtain their shares by borrowing directly from the bank. This easy payment plan permitted eligible employees to repay the fund over 24 months through payroll deductions. The collateral for the loan was the underlying stock.[6]

PRICING. The task of arriving at the "right' price for the shares revealed the inherent tension between pricing low enough to ensure a strong response to the offering, and high enough to satisfy the government's desire to maximize revenue from the transaction. Prime Minister Seaga had publicly stated that a primary objective of the government was to ensure wide distribution of the NCB shares. However, if the shares were priced too low, critics would claim that the NCB offering was a "give away" in order to attract a large number of shareholders. Yet if the shares were overpriced, there was a possibility that less than the full amount of the stock would be sold. This would trigger a different set of criticisms.

---

5.   Although some measures in the scheme were unique to the NCB transaction, it bore the mark of Rothschild's previous experiences with privatization in the United Kingdom, as well as other countries. In the British Telecom transaction, for example, all company employees were offered a specified number of free shares, plus some additional shares at half price, and a further amount at the issue price. Approximately 96 percent of British Telecom's employees took further amounts at the issue price. Approximately 96 percent of British Telecom's employees took advantage of the scheme.

6.   Although no data are available, many other banks also offered attractive loan terms to purchase NCB shares on margin.

The pricing decision was also clouded by doubts about whether the transaction would succeed. The sale would require the Jamaican stock exchange to absorb more shares than had ever before been sold in the market's history. The capacity of the exchange to handle the volume was uncertain, and the public's response to this relatively unknown investment vehicle was also unknown.

Another variable that influenced the pricing decision was the government's long-term privatization strategy. The privatization team was conscious of the linkage between the offer price of NCB and the future prospects of their privatization program. If the NCB offering was well received, the outlook for future privatization transactions would be enhanced.

On balance, the team decided that the most important objective was to ensure broad share distribution and demonstrate the merits of privatization to the public, rather than to maximize government revenues. A financial analysis was conducted to assess the company's past performance and future prospects. The Bank of Nova Scotia, a bank of comparable size, was used as a benchmark. At the same time, the team held discussions with local stockbrokers and institutional investors to obtain their best professional judgment on the price that would attract the small investor. The team concluded that the NCB shares should be priced at a discount from the share price of NCB's principal competitor to reflect the fact that the NCB offering represented new merchandise. It also was a recognition that the appropriate financial indicators revealed that the Bank of Nova Scotia had been performing better than the NCB in recent years.

The final decision was to price the shares at J$2.95, which represented a price/earnings (P/E) ratio of approximately 7.6, based on earnings per share of J$0.39. This compared with a P/E ratio of over 14 for Bank of Nova Scotia shares at that time, and an average of 9.3 for other major commercial banks in the private sector.

Results

The public offering lasted for ten working days in late November and early December. More than 30,000 Jamaican citizens and institutions applied for shares, and the offering was 170 percent oversubscribed. The strong investor demand surpassed most expectations.

On December 23, the first day the NCB shares traded on the Jamaican stock exchange, 170,000 shares exchanged hands and the stock closed at J$4.94, an increase of 67.5 percent from the J$2.95 offer price. This enormous price increase raised questions about the prime minister's assessment that the NCB privatization was a "fabulous success," and it appeared to substantiate the view of one NCB official who speculated that "the shares could just as easily have been sold at J$3.50 as J$2.95."

Nevertheless, this pilot privatization project—the first public offering of its kind in Jamaica's history—did achieve a number of government objectives. In terms of the public's perception, the privatization program was off to a good start. The stock market was boosted by the substantial increase in capitalization, and by the introduction of tens of thousands of first-time shareholders. NCB, with a new and independent board, was poised to compete more effectively in the market place. Politically, the privatization served as an endorsement of the prime minister's strategy for development, and public skepticism about privatization diminished. Finally, the privatization team learned a great deal that could be applied to future transactions of a similar nature.

The CCC Public Offering

In the wake of NCB's privatization, the government wanted to proceed immediately with plans to privatize a second state-owned enterprise via the public offering route. Even before the NCB transaction was completed, the Rothschilds team had agreed informally with Downer that the logical second candidate would be the Caribbean Cement Company. The transaction would be large enough to warrant a public offering, which would further promote the government's objective to develop the capital market; the management and employees of CCC were expected to support the privatization; the company reported strong earnings at the end of 1986 and projections for future profitability were encouraging; and the company was not operating in a politically sensitive sector such as telecommunications or air transport.

Once the team and Downer were in agreement and the prime minister's support was assured, they moved quickly to gain the backing of key USAID officials. As with the NCB transaction, they counted on a grant from USAID to pay Rothschild's technical advisory fee. USAID officials were strong supporters of Prime Minister Seaga's privatization objectives, and they wanted to ensure that the program did not lose momentum. As a result, an acceptable agreement was quickly reached with USAID even though the Rothschild fees were considerably higher than the standard rates USAID was accustomed to paying.

In February 1987, Downer presented the prime minister with a memorandum outlining the key characteristics of the proposed offering and the adjustments in government policy that would be necessary to facilitate the sale. The prime minister approved the memorandum, including the proposal to schedule the offering in June 1987.

The Company

The Caribbean Cement Company, the only producer of cement in Jamaica, began commercial operations in February 1952 as a private company. During the subsequent 15 years, the company gradually expanded its capacity. CCC was sufficiently well established by 1969 that its shares were publicly traded when the new Jamaican stock exchange first opened. By the mid-1970s, the company had the capacity to produce 400,000 tons per year of clinker, the intermediate product that is mixed with gypsum to produce cement.

In January 1977, the government announced its intention to nationalize CCC. The takeover was triggered by a controversy over the company's future capacity. The government wanted CCC to undertake a major expansion, but was unwilling to accede to CCC's request for an increase in the price of cement, which was government controlled. When the two sides reached an impasse, the government moved to take over the company.

In addition to the immediate controversy, the company was a logical choice for nationalization from the perspective of the Manley administration. It was well known that the prime minister was intent on capturing for the government the so-called "commanding heights" of the economy, and cement was considered a vital industry for the nation's development. Moreover, the company had been consistently profitable during the 1970s, and the electorate knew that CCC was controlled by a handful of the island nation's wealthiest families.

Negotiations dragged on for three years before the nationalization was consummated. Not surprisingly, the plant, equipment, and operations had began to deteriorate markedly almost from the day the negotiations began. Finally, in 1980, CCC shares were turned over to the government-owned National Investment Bank of Jamaica (NIBJ) in exchange for NIBJ debentures. Eventually, NIBJ acquired more than 99 percent of the outstanding shares.

In the five-year period after the nationalization (1979-83), the company was profitable in only one year, and its cumulative losses totaled over J$17 million. Although pinpointing the precise causes of this poor performance is difficult, sluggish economic growth and price controls had an adverse effect on the company's financial performance.

In 1981, the government signed a bilateral agreement with the Norwegian government that stipulated that A/S Norcem, Norway's only cement company, would provide technical services to CCC. Norcem, which eventually became a major shareholder in the privatized CCC, played a crucial role in rehabilitating the company in the mid-1980s. That same year, the government-owned CCC began negotiations with the Inter-American Development Bank to obtain financing for a US$90 million expansion and modernization program. In 1982, the first of two loan agreements were signed with the Inter-American Development Bank that resulted in more than US$57 million of funding for CCC, which it used to double its capacity to 800,000 tons per year. After the expansion, the company would have had to export 30 to 40 percent of total production in order to utilize its capacity fully.

CCC's financial performance began to improve, and in 1984, after five years of almost continuous losses, the company entered a period of profitability that continued until the privatization in June 1987 (table 5.1)

Table 5.1 Summary of CCC's Financial Performance, 1983-86 (J$ million)

Sales and profit /loss)	1983	1984	1985	1986	1987*
Sales	66.5	97.5	113.5	122.0	71.6
Net profit /(loss)	(1.9)	6.7	3.1	17.5	11.6

*Half year ended June 30, 1987

While in government hands, CCC continued to be Jamaica's sole cement producer. Although starting up a second producer was not prohibited, the combination of a relatively small domestic market and the high investment cost of launching a cement production facility created formidable entry barriers. Even low-cost foreign producers were not inclined to compete in the Jamaican market, even though the duty on imported cement was small, because of the high transport costs.

Support for Privatization

The combination of a new management team, a reputable foreign technical partner, and a capital infusion from the Inter-American Development Bank contributed to a sense that CCC was ready to be

The combination of a new management team, a reputable foreign technical partner, and a capital infusion from the Inter-American Development Bank contributed to a sense that CCC was ready to be privatized in 1987. CCC management acknowledged that during the Seaga administration there was minimal government interference in the company. Nevertheless, privatization was expected to eliminate a number of constraints that affected how CCC operated. For example, salary negotiations were strained because the government insisted that management maintain parity between CCC salaries and those paid to individuals with comparable skills in other public sector jobs. Consequently, salaries in CCC were consistently lower than in many similar private companies. There was also concern that government ownership hampered the company's ability to manage its financial affairs efficiently. As a state-owned enterprise, for example, credit transactions with banks had to conform to the standards established for other government enterprises. Even bank overdraft facilities, which were essential for CCC's operations, were subject to government approval. Thus, CCC's management strongly supported Prime Minister Seaga's privatization program.

Preparing for the Offering

On March 20, 1987, the prime minister announced the government's intention to privatize CCC. "Once again," he said, "the allocation mechanism for the shares will, as was the case with the NCB privatization, favor the smaller investors." He went on to emphasize that the government was committed to "putting into the hands of the Jamaican people, directly, enterprises for which there is no special advantage in state ownership, and which, on the contrary will benefit by divestment" (JAMPRESS, March 20, 1987). In addition to democratizing ownership, he emphasized that a limit would be placed on the amount of shares that any single investor could purchase to safeguard against a company takeover by one or two wealthy investors.

The offering was scheduled to take place three months after the prime minister's announcement. The goal was to raise about J$214 million, compared to the J$90 million raised by NCB a few months earlier. Although the CCC stock issue would be more than double the size of any public offering in the history of the Jamaican stock exchange, Downer and the Rothschild team reasoned that because the NCB transaction had been 170 percent oversubscribed, there was considerable absorptive capacity in the local market.

A privatization team similar to the group that had prepared the NCB transaction was formed. Downer was again responsible for the overall effort, the Jamaican Information Service was given responsibility for coordinating the marketing campaign, and a number of the same attorneys were involved. There was, however, one important change. Although Rothschilds had again been designated as the foreign technical adviser, the personnel from the merchant bank were not the same as had worked on the NCB transaction. Both Redwood and another executive were preoccupied with the upcoming parliamentary elections in Britain as both were running for office. As a consequence, a new individual from Rothschild's office in London was assigned to the task.

Some of the most important aspects of the preparations for the offering are discussed below.

MARKETING. Pleased with the enormous success of the NCB marketing campaign, the architects of the CCC effort were reluctant to alter their basic strategy. As one leader of the marketing effort explained: "NCB was the model." Although minor adjustments were made, there was an understandable hesitancy to tamper with a successful formula.

The campaign moved forward on two fronts simultaneously. First, the Jamaican Information Service spearheaded the effort to focus media attention on the privatization process by preparing advertisements, holding press conferences with important interest groups, and getting feature stories published in *The Daily Gleaner*. As with the NCB campaign, the objective was to educate the public about the stock market and encourage people to participate in the offering. Second, a private advertising agency in Kingston was hired to increase public awareness of CCC. In an effort to appeal directly to nationalistic pride, many of the advertisements prominently displayed the CCC motto, "Helping to Build a Better Jamaica." The task, however, was formidable. As one of the campaign's leaders explained, only half in jest: "It's difficult to love cement."

There were, however, some significant differences between NCB and CCC that were important from a marketing standpoint. Unlike NCB, CCC was not a household name in Jamaica, nor did it have a long, established record of profitability. During 1975-84, CCC lost money more often than it was profitable. Moreover, uncertainty surrounded the company's costly restructuring and expansion. In addition, investors had no assurance that the domestic and export markets could absorb CCC's additional output at acceptable prices. The marketing team had to convince the public to buy CCC stock based on the company's future earnings potential rather than its past performance.

Another factor was the vigorous opposition to the privatization by former Prime Minister Michael Manley's People's National Party. One of the party's leading spokesmen called the CCC privatization "a sordid transaction that never should have been permitted." The week before the CCC shares were to be offered for sale, a national newspaper, *The Star*, protested that the divestment "does a great injustice to the Jamaican consumer and taxpayer by transferring at discount prices the benefits they should derive to a few investors and speculators who will number no more than 10,000 to 20,000 people" *(The Star*, June 13, 1987).

Although the marketing campaign did not respond directly to the People's National Party's criticisms, one of the principal themes emphasized that the Jamaican people would be the major beneficiaries of the divestment. Prime Minister Seaga's public comments stressed that the sale would "favor the small investor," and that a major objective of his government's privatization program was "to ensure that ownership would be democratized." (JAMPRESS, March 20, 1987). In addition, as with the

NCB campaign, a number of endorsements from labor union leaders were prominently mentioned in the press.

The upcoming sale also received some welcome publicity when a number of local financial journalists wrote columns about the offering and recommended the CCC stock as an attractive buy at the rumored price.

THE FOREIGN INVESTOR. Scancem (formerly Norcem), the Norwegian cement producer, had been providing technical assistance to CCC since 1981. As one official from CCC explained: "The Norwegians had played a crucial role in rehabilitating the plant and getting CCC back on its feet." They had come to know CCC extremely well, and personnel selected from Scancem were occupying four of the most important positions in the company at the time of the divestment (deputy technical director, marketing director, spare parts engineer, mechanical maintenance manager).

The privatization team and CCC's management agreed that having Scancem as an equity partner would be desirable. Participation by the foreign technical adviser would, they believed, ensure a high standard of performance in CCC. Moreover, Scancem might help the company to establish a presence in the export market, where Scancem had considerable experience. They also hoped that prospective investors would perceive Scancem's participation as a stamp of approval of the public offering. In short, according to one member of the privatization team: "We considered the involvement of Scancem as one of the keys to the success of the deal."

For its part, the Scandinavian company was interested in buying a stake in the enterprise that it had successfully rehabilitated. After protracted negotiations between Scancem and the government, they reached agreement whereby the foreign company would subscribe for 10 percent of the offered shares at a price of J$2.00 per share.

LIMITED OWNERSHIP. The prime minister emphasized, as he had with NCB, that share ownership by individual purchasers of CCC would be limited this time to 10 percent of the total stock offered. This ruling effectively limited Scancem's investment in CCC to 10 percent.

EMPLOYEE PURCHASE PLAN. Just over 4 percent of the total stock offered for sale, or 4.84 million shares, were reserved for purchase by the company's 400 full-time employees. As with the NCB transaction, the employees were offered attractive terms. In this case, employees would get one free share for each of the first 6,000 shares they bought, and another 6,000 shares on a priority basis at the offer price. On top of this, employees buying shares under the scheme were offered 100 shares free.

If all the shares set aside for employees were not purchased in the initial offering, they would be placed in a trust account to be administered by the company. An easy payment plan allowed employees to pay for the shares through monthly salary deductions over a two-year period. Deputy Prime Minister Hugh Shearer, who also served as the president of the Bustamante Industrial Trade Union that represented most of the workers, urged the employees to buy CCC stock: "Share ownership in the cement company will mean additional incentives for production, efficiency, and profitability" (JAMPRESS, May 29, 1987).

FINAL RESTRUCTURING. About one month before the public offering a number of significant measures were taken that were designed to make the company more attractive to prospective investors. To begin with, the government agreed to assume the foreign exchange risk on the approximately US$62.3 million that CCC owed to foreign creditors. The government also arranged to strengthen the company's debt to equity ratio prior to the offering by purchasing 16.5 million shares of CCC stock at the same share price paid by Scancem. The temporary capital injection, which would be repaid to the National Investment Bank of Jamaica from the proceeds of the public offering, was an effective device to strengthen the company's balance sheet at a time when prospective investors were scrutinizing it.

Finally, the government ensured that the privatized CCC would continue to benefit from a temporary moratorium on the payment of approximately J$80 million of duties that it owed the government on the importation of machinery and capital goods for the expansion project. According to the concession, which predated the privatization decision, the company would be allowed to defer payment (interest free) until January 1988, and would then make ten equal installment payments on an annual basis. The government reasoned that the financial cost of these concessions was relatively insignificant compared to the importance of enhancing CCC's attractiveness to prospective investors.

The divestment team was confronted with two related decisions: what percentage of the company's shares to sell, and at what price per share. Not surprisingly, both decisions were heavily influenced by the market response to the NCB privatization. The advisers reasoned that since the

NCB stock sale had been 170 percent oversubscribed, the local stock market had considerably more absorptive capacity than they had thought.

Another lesson they took away from the NCB experience was concern for the "overhang" created by the 49 percent of NCB stock that remained in government hands. According to the NCB prospectus, these shares would be sold at some time in the future as market conditions permitted. However, there was persistent market nervousness that the price of the stock in the secondary market would be depressed by the prospect of a large volume of new NCB shares entering the market at some future date. This threat could be eliminated in the CCC offering if the decisionmakers believed that the market could absorb 100 percent of the shares. In addition, both the chairman of CCC and Scancem management were strongly in favor of selling 100 percent of the shares.

The divestment team also noted that the NCB shares had jumped to a 67 percent premium on the first day that the stock was open for trading on the Jamaican stock exchange. Although there had been surprisingly little adverse public reaction to this bonanza for NCB shareholders, the decisionmakers wanted to avoid the possibility of charges that they had underpriced the CCC shares. However, gauging the appropriate offer price for CCC was extremely difficult. Not only would the team have to overcome the public's lack of knowledge about the company, but also its past financial performance. Thus, there was an understandable desire to price the shares to reflect the company's future earnings potential instead of its historical record. Yet if they opted for this strategy, investors might view the price as unrealistically high.

Another difficulty was that Jamaica had no companies that served as obvious comparators to CCC. The team tried to undertake a comparative analysis with Jamaica Flour Mill Ltd., a company of similar size and financial performance that was also the sole producer of a single commodity. In the end, however, the advisers set the price so that it roughly reflected a price/earnings ratio somewhat lower than the average price/earnings ratio of companies listed on the Jamaican stock exchange.

An additional determinant was the price agreement reached earlier with Scancem and the National Investment Bank of Jamaica. The advisors had wanted to extract the highest possible price from Scancem and NIBJ, but recognized that the price for these two large buyers was likely to become the offer price for the general public. They rightly worried that if prospective investors were disenchanted with the price paid by the foreign investor and the government, the public sale might be undersubscribed.

The final price set was J$2.00 per share, which represented a price/earnings ratio of 8.6 based on projected 1987 earnings of J$26 million (compared to J$17.5 million the previous year).

WARRANTS. Another important step was the decision to offer warrants, which grant the buyer of a particular stock issue the opportunity to purchase additional shares at a specified price within a prescribed period. Warrants are normally offered as an incentive, and are designed to enhance buyer interest in the stock offering. The advisers decided to "attach" the warrants because of concern that the J$2.00 offer price would not be sufficiently attractive to sell 100 percent of the issue. With the warrants, for each five shares of stock purchased the buyer would have the right to buy an additional share for J$2.30 at any time before December 31, 1988.

The decision to include the warrants presented additional risks for the advisers. In a market environment where most of the participants were barely accustomed to the idea of investing in the stock market, the mechanics and the potential advantages of the warrants had to be carefully explained to prospective investors. A backlash could result if this additional marketing task resulted in investor confusion or uncertainty. Moreover, they ran the risk that investors would interpret the warrants as an incentive to compensate for an unattractive offer price.

Results

In June 1987, 107 million shares of CCC were offered to the public for sale at the J$2.00 price, with warrants. By the final day of the sale, 72 percent of the offered stock, or 78.69 million shares valued at J$157.38 million, had been sold. Approximately 23,000 investors, or more than 1 percent of the nation's population, became owners of CCC stock. In addition, 99 percent of the company's employees elected to purchase shares, although the volume purchased was lower than expected. The 28 percent that remained unsold was retained by the issuer, NIBJ, as nonvoting stock that would be sold in the future as market conditions permitted.

All public offerings are influenced by exogenous events that are beyond the control of the principal participants, and the CCC transaction was no different. The advisers were understandably concerned, for example, that interest rates were unusually high in June 1987. An investor could obtain an annualized real return of about 12 percent (18 percent nominal) by purchasing a six-month treasury bill issued by the Bank of Jamaica. The alternative of investing in the stock market appeared considerably less attractive, given the relative risk profiles of the two investments.

Conditions in the stock market were also unfavorable. For a variety of reasons related to domestic and international economic events, the stock index had declined steadily from a record high of 1,940 in February to 1,816 in June. As with any attempt to raise new equity in a retreating market, this was cause for concern.

The advisers also had to contend with a potentially dangerous communications breakdown within the country's central bank, the Bank of Jamaica. One week before the CCC offering, the Bank of Jamaica rolled over about J$400 million of government-guaranteed six-month certificates of deposit. The privatization advisers attempted to persuade the bank to defer the rollover until after the CCC offering had been completed. Their understandable concern was that the government's sale would divert attention and investor funds from the CCC transaction. Although it was not possible to gauge the precise effect on investor behavior, the government action was not likely to work in CCC's favor, particularly among large institutional investors that were regular purchasers of government certificates of deposit.

Despite these hindrances, CCC raised more capital than any other public offering in the nation's history, but the public's expectations, based partly on publicity created by the advisers, was that 100 percent of the issue would be sold. The predictable conclusion of the public was that the offering was undersubscribed because the share price was too high. When the CCC stock opened for trading two weeks later on the stock exchange, the price was J$1.90, but it soon plummeted to J$1.55, a 20 percent discount from the offer price (The price later moved slightly higher, but remained considerably below J$2.00 in December 1987.)

NCB, CCC, and the Conventional Wisdom

As an alternative to conventional development, privatization is too new and untested a strategy to be able to draw definitive conclusions about how it should be done. Conditions affecting the outcome of privatization vary tremendously from country to country; different financing techniques significantly influence the appropriate divestment strategy; and requirements change from sector to sector. Nevertheless, a conventional wisdom has emerged about privatization in developing countries, and in a number of respects the Jamaican experience does not fit the mold.

Candidates for Privatization

Development practitioners generally believe that a major impediment to privatization, particularly in developing countries, is governments' understandable reluctance to sell profitable SOEs, and the difficulty of selling poor performers. For example, the Overseas Development Institute in London has stated that "the desirability to [any] government of getting rid of a particular enterprise will be inversely correlated with its saleability" (Commander and Killick 1986, p. 32). Contrary to this hypothesis, NCB had a lengthy history of profitability and was considered to be one of the most valuable assets in the government's portfolio. Although CCC's historical performance was more erratic, at the time of privatization, the company had a three-year record of increasing profitability, and its future prospects were encouraging. Thus, the Jamaican experience illustrates that it may be advisable for governments to sell one or two attractive assets in the beginning to create a demonstration effect and build momentum in the public arena for privatization.

Privatization and Increased Efficiency

Privatization, according to most economists, only makes sense when there is plausible evidence that the enterprise will become more efficient as a result. One economic analysis of SOE divestiture, for example, opined that "there is little to be gained from divestiture unless enterprise behavior changes in the direction of cost efficiency and heightened entrepreneurial initiative" (Jones and others 1987, p. 7).

Although some efficiency gains may occur over the long run in the case of NCB, there was no clear evidence that privatization would have a significant effect on operations. One year after privatization, the bank's competitive position remained the same, no major changes in management had occurred, staff reductions were not found to be necessary, and no financial restructuring that would affect earnings had taken place. Although the bank's profits had increased substantially, the same was true for most of NCB's competitors. Apparently the principal explanation was Jamaica's improved macroeconomic environment.

The privatization of CCC entailed transforming a public sector monopoly to one in the private sector. Eventually, CCC's board of directors may become more independent, labor relations may improve, and small changes may enhance operational performance, but as with NCB, there was scant justification for privatization on the basis of its likely effect on the company's efficiency.

Nevertheless, both privatizations were likely to benefit the country in other ways. Particularly in the case of NCB, the demonstration effect was considerable, firmly establishing a public perception that privatization was a desirable national goal under certain circumstances. Although the problems CCC encountered were a setback to the government's efforts to create a positive public image for the privatization program, the foundation had been laid for future transactions. In addition, the developmental impact on the stock market was considerable. Thus, designers of privatization strategies are cautioned to view the potential benefits more broadly than simply the impact on the enterprise itself.

Management Resistance to Privatization

On the assumption that privatization threatens the protected status state-run companies traditionally enjoy, management is expected to oppose efforts to subject the enterprise to the rigors of the private sector. Thus, "in practically all cases, the existing managers of the SOEs will wish to have the government retain a significant interest in the enterprise in order to protect their tenure" (Vernon 1987, p. 3).

In both the NCB and the CCC cases, because management jobs were not in jeopardy, the privatization scheme had widespread support. The managing director of NCB and the chairman of CCC became principal spokesmen for the government on behalf of their enterprises, and most of their management were equally enthusiastic. This suggests that, whenever possible, at least some key members of the management team should be retained, and that incentives should be created to ensure their support for the transition.

Capital Markets and Privatization

An IMF report on privatization in developing countries declared that: "The thinness of domestic capital markets necessarily places limits on the ability to finance privatization from domestic resources" (Hemming and Mansoor 1987, p. 15). According to this widely held view, raising sufficient amounts of equity capital in the absence of a well-established stock market is extremely difficult. The Jamaican stock market had fewer than 40 listed stocks in 1986, its trading volume was thin and erratic, and it was open for trading only twice a week for two hours per session. Moreover, prior to the NCB offering, stock trading was heavily dominated by a few large institutions such as insurance companies and pension funds, with the public at large relegated to an insignificant role.

The two privatization transactions, the largest in stock exchange history, increased the value of the equity market by about 15 percent and introduced tens of thousands of new shareholders to an alternative conduit for their savings. As one of the government's advisers noted: "The offer has shown that the liquidity is there underneath people's mattresses, and that the scope of the capital market can be significantly increased by sophisticated privatization, even in a developing economy."[7]

These two transactions demonstrate that (a) the so-called savings rate may be an imperfect barometer of the public's willingness and ability to commit capital to the stock market; (b) the public may respond to new opportunities that hold the potential to increase their savings; and (c) investing in the stock market need not be an enigma to the small investor. Thus, these transactions suggest that underdeveloped capital markets in themselves are not necessarily an impediment to privatization.

Privatization and Wealth Redistribution

Economists generally believe that when domestic savings rates are low, privatization will entail the transfer of assets from one privileged group (the government) to another (either local big business interests or foreign investors). As the Overseas Development Institute warns: "If ownership remains in national hands, it will pass to an already wealthy elite, thus tending to perpetuate inequalities" (Commander and Killick 1986, p. 11).

The two transactions demonstrate that this undesirable outcome is not inevitable. The privatizations created thousands of new Jamaican

---

7. This comment, however, is somewhat misleading because no one has determined what portion of the J$280 million raised in the two transactions came from "under the mattress," compared to the amount that was simply transferred from one financial instrument to another.

shareholders, not one of whom controlled a dominant block of voting shares. In the NCB case, according to the stock allocation system, shareholders owning up to 5,000 shares controlled 49 percent of the voting rights. Combined with the bank's employees, who controlled another 12.8 percent, these two groups controlled 61.8 percent of the voting power, and could effectively thwart institutional domination. In CCC, the 10 percent limit on share ownership also made it extremely difficult for a small shareholder group to seize control of the company. The results of the offerings suggest that if safeguards are in place to ensure broad stock ownership, there is no reason why privatization should perpetuate inequalities.

Trade Unions and Privatization

Most studies of SOEs stress overstaffing as one of the primary causes of inefficiency. Insulated from competition and protected by government labor laws, unionized employees understandably are threatened by the prospects of privatization. Although NCB's staff costs were high relative to those of the Bank of Nova Scotia, payroll was not a significant drag on earnings, and privatization did not result in layoffs. Similarly, CCC was not overstaffed, and no workers were displaced as a result of privatization.

More important, the carefully designed employee purchase plans stimulated widespread employee support for privatization. Most employees in both companies chose to participate. In each case the staff association publicly supported the ownership transfer. The architects of the transactions, taking their lead from the British experience with privatization, discovered that the most effective means for mobilizing the support of organized labor was to demonstrate through a stock ownership plan that employees have much to gain from the transaction. Although this may represent a cost to government (in the form of foregone revenue), it seems a small price to pay for worker support.

Long-Range Strategy Versus the Case-by-Case Approach

In recent years, privatization has become a priority for many key development institutions. The preferred approach, particularly for the World Bank, is to fund elaborate planning exercises that carefully analyze and establish government priorities, adjust relevant regulations and policies, and methodically move forward step-by-step under close Bank supervision. For example, this has been the approach in numerous Sub-Saharan African nations and in Turkey, which was a major recipient of technical assistance funds from the World Bank for privatization.

Once again, the NCB transaction seems to go against the grain. Although the government gave considerable forethought to privatization as an important component of its overall development objectives, it did not have a well-defined, long-term strategy, nor did it undertake numerous financial analyses to determine which enterprises were most saleable. The preferred approach in Jamaica was to move ahead enterprise by enterprise. One internal assessment of the government's privatization program noted: "An effort to address the longer-term [strategy for privatization], other than a broad overview, will in all likelihood prove to be a wasted effort. This assertion is based not only on pragmatism, it is also based on experience, and was the consensus at the [USAID] conference on privatization held in February 1986" (internal government memorandum).

The Jamaican transactions suggest that one effective strategy is to select a relatively attractive state-owned enterprise, move quickly to complete a transaction amid close public scrutiny, and hope that the demonstration effect will provide the necessary momentum to move forward with additional, albeit more difficult, transactions.[8] According to this model, the donor agencies should be prepared to provide the relatively modest amounts of foreign exchange necessary to pay for the type of hands-on technical assistance that is not likely to be available in developing countries.

External Pressure to Privatize

Observers often contend that governments promote privatization because of pressure from the aid agencies. For example, one observer wrote: "Appearance of privatization on the development agenda is largely due to external pressures from international aid donors and banking agencies" (Aylen 1987, p. 15). The connotation is that governments are

---

8.   Of course, this approach also has its pitfalls. For example, there is a danger that the first privatization will exhaust the nation's absorptive capacity. Or an early failure could undermine the credibility of future privatization efforts. Only time will tell if the CCC undersubscription will adversely affect the country's long-term privatization plans.

reluctant advocates of privatization, and pay lip service to the objective to gain access to much needed foreign exchange.

There is no question that both the World Bank and USAID were strong supporters of privatization in Jamaica, and both institutions linked future lending to progress on the privatization front. Nevertheless, it is equally apparent that Edward Seaga and his aides were genuinely committed to privatization as an integral link in the administration's development strategy. Two years before Michael Manley was defeated at the polls, Seaga publicly revealed that privatization would be one of the themes of his campaign. Although his views on the most effective strategy changed over the years, there is no evidence to suggest that his advocacy of privatization was halfhearted or resulted primarily from external pressures.

The Transactions in Hindsight

With hindsight, a few lessons can be gleaned from the two transactions.

The Government's Role as Promoter

The marketing of shares in the two state enterprises magnified the inherent conflict of interest for a government selling state-owned assets to the public. From a market perspective, the offerings were very successful. Nevertheless, the publicity campaign may have suffered from overzealousness. None of the literature, for example, made specific mention of the volatility of the stock market, or the possibility that a large portion of an investor's principal could be lost if the stock price suddenly declined. Less sophisticated investors were probably unwittingly caught up in the frenzy to participate in a get rich quick scheme.

Once the decision had been made to sell a state-owned enterprise, as with the sale of any new product, the objective was to convince prospective buyers that the assets were worth owning. However, the government also had a broader responsibility to the public: to ensure that those citizens interested in purchasing the stock were presented with a balanced assessment of the risks and awards attendant to the sale. These two roles—promoter and regulator—are inherently in conflict, and require that the government take extraordinary precautions to ensure that it acts prudently, and always with the public welfare in mind.

Pricing

"Getting the price right" proved to be as contentious in these transitions as in most privatizations. Given the government's multiplicity of objectives, striking the precise balance and deriving the equilibrium price may have been virtually impossible. Nevertheless, in the NCB case there was a legitimate question of whether the government's broader objectives could have been achieved at a price level that rewarded shareholders with, say, a 27 percent overnight capital gain rather than 67 percent. If, for example, the shares had been offered at J$3.50 per share, the government would have earned an additional J$15 million.

This question of the right price is particularly elusive in the context of a developing country with a thin capital market. Price/earnings ratios, stock market trading volumes, and share prices obscure the reality of the moment when the pricing decision is made. The NCB and CCC transactions were unprecedented events, and even the most sophisticated advisers were plagued by doubt and uncertainty about the outcome. One key participant in the NCB decision acknowledged later that "we would have priced the shares higher if we had known the extent of the demand."

Buying on Margin

A substantial portion of stock was purchased with borrowed funds. Although no aggregated data exist to substantiate this claim, in the NCB case, management acknowledged that most of its employees took advantage of the easy payment plan. Other brokers and local bankers also concede that they arranged similar loan packages. This arrangement works to everyone's benefit so long as the stock price increases in the secondary market. However, if prices decline, the government's ultimate purpose could be defeated entirely. At a certain price level lenders would call in the loan or take possession of the stock. This would have occurred in the CCC case, and Prime Minister Seaga would have been confronted with a negative demonstration effect: the public would have blamed the government for their losses, the broad distribution of the stock would have been lost as creditors accumulated more and more stock, and the political opposition would have been handed the perfect opportunity to proclaim the government's privatization program a failure.

Some of these adverse consequences occurred in the aftermath of the CCC offering. Governments must carefully weight the advantage of easy payment plans and generous margin accounts against the risk of a sudden price reversal that could undermine their objective of developing the capital market and broadening share ownership.

The Economic Impact of Privatization

The advisory team made virtually no attempt to measure the impact of either of the transactions on the public treasury. Their concern was to get the deal done rather than to measure economic and financial costs and benefits for the government, which they viewed as a futile, imprecise exercise. As a result, the prime minister's pronouncement that the NCB transaction was an outstanding success could not have been based on the net economic benefit for the government.

The advisers were justifiably concerned about the methodological and practical problems associated with determining the ultimate fiscal impact of the sales on the government. They felt uncomfortable, for example, making assumptions about how the government would apply the revenues received from the sale, the amount and effect of future tax revenues on both the government and the enterprises, and the appropriate discount factor to be applied to determine the present value of future earnings.

Key members of the privatization team agreed that the probable fiscal impact of the transactions would be negligible, and therefore chose to devote their energies to more practical matters. The enterprises would continue paying taxes on the same basis as when they were government owned; significant near-term efficiency gains were not apparent; and since NCB had not generated losses that had to be covered by government expenditures, privatization would not result in direct savings for the public treasury. Thus, except for the immediate capital gain resulting from the sale, the privatization team assumed that the economic impact would be insignificant. However, this hypothesis was never put to the test.

External Assistance and Privatization

The transactions raise difficult questions about the role of external assistance in implementing privatization strategies. To what extent, for example, was pressure from external aid agencies such as the World Bank and USAID a key factor in stimulating the Jamaican government to privatize? How important were external financial resources to the success of the privatization effort? Are foreign technical advisers necessary, and if so, how should their performance be monitored and assessed?

For the recipient government, the challenge is how to benefit from the financial resources and technical knowhow that are usually needed to implement privatization strategies, without succumbing to unpopular external pressures. This issue is particularly acute in the case of privatization because the process is fundamentally political, and government leaders are particularly sensitive to the appearance of foreign meddling in domestic affairs. In Jamaica, both the government and USAID agreed that the aid agency would have to keep a low profile if it was going to play an effective role and eschew any public credit.

Defining "Success"

Despite the record amount of capital raised in the CCC public offering, disappointment that the sale was not more successful was widespread. Success was measured in the public arena primarily by two related factors: the percentage of the total offering that was sold and the opening price in the secondary market. Unfortunately, various other aspects of the sale that pointed to a positive outcome were largely ignored, such as the marketing campaign that induced more than 23,000 Jamaicans to purchase shares, the successful transformation of CCC into a publicly held corporation, the contribution of the offering to capital market development, and the approximately J$190 million (gross) raised for the government.

As one adviser pointed out: "Our biggest mistake was deciding to sell 100 percent of the shares. If we had opted for less, the transaction would have been perceived as a tremendous success." The unstated corollary to this view was the implicit tradeoff between price and volume that the advisers had to consider. Would the results have been different, for example, if 100 percent had been offered at a lower price? Or, would the transaction have been oversubscribed if only 70 percent was offered at the J$2.00 price?

These questions raise an issue that is critical to the privatization process, namely, the public's perception of success. In the case of CCC, it should not have been necessary to sell 100 percent of the company for the public to perceive the transaction as a success. Revenue maximization was not the government's primary objective, nor was a 100 percent sale important to other key privatization goals. Thus, a lower offer price would probably not have affected public opinion adversely.

Previous Experience Is a Mixed Blessing

The CCC transaction benefited immeasurably from the hands-on experience that most of the key participants had gained from working on the NCB privatization six months earlier. However, the fact that the NCB offering was 170 percent oversubscribed may have led them to conclude that the stock market would be capable of digesting all the CCC shares at once at the J$2.00 price. If the NCB transaction had not loomed large as the comparator, the advisers might not have concluded that the market would respond as enthusiastically to the cement company as it had to the nation's largest and best-known commercial bank. In addition, NCB cast a shadow over the pricing itself. As one adviser acknowledged: "We wanted to avoid charges later on that we underpriced the stock, as was the impression left in some quarters after the NCB offering."

Preoccupation with the "Overhang"

The government was understandably concerned that disposing of unsold CCC shares in the future might be difficult if it decided to sell less than 100 percent. A new government might be reluctant to sell the remaining shares; the stock market could enter a period of protracted decline; or the company might perform poorly, which would depress the value of the stock for a sustained period of time. Nevertheless, the government had to balance these risks carefully against the adverse effects for its future privatization agenda if the CCC offering was undersubscribed.

Another factor, more difficult to weigh, was the pressure the prime minister felt to generate revenue from the privatization program. He had raised expectations that his divestment program would help reduce the fiscal deficit.

The Warrants

One of the advisers conceded that "the warrants did not help as much as we had expected." One of the brokers, stating a view that was repeatedly expressed in the months after the offering, indicted the warrants with the claim that "they were an attempt to correct the price of the stock." One alternative to the warrants, which apparently never received serious consideration, was an offer price substantially lower than J$2.00.

The Brokers

In countries with well-developed financial markets, it is customary to rely heavily on the judgment of the brokers and dealers when it comes to the price decision. These individuals are in the optimal position to supply timely and accurate information on this all-important issue because they are actively involved in buying and selling securities on a day-to-day basis.

None of the brokers dissented in the decision to sell the CCC shares at J$2.00. Possibly this was because the relatively underdeveloped state of the domestic financial market made it difficult for the brokers to obtain and interpret the information needed to arrive at an accurate pricing decision. Another possibility is that they believed demand for the CCC stock at J$2.00 per share would be sufficient to warrant a 100 percent sale. Regardless of the reasons, the CCC pricing highlights the difficulty of obtaining accurate, market-based information in a rudimentary financial market.

Conclusion

On the surface, the outcome of these two transactions was different. One was heralded as a success by both the government and the press; the other was considered a disappointment, largely because it was not fully subscribed. However, closer analysis suggests that the similarities between the two transactions outweighed the differences. The initial assessments of the two transactions overstated both the success of the NCB privatization and the shortcomings of the CCC deal.

The government chose to laud the NCB transaction for a number of reasons. The ultimate measure of success was that the offering was 170 percent oversubscribed and the shares reacted favorably in the secondary market. In addition, the prime minister and his associates were genuinely pleased by the impact of the public offering on capital market development. They were also pleased that the NCB transaction paved the way for future privatization, defusing public suspicion that the sale would do little more than transfer public assets from one wealthy elite to another. The widespread publicity surrounding the NCB transaction contributed to the government's objective of changing public attitudes about privatization in general, and the stock market in particular. Finally, a privatization team was successfully organized and began to acquire expertise that would be useful for years to come.

However, this positive assessment hinged largely on what the government aspired to accomplish with the privatization. The transaction did not maximize the government's revenues, since by most standards the NCB shares were underpriced; the change in ownership did not precipitate major changes in the bank that would justify a conclusion that privatization enhanced NCB's efficiency; and no serious attempt was made to measure the impact of the transaction on the fiscal deficit, although the IMF has cautioned that: "If an asset sale is used to reduce the overall deficit, while other revenues and expenditures are held constant, there will be no financial impact in the medium term, provided the asset is sold at market value" (Hemming and Mansoor 1987, p. 28).

Yet despite indications that the CCC transaction results were not optimal, the government achieved many of its privatization objectives: with 78 million shares trading on the Jamaican stock exchange and thousands of new participants, the offering did contribute to capital market development; share ownership had been broadened and democratized as the prime minister had hoped; the government had one less state-owned enterprise to administer and monitor; and the public treasury was richer by about J$182 million, less the expenses incurred in executing the transaction.

Although a number of useful lessons can be gleaned from the NCB and CCC cases, the relevance to other countries and sectors must be carefully weighed. For example, the issues involved in privatizing a bank are somewhat different than for a manufacturing enterprise or public utility. Also, privatizing an SOE that has a history of profitability is obviously less difficult, as was the case with NCB, compared to one that has experienced perennial losses, such as CCC. The issues differ somewhat when the targeted enterprise is being returned to private ownership, as opposed to a candidate that is being privatized for the first time. Both NCB and CCC had been nationalized by the Jamaican government in the mid 1970s, and thus they were reprivatizations, which slightly changed the nature of the deals. While these and a number of other features of the two transactions are not unique, they do illustrate that each privatization transaction must be viewed carefully to determine its relevance to other cases.

Nevertheless, the two transactions provide some useful insights that are applicable beyond Jamaica. Doubt should be cast, for example, in the minds of those who view the execution of a privatization transaction as simply another form of technical analysis leading to the correct valuation, pricing, and sale of assets. These cases illustrate that decisions must be made along the way that also require a high quotient of vision and good judgment: selecting technical advisers, determining the optimal timing of the transaction, designing and implementing a marketing campaign, ensuring employee support for the privatization, defusing political opposition, and so forth.

The Jamaican experience also illustrates several techniques for mobilizing support for privatization among various interest groups that are not country specific:

- for a relatively low financial cost, employees can be induced to support privatization with special share purchase schemes;
- bureaucratic resistance to privatization can be reduced by transferring the implementation process to private sector agents who are loyal to the political leadership;
- creative marketing and a well-orchestrated public relations campaign can effectively mobilize public opinion for privatization;
- broad public participation in the privatization process through share distribution is an effective foil against political opposition.

The most striking conclusion about privatization in countries such as Jamaica, therefore, is that many of the key decisions that determine success or failure are based on calculated subjective judgments. No amount of quantitative analysis, for example, can identify the "right" price. No market survey can measure with precision the effective demand or the likely effect of adding warrants. No formula exists that can establish the correct tone for an advertising campaign. These matters depend on experience, judgment, and good fortune. The Jamaican program benefited from each of these elements, and the government established a solid foundation for future privatization initiatives.

References

Aylen, Jonathan. 1987. "Privatization in Developing Countries." *Lloyd's Bank Review* 173 (January):15-30.

Commander, Simon, and Killick, Tony. 1986. "Privatization in Developing Countries: A Survey of the Issues." Paper presented at the conference on Privatization in Developing Countries, University of Manchester, U.K., December.

Cowan, Gray L. 1983. "Divestment and Privatization of the Public Sector: Case Studies of Five Countries." Report submitted to the Agency for International Development, Washington, D.C.

Hemming, Richard, and Ali M. Mansoor. 1987. *Privatization and Public Enterprises*. IMF Working Paper. Washington, D.C.: IMF.

Jones, Leroy P., Pankaj Tandon, and Ingo Vogelsang. 1987. "The Economics of Divestiture: Ex Ante Valuation and Ex Post Valuation." Draft.

Vernon, Raymond. 1987. "Enterprises Jointly Owned by the Public and Private Sectors." Paper prepared for discussion at the Council on Foreign Relations. Draft.

6

PRIVATIZATION THROUGH PRIVATE SALE: THE BANGLADESHI TEXTILE INDUSTRY

Klaus Lorch

Privatization currently ranks high on the agenda of developing country governments and international development agencies (see, for example, Vernon 1988). Their motives are many and diverse, but the hope for higher economic efficiency underlies many of their expectations. Yet few researchers have carefully assessed efficiency and other long-term effects of privatization. Studies concerned with this question in the context of developed countries often limit themselves to the impact of privatization on stock prices and financial profits. Those set in developing countries have focused largely on the planning and implementation of recent privatizations rather than on their longer-term consequences (see, for instance, Asian Development Bank 1985; Chowdhury 1987; Nankani 1988). In contrast, this study is largely about the consequences of privatization, and focuses on the textile industry of Bangladesh.

The Bangladeshi textile industry was in many ways an ideal setting for exploring the impact of privatization. First, it permitted a comparison of efficiency across public and private firms because after privatization in 1982-83, both public and private mills participated in the industry. The mills were comparable in plant size, location, age, technology, products, and management at the time of privatization, except that the privatized mills

The financial support provided by the World Bank for an earlier study of privatization in Bangladesh (Lorch 1987, 1988) on which large parts of this article are based is gratefully acknowledged. This research was conducted while the author was on the research staff of the Harvard Institute for International Development. The findings and conclusions expressed in this article are, however, entirely those of the author and should not be attributed to those institutions.

included fewer very old and very new mills. Second, each ownership category had more than 20 firms, thus eliminating the small numbers problem that often makes comparing the performance of public and privatized firms difficult. Finally, at the time this study was conducted, more than four years had elapsed since privatization, so its impact on performance could begin to be assessed.

Ideally, an *ex post* evaluation of privatization would quantify, aggregate, and discount all economic costs and benefits, including income distribution effects, and compare the results with the counterfactual case where the firms had remained in government hands (see Chapter 2 for such an approach). However, a rigorous approach of this sort runs into severe empirical limitations in a case like the Bangladeshi textile industry, where published data are unreliable and unrecorded activities such as smuggling and side payments play a key role. Therefore, a less sophisticated but more practical approach suggested by Vernon (Chapter 3) was employed. This approach calls for a partial analysis of performance along several dimensions relevant to policymakers, such as static efficiency, dynamic efficiency, and the impact of privatization on income distribution and public finance. This study also benefited from Ayub and Hegstad (1986), Commander and Killick (1986), Hemming and Mansoor (1986), Millward (1986), and Pack (1987).

Background

When Pakistan became an independent nation in 1947, it consisted of a western part, which is today's Pakistan, and an eastern part that split away from Pakistan in 1971 to become Bangladesh. Between 1947 and 1971, industries in East Pakistan were largely integrated into and owned by West Pakistanis. Only in the 1960s did local Bengali entrepreneurs begin to set up their own large firms, mostly in the textile and jute sectors. Independence severed Bangladesh's access to capital, technical expertise, management, raw materials, and foreign exchange from West Pakistan. Moreover, West Pakistanis abandoned many firms in Bangladesh, and the state took them over. However, in 1972 the socialist government of President Mujibur Rahman decided to take over all large and medium-sized private firms, including those owned by Bangladeshis. All the textile mills were nationalized and placed under the control of a new state sector corporation, the Bangladesh Textile Mills Corporation (BTMC) (see Yusuf 1985).

By 1981, about 300 companies, many of them small ones, had been denationalized, and most industrial sectors were reopened to the private sector, but the state still owned 85 percent of the fixed assets of medium and large industry, including all 59 cotton spinning mills (Ameen 1987; Chishty 1986; Humphrey 1987; Sobhan and Ahsan 1984). By the early 1980s, changes in political leadership and economic conditions led to a marked shift in official policy in favor of private enterprise.

For several years, Bangladesh's industry had experienced little or no growth, and the state's ownership of enterprises was believed to be one of the causes of this stagnation. The BTMC, for instance, never matched the pre-1971 output, capacity utilization, or productivity of its spinning plants, and lost money every year after fiscal year 1975/76. Several attempts at reform failed, and during the recession of 1981-82 the BTMC group lost Tk681 million (US\$34 million), or almost 20 percent of sales.[1] International agencies and donors pushed for economic reforms in Bangladesh, but sweeping reforms had to wait until General Ershad seized power in 1982. His new industrial policy aimed to expand the role of the private sector and reduce government intervention in the economy (People's Republic of Bangladesh 1982). As part of this new policy, more than 20 state-owned textile mills that locals had formerly owned were slated for privatization. The move was significant because textiles accounted for 15 percent of Bangladesh's industrial output.

President Ershad carried out privatization with surprising speed, presumably to preempt resistance from opponents, who were at that time still ruled by martial law. Several interministerial committees, most of them chaired by officials from the Ministry of Industry and Commerce, implemented the program. Even key parties such as the Ministry of Finance, state-owned banks (which had loaned the state textile mills

---

1.   Calculated from annual reports and other data obtained from BTMC. Note that import duties (without surcharges) were only 10 to 20 percent on cotton but 35 to 50 percent on yarn, 100 percent on gray cloth, and 150 percent on finished fabric. However, smuggling was rampant, BTMC's prices were controlled, and the state levied a special sales tax (see Mallon 1984). The loss of all public enterprises together rose to Tk1.5 billion (US\$75 million) in 1981/82.

substantial sums of money), and the labor unions played only a limited role.

To simplify the transaction, all former Bangladeshi owners of textile mills received the same terms: they were offered their original shares, plus any additional shares required to attain at least a 51 percent majority, at the same price that they had received as compensation at the time of nationalization a decade earlier. The enterprises were transferred "as is" with all assets, liabilities, and personnel. There was a one-year ban on dismissal of personnel. Financial or physical restructuring was not part of the agreements, but its prospect was held out by government officials (see *Bangladesh Gazette* 1982; Lorch 1988). By April 1983, ten months after the government decision to denationalize the textile industry, 22 mills had been returned to their former owners, leaving 37 in the public sector. Thus, by mid-1983, 40 percent of the spindles and 45 percent of the looms in Bangladesh's modern textile sector were in private hands, up from zero percent in both categories just one year earlier.[2] In 1984-85, two more mills were divested.

Static Efficiency

How did the change in ownership affect the performance of the Bangladeshi textile industry? We turn first to the question of static efficiency, by which we mean the efficiency with which current outputs are produced. Rather than compare the efficiency of the same mills before and after privatization, we conduct a cross-sectional comparison of public and privatized mills in the post-privatization years (1983-86). The analysis is largely confined to spinning operations. Static efficiency is assessed in four functional areas: procurement, production, sales, and support functions. In the first step, the cost advantage of private mills relative to state-owned mills is roughly estimated in financial terms in each of these areas and expressed as a percentage of yarn cost.[3] Financial measures

2. This excludes powerloom units and small, specialized weaving mills. Note also that the sale of the assets of four liquidated BTMC mills to investors (who thereafter operated them under new company names) increased the private sector share to 45 percent of spindles and 66 percent of looms by 1984 (data from personal interviews and BTMC annual reports).

3. The underlying cost structure is that of BTMC's spinning mills of pre-1982 vintage in 1985/86, adjusted for cotton price changes: raw materials 52.5 percent, labor 18.3 percent, administrative expenses 4.7 percent, power and fuel 6.8 percent,

reflect the prices actually paid or received by firms for inputs and outputs. Subsequently, financial costs are converted to economic costs using a set of conversion factors for salaries, skilled and unskilled wages, electricity, gas, cotton, interest charges, and foreign exchange.[4] Table 6.1 summarizes the findings, which are discussed in detail below.

Procurement

Raw cotton and manmade fibers accounted for 50 to 60 percent of the total unit cost of yarn. Moreover, imports accounted for most of the supplies. Thus, differences in procurement efficiency between public and private mills could potentially have a large impact on both their financial and economic costs. As shown in table 6.1, private mills appeared to have no significant net advantage in this area in financial terms, but a disadvantage of about 1.5 percent of yarn cost in economic terms (based on the midpoint of the subtotal range).

Privatized firms appeared to be able to buy cotton at lower prices, especially after adjusting for differences in quality and delivery terms, for a number of reasons. The first reason was the private mills' eagerness to obtain the best prices and their ability to move swiftly in response to changing market prices. By contrast, their public counterparts were not as concerned with minimizing costs or as flexible in procurement. For instance, cotton procurement was centralized in BTMC, and individual mills therefore had great difficulties altering their procurement or production plans to match changing prices of various fibers or changes in consumer demand. BTMC tended to buy cotton in large quantities, up to half its annual requirements. Given the level of expenditure, most purchases required cabinet approval. Public sector rules required procurement through time-consuming bids. These bids also made more demands on bidders, such as requiring a 10 percent performance bond. Many suppliers found this burdensome and did not submit bids.

A second reason why BTMC may have been at a disadvantage relative to private mills was its relative lack of expertise and the short time horizon

---

auxiliary materials 2.6 percent, cotton waste 4.7 percent, depreciation 2.6 percent, and interest 7.8 percent (based on annual reports and other data obtained from BTMC).

4.   Conversion factors were roughly estimated as 0.82 for officers and skilled workers, 0.73 for unskilled labor, 1.20 for electricity, 0.60 for gas, 1.35 (at shadow exchange rate) for cotton, 1.30 for interest, and 1.50 for the exchange rate (People's Republic of Bangladesh 1985, 1986; Wasow and others 1984).

of officials involved in procurement: BTMC had four different directors of procurement in 1983-85, three of whom came from the military.

Finally, corruption was reported in both the public and private sectors, but may have affected BTMC's costs, delivery terms, and quality of raw materials more adversely because managing directors of private mills had to strike a balance between personal profits resulting from any irregularities on the one hand, and maintaining their companies' competitiveness and their partners' goodwill on the other hand.

The government also regulated procurement by private mills in the form of foreign exchange controls. For instance, to take advantage of the overvalued exchange rate, private firms had to apply for import entitlements, which were issued infrequently and had a short validity. Thus, privatized mills also found themselves buying excessively large shipments of cotton or buying at the wrong times. All things considered, however, private mills appeared to do better than public mills in the procurement price and terms for cotton and manmade fibers.

However, the disadvantages of public procurement were more than offset by the scale economies BTMC enjoyed through central procurement for its 35 mills. Transaction costs were lower per unit of raw material because they were spread over a larger volume. Shipment costs and cotton stocks were lower for the same reason. For instance, raw materials inventory, measured in months of consumption, was about half as large in BTMC as in private mills in 1984/85: two months versus about four months. BTMC may also have enjoyed a quantity discount compared to private mills. Private mills procured independently, as only two of the privatized mills belonged to the same owner. Ownership in the private sector did not become concentrated to any degree as the mills had been returned to their former owners who had generally possessed only one textile mill each, and the resale of shares was restricted. Moreover, independent mill owners did not cooperate in procurement because of differences in requirements, or because joint purchases made overinvoicing more hazardous. Thus, despite inefficiencies in procurement and a failure to exploit scale advantages fully (for instance, through active intermill transfers of cotton) BTMC's overall cost of fiber procurement, covering purchase, shipment, and storage, was probably somewhat lower than that of privatized mills in financial terms.

Table 6.1 A Comparison of the Static Efficiency of Public and Privatized Textile Spinning Mills in Bangladesh, Fiscal Year 1985/86

Function	Sources of difference[a]	Net financial advantage of private over public[b] (percentage of yarn cost)	Net economic advantage of private over public[b] (percentage of yarn cost)
Procurement			
Cotton and manmade fiber	-Higher cotton stock because of small scale and rigid import entitlement procedures	(1.5) - (2.5)	(2.0) - (3.3)
	-Higher transaction cost because of small scale	(0.6) - (1.2)	(0.6) - (1.2)
	+Better cotton price, quality, and terms due to better incentives and no tender requirement	1.3 - 2.0	1.7 - 2.7
	+Evasion of local and barter cotton purchases	1.1 - 1.7	0.0 - 0.0
	Subtotal[c]	(1.3) - 1.6	(2.8) - 0.1
Production			
Power supply	+Less production loss and higher quality through generators and special arrangements with power stations	2.0 - 3.0	1.1 - 1.7
Labor	+Reduction of workforce	0.4 - 0.6	0.3 - 0.5
Machinery	+Better incentives in procurement	n.a.	n.a.
Quality control	-No central testing facility because of small scale	(0.5)	(0.6)
	+Stronger incentives to focus on quality	1.0 - 2.0	1.0 - 2.0
Wastage	+Stronger motivation to control waste and its use	0.3 - 0.5	0.1 - 0.2
	Subtotal[c]	4.4 - 7.5	2.4 - 4.6

Sales			
Distribution	+Lower transaction cost due to few, close dealers	0.3 - 0.5	0.3 - 0.5
	+Higher interest on dealer security	0.3 - 0.5	0.0 - 0.0
	+Price premiums going to owner group (or mill), and tax lowered through transfer pricing	1.0 - 1.5	0.0 - 0.0
Pricing and planning	+Lower yarn stock	1.0 - 1.5	1.3 - 2.0
	+Flexible adjustment to changing demand	0.6 - 1.0	0.3 - 0.5
Marketing	+Lower transaction cost and buyer risk due to label's quality image	0.5	0.5
	Subtotal[c]	3.7 - 5.5	2.4 - 3.5
Support Functions			
Staffing	+Retirement of officers and staff	0.9 - 1.2	0.7 - 1.0
Finance	+Default and delay of service of transferred debt	3.5 - 6.0	0.0 - 0.0
	+Low depreciation as few privatized mills are new	1.5 - 2.0	0.0 - 0.0
	Subtotal[c]	5.9 - 9.2	0.7 - 1.0
Total		12.7 - 23.8 Midpoint: 18.2	2.7 - 9.2 Midpoint: 6.0

a. The signs indicate whether the private sector had an advantage (+) or a disadvantage (-) over the public sector in that function.

b. Negative numbers (shown in parentheses) imply that the cost for privatized mills was higher than that for BTMC mills. The opposite is true for positive numbers.

c. The low and high ends of the range are obatined by adding the lowest and highest ends, respectively, of the range for each component.

Source: Author's estimates based on interviews and other sources as explained in the text.

The last column of table 6.1 shows the cost differences between BTMC and the private mills in economic terms, after correcting for the real price of foreign exchange, the social opportunity cost of capital, and the cotton price before import duties. BTMC still had a net economic cost advantage over private mills equal to roughly 1.5 percent of yarn cost.

One final factor eroded BTMC's financial cost advantage. The government required that all textile mills buy 10 percent of their annual cotton requirements locally and another 10 percent under a long-term barter agreement with COMECON countries. Under the barter agreements, Bangladesh bought cotton in exchange for its main export, jute. The private mills largely ignored these requirements, while BTMC often exceeded them to absorb the remaining quantities.[5] Most private mills bought almost no cotton locally and less than 5 percent of their total requirement under barter. Since cotton bought locally or in barter deals was more expensive than cotton purchased in international markets, private mills enjoyed a financial advantage of 1.1 to 1.7 percent of yarn cost over BTMC. However, this practice produced no net benefit for the country since the burden was merely shifted from one part of the Bangladeshi economy (private mills) to another (BTMC).

Production

In the production function, privatized mills had a net cost advantage over public ones in both financial and economic terms. The main sources of cost advantage for private firms were a more reliable power supply, slightly lower wage costs per unit of output, lower wastage rates, and superior quality. BTMC's only major competitive advantage was its large overall scale, but it failed to exploit this potential strength in all areas but quality control (table 6.1).

Both public and privatized mills consumed similar amounts of energy, were supplied by the same primary source (the Bangladesh Power Corporation), and paid basically the same rates. Both were also severely hurt by frequent, unplanned power outages and up to four hours per day of planned outages. Irregular and inadequate power reduced output and, because the air conditioning stopped, also lowered product quality by

---

5. In some years, however, even public mills bought less than 10 percent locally because only 3 percent of the country's cotton requirements were available locally (information from author's interviews and BTMA annual reports).

permitting temperature and moisture changes, which alter the properties of cotton. Altogether, power outages shrank the industry's revenues by an estimated 10 percent of sales. Comparatively speaking, however, private mills were hurt less, either because they worked out special arrangements with local power authorities, such as an exclusive power line to the mill, or because they used standby power generators. Public mills lacked the incentive and the capacity to make special arrangements with officials in the power authority. However, from the policymaker's perspective, such agreements only transferred the burden of load shedding to other industries.[6] With regard to standby generators, BTMC had only two units in its mills compared to six to eight in the private sector. The government was reluctant to sanction foreign exchange to import generators when power could be produced more economically in large power plants. However, private mills could buy foreign exchange in the open market to import generators.

Both public and private mills operated with excess labor. When the textile industry was state owned, the workforce was excessive for all the usual reasons: political concern for the organized urban labor force, inflexible work rules imposed by unions, political appointments, and so on. At the time of privatization, the government imposed a one-year ban on dismissals in the divested enterprises. Even thereafter, however, powerful unions and high severance pay requirements prevented private mill owners from laying off surplus workers on a large scale. As only two privatized mills invested in additional capacity, excess workers could not be absorbed through growth in output. Wage reductions were also close to impossible in both sectors. After privatization, the country's leadership called on private employers to follow strictly each pay rise of the public enterprises. Under the circumstances, privatized mills used early retirement and golden handshakes to get rid of nearly one in three managers by 1986. During the same period (1981-86), total employment in private mills shrank by only 4.6 percent, including a mere 2.8 percent contraction in permanent factory workers (mostly through attrition, turnover, and early retirement). BTMC also registered some decline in the corresponding numbers, but to a lower

---

6. The country was better off only if power interruptions were indeed more detrimental to textile production than to other industries. This might have been the case with spinning due to high fixed cost and vulnerable product quality.

degree in all categories: executives fell by 5 percent, permanent workers by 0.4 percent, and total employment by 0.5 percent.[7]

Another trick the private sector used to contain wage costs was to use fewer workers classified as skilled, so that the ratio of skilled to semi-skilled workers was significantly lower than in public mills: in 1986, the ratio was 1:1 in privatized mills compared to 3:1 in BTMC. In some cases, private mills merely reclassified workers and tasks; in other cases, they got less-skilled people to do what more-skilled employees had done in public factories. Of course, only this latter created real economic gains for the country.[8]

Employee relations were strained in both sectors. Unions were militant and affiliated with political parties. Their local leaders fought hard to gain control of the workforce and, at times, the mills themselves. Mill directors and managers were frequently beaten, locked up in their offices for days, and denied access to their own mills for weeks. These practices affected labor discipline and motivation in both the public and privatized companies. Although BTMC mills were occasionally closed because of labor violence, the mills' managers were generally reluctant to take on the unions.[9] Private firms, however, adopted varied strategies. Some allowed unions to dominate, while others gave workers generous benefits to weaken union control. Other private owners built up massive security forces (up to one guard for every ten workers) to control labor violence, and a few chose to close down their factories.

Incentive pay systems existed in both sectors, but performance bonuses were less common in private mills than in BTMC. However, the performance incentive system in BTMC was not very effective because unions pressurized management to pay despite underperformance.

---

7. Public mills cut temporary employment more rigorously than privatized ones, however (54 percent versus 29 percent, between 1981 and 1986). Moreover, if one chooses to believe the low production figures reported by privatized mills, their labor productivity became about 8 percent worse than BTMC's.

8. Those economic gains were about 0.5 to 0.8 percent of the cost of yarn under the assumption that half the cases were just reclassification.

9. The country's leadership sought the support of the workforce, and public managers had little incentive to oppose powerful and politically connected labor leaders. Note also that 1 out of 50 employees of the BTMC group were work-exempt union representatives. In 1983/84 BTMC sold four factories that, its managers told the author, were liquidated because they had become "unmanageable." On labor relations in SOEs, see Vermeulen and Sethi (1982).

Privatized firms also enjoyed a quality advantage relative to BTMC mills in the production function. Yarn of very good quality (within each thickness grade) commanded a 10 to 15 percent price premium, largely because it reduced weavers' production costs. A supplier with a reputation for selling consistently excellent quality yarn might command an additional premium of 5% or more as the buyer faced less risk. Private mills were more inclined to emphasize quality so as to capture these higher margins, except those among them that operated with a short time horizon.[10] By contrast, public mills were more likely to compromise on quality: in procurement because of possible corruption, and in production because of more frequent interruptions and because managers were judged by the volume of production and cost of manufacturing rather than by the profits they helped generate. Further, many of these managers felt that BTMC's mission was to produce basic cloth for the population at large. As a result, privatized mills, as a group, probably produced yarn that commanded a 2 percent price premium over BTMC's yarn.

Repair and maintenance were poor in both public and private mills. Good technical supervisors were rare in either sector. Likewise, imported spares were seldom available in a timely fashion in both sectors, although delays were slightly greater in BTMC because of centralized procurement and personal rent seeking. Managers in both sectors tended to neglect the maintenance function, although for different reasons. In BTMC, mill managers were rotated every three years or so, and therefore took a short-term view, whereas in private mills, the possibility of renationalization diminished owners' willingness to invest in maintenance.

One area in which BTMC would have been expected to enjoy an advantage over denationalized mills was scale economies in production, but that appeared not to be the case. First, with respect to operations at the level of the individual mill, BTMC had no scale advantage because its average mill (in 1982/83) had about the same number of spindles (18,850) and looms (260), for those that had a weaving section, as the average privatized mill. Second, BTMC did not appear to enjoy economies associated with multi-plant operation in any area other than quality control, where a central laboratory and five regional testing centers served about

---

10. By 1987, some privatized mills spent heavily on quality control, while others still lacked all but the most basic testing facilities.

seven mills each. In other areas, BTMC did not achieve scale economies despite its control over 37 mills. In staffing, for instance, work rules made it difficult for BTMC to allocate human resources optimally across the mills: unions would not permit workers to be moved freely between plants to even out imbalances in workloads. In manufacturing operations, BTMC mills did not specialize in individual varieties of yarn or cloth because most of the mills had been built before nationalization by investors who had installed nonspecialized equipment to reduce their risks and maximize flexibility. As concerns maintenance, a large central workshop was hard to control and therefore did not yield the scale economies that might have been expected. Finally, under union and political pressure, BTMC usually cut production across all mills during a recession rather than closing the least efficient mills first and running the better ones at full capacity.

Private mills, for their part, had little success in securing the benefits of scale through voluntary cooperation. As with procurement, the desire to maintain secrecy and independence, as well as historical rivalry and mistrust between families, prevented cooperation among privatized mills. Moreover, only one private group operated more than one plant. When privatized mills expanded their capacity after privatization—which happened in only two cases—they did so in the same location rather than at a new site. Apart from financial reasons—insufficient funds for a whole new mill—this seems to have been prompted by the desire to retain close, family supervision of operations. Moreover, unlike public enterprises, private mills were able to squeeze scale economies out of larger plants and, therefore, preferred to expand at the same location. Among privatized mills, larger plants were actually more profitable than smaller ones, while the opposite was true for public mills. Thus, privatized mills were more successful than public mills at exploiting scale economies at the level of the individual plant, while BTMC was unique in having potential economies of multi-plant operation, most of which, unfortunately, were not actually exploited.

Sales

Privatized mills had a clear advantage over public mills in sales and marketing—estimated at 2.4 to 3.5 percent of the economic cost—of yarn because of lower transaction costs, lower inventories of finished goods, and greater flexibility in responding to changes in demand.

The transactions on the output side of each BTMC mill were handled through arms-length bids with 15 to 50 wholesalers appointed by the head office, compared to just 2 to 4 dealers per mill in the typical private mill. BTMC used many wholesalers to minimize the risk of corruption, to avoid dependence upon a few dealers, and at the same time to encourage small dealers. In practice, it did not consistently realize any of these objectives. Small dealers were often fronts for established, large dealers. Moreover, BTMC's prices, which were overly rigid because they were set by the head office with approval from the cabinet, failed to reflect quality differences across different batches of yarn or changes in market conditions.[11] The prices of a typical state-owned mill, for example, were changed only once every six months. Consequently, BTMC yarn was underpriced when market prices rose and overpriced in a slump. This promoted personal rent seeking inasmuch as dealers were anxious to pick up BTMC yarn when it was underpriced. Similarly, fraud was encouraged by the fact that BTMC prices were generally a bargain for better batches of yarn but excessive for poorer quality lots. Inflexible prices meant that stocks piled up in certain grades of yarn. BTMC tried to solve that problem through "bundling," that is, requiring dealers to take both "slow-moving" and "fast-moving" yarn, and to pick up the same weekly amount when prices were high and when they were low. However, this was not very effective because the incentive for noncompliance was very high (see, for example, Tariff Commission 1987).

Privatized mills, in contrast, changed their prices frequently, often daily. Each of them had close ties with the two or three dealers who bought all their output. Their steady relationship with these dealers ensured that the dealers lifted all the output, maintained the quality reputation of the products,[12] and helped to manipulate market prices in conjunction with

---

11. Price controls were lifted in the early 1980s, but the cabinet continued to set the prices of state-owned mills, apparently to keep some control of textile prices and to avoid fraud. In 1987, public mills got permission to give small discounts, but few took the initiative to do so.

12. Some privatized companies also strengthened their label through active marketing toward dealers, weavers, or consumers. BTMC officers, by contrast, deemed marketing unnecessary, stressing that BTMC was "no marketing agency" (personal communication with author, 1987).

other private mills.[13] Privatized mills were also very flexible in changing their production plans—at times within hours—based on market intelligence flowing back speedily through their dealers. BTMC, in contrast, set detailed production plans for each mill as part of its annual budget exercise, approved by the government, and could not make changes easily or quickly.

The combined effect of these differences was that transaction costs and inventory carrying costs were significantly lower for private mills. The average privatized mill, for instance, held only about three weeks of yarn output in stock (while some operated with as little as a week's output), compared to 2-1/2 month's stock in BTMC, in 1984/85. In 1986, some BTMC mills had as much as six month's output in finished goods inventory, which was eventually sold off at a discount. The advantages of privatized mills in the sales area were partly economic gains, and partly financial gains realized at the expense of the less nimble state-owned competitor. In addition, private millowners enjoyed a financial advantage over BTMC mills in sales because they were able to require dealers to place larger security deposits with them than the dealers did with public mills. Further, private mill owners were able to siphon off profits from their factories at the distribution stage, and thus reduce their taxes to the government, when the dealers involved were relatives, as was often the case. Such transfer pricing could increase the after-tax profits of the owner families, but from a public policy standpoint did not benefit the country as a whole.

In about half the spinning mills, part of the yarn output was not sold but processed further in a weaving section. Such forward integration saved substantial handling, transport, and transaction costs. Yet in public and private mills alike, these economies were offset by the problems of controlling large enterprises, by the existence of organizational slack due to the availability of an internal market within the firm, and by depressed market prices for cloth. Most integrated mills in the private sector also had dyeing and printing operations. In the post-privatization period, many private mills modernized these units, often adding large design sections as well. BTMC, in contrast, did not overhaul its old dyeing units. Instead it

---

13. Apparently, communicating with competitors about prices was common. In the longer run, market prices were, however, determined by the world market, tariffs, and border controls against smuggling.

planned to build one giant dyeing and printing plant. That central plant, unfortunately, was delayed for years because of procurement problems.

Support Functions

Privatized mills had a substantial financial cost advantage over BTMC in the support functions, particularly in administration and finance. In administration, their advantage stemmed from the smaller bureaucracy in private mills. Whereas the new private owners had initially absorbed all the workers previously employed under BTMC, they had not taken any managers from BTMC's central head office, although they had earlier agreed to do so. Private mill owners cut management staff in their mills to two-thirds of the number under state ownership through golden handshakes and early retirement. Initial expectations that capable managers might leave the BTMC group to earn more in privatized mills turned out to be wrong. Authoritarianism, familism, centralized decisionmaking, and little scope for personal side-benefits in privatized mills made them unattractive for managers who were not related to the owners.

In finance, privatized mills had a big edge over BTMC because they defaulted continually on huge liabilities to the government and state-owned banks, yielding the mills a financial cost advantage of 3.5 to 6.0 percent of yarn cost. The private investors never accepted the position that the debts they assumed at the time of privatization were their responsibility, and they insisted on the debt relief that government officials had promised when the mills were transferred. While the controversy on this issue continued, private mills refused to service most of their outstanding debt (Lorch 1988). They also faced lower depreciation charges than state-owned mills because none of the privatized mills were new. Of course, these financial cost advantages the privatized mills enjoyed did not translate into real economic gains for the country.[14]

Dynamic Efficiency

Dynamic efficiency refers to the potential for changes in efficiency over time. The question of interest was whether privatized mills had a stronger

---

14. However, the protracted dispute over old debt also made it harder to obtain funds from foreign donors for rehabilitation or expansion. Thus, Bangladesh forewent concessionary foreign credit, unless donors substituted their blocked lending to the textile industry with additional lending to other sectors.

inclination and capability than public mills to increase efficiency and mobilize resources in the long run. Our finding in Bangladesh, in a nutshell, was that privatized mills were no more likely than public mills to promote dynamic efficiency. The study explored three critical sources of dynamic efficiency: investment in new capacity, technological upgrading, and the development of human capital.

Fully five years after privatization, only two private mills had expanded their capacity significantly, and half a dozen others had replaced or added a small number of spindles. Most privatized mills did not expand their capacity or adopt new process or product technology. While more privatized mills than public ones attempted to attain international standards of quality (to cater to the growing garment export industry in Bangladesh) or attain domestic cost leadership, many privatized mills did not do so. In the BMTC group, innovation was stifled by the lack of flexibility, autonomy, market information, and profit incentives, but it was equally hindered in most private mills by the lack of scale, intermill cooperation, credit, and confidence in government policies.

One reason why the private sector hesitated to invest in new technology was the difficulty of raising new funds. As mentioned earlier, privatized mills were enmeshed in a conflict with the government about how much of their mills' debt they should be held responsible for. At the time of privatization, private mill owners assumed a total debt of Tk1.3 billion (US$56 million), a sum larger than the annual sales of all their mills. Close to two-thirds of this was the result of working capital loans taken by the mills while they were state-owned; another one-fourth resulted from cash infusions over the years by the government to cover operating losses; the balance consisted of unpaid principal, interest, and penalties on long-term loans obtained from state-owned banks. The principal owed in foreign currencies had also swelled because of devaluation (between nationalization in 1971/72 and denationalization in 1982/83, the taka lost about 80 percent of its value against the U.S. dollar). Private mill owners wanted the government and its banks to write off most of this debt. From their point of view, they had little to lose and much to gain by being uncompromising; after all, it would be embarrassing for President Ershad's government to renationalize the mills or to force them to close down. Not only was the urban industrial workforce politically very important, but the government had plans to extend the scope of its privatization policy. Some investors even seemed to just harvest their mills without reinvesting, strip off assets, and eventually close down.

The government, for its part, found it politically difficult to admit that past irregularities and inefficiencies had contributed to the indebtedness of the now privatized mills when they were still state owned. It was equally difficult for the government to write off loans and give the appearance of caving in to the demands of private mill owners, even though some financial relief had been promised unofficially in 1982 and auditors appointed by the government had found that liabilities were lower than claimed by the government and its banks (Lorch 1988). State-owned development banks were already in deep trouble with their loan portfolios at that time—with the largest industrial bank, the Bangladesh Shilpa Bank, being able to collect only 16 percent of amounts due between 1983 and 1985—and, therefore, were not in a position to accept major losses on their textile loans (Lorch 1988). At any rate, because of this deadlock, private mills were blacklisted by state-owned banks, and thus cut off from foreign donor credit. They were left only with internal resources to finance investments. The underdeveloped Dhaka stock exchange was not a viable source of funds either because potential buyers of shares worried about price manipulation and phony accounting practices in the private sector. Only six textile mills were listed on the exchange in 1987, and the shares of even fewer were traded regularly.

There is no certainty, of course, that even if funds had been available, private mills would have invested heavily. First, smuggled textile goods continued to offer fierce competition to local production. Second, mill owners were concerned about government intervention—the privatization agreement gave the government the "right to intervene" (People's Republic of Bangladesh 1982)—or political instability, perhaps entailing renationalization. Hence they preferred to invest in areas that promised faster returns. BTMC, however, commissioned seven new mills between 1982/83 and 1987, although all of them had been conceived before the privatizations took place. The private sector, in contrast, had commissioned only 30,000 new spindles half way through the country's third five-year plan, compared to a target of 600,000 for the entire plan period.

Privatized mills also had an uneven record with respect to the development of human capital. Whereas public mills trained about 500 managers and workers every year in an institute set up with international assistance and supervised by BTMC, only one in four privatized mills sent participants to this institute because of their adversarial relationship with the government, and hence with BTMC. In some cases, privatization actually worsened the quality of management: six mills reverted to families that had never run a textile mill before, even though they had been involved in planning and constructing their mills until the government nationalized them in 1972. Some other mills were taken over by inexperienced heirs of former owners. A tendency to rely on family members to man all key positions also hurt the development of managerial talent in private mills.

Effects on Other Government Objectives

As one might expect from reading the section on static efficiency, privatization affected income distribution in Bangladesh in a number of ways, but the levels involved were quite limited. Aside from the impact on public finances, which is discussed later, privatization transferred income from employees and traders to mill owners. As mentioned before, the private employers retired many executives and shifted to less-skilled workers.[15] These practices lowered payments to employees by some 10 percent of the wage bill. In addition, family-based control in the privatized mills seems to have sharply reduced employee theft; for example, official BTMC policy paid little attention to waste cotton, but it was carefully controlled in private mills.[16] The reduction in the workforce and in employee compensation, including fringe benefits, might have been more severe had the government and trade unions not put up resistance.

Traders also suffered from privatization because private producers were more successful than BTMC at capturing price premiums associated with higher quality products or shifts in market demand. One exception to this was the case of dealers who were relatives of mill owners, in which case it

---

15. In addition, three privatized mills had laid off their workforce by 1988; however, BTMC had also closed down four mills in the early 1980s.

16. If all collectable waste cotton were sold, the revenues would equal about 1.5 percent of yarn sales. BTMC annual reports from 1983/84 to 1985/86 did not mention waste cotton sales. According to BTMC officers, waste cotton was supposed to be sold by tender, but often the floor price set by BTMC was not met.

was sometimes desirable for owner families to capture profits at the distribution stage rather than the production stage. The losers in this case were the minority shareholders of privatized mills and the creditors who were told that the mills were unable to service their debt. The government was most disappointed that privatization did not lower prices for final consumers or handloom weavers, who bought much of the yarn. Prices continued to be determined by tariffs and border controls because the local cost and output gains were insufficient to crowd out imports.

Privatization affected public finances in several ways. On the positive side, it reduced the grants and subsidies flowing to the textile industry to cover operating losses: in the three years prior to privatization, the mills had lost US$10 million annually. Although the mills BTMC retained made an overall profit in the three years after 1981/82, privatization itself may have contributed to that result. The increased government scrutiny, fear of further privatization, and a new sense of competition apparently boosted the performance of BTMC mills for a while, but it dropped back to lower, more familiar levels in 1985/86 (Lorch 1987). The government also realized money through the sale of the mills, although the amount was a paltry US$1 million for all 22 mills.

On the negative side, debt service payments from the privatized mills to the government, including state-owned banks, were lower after privatization than before. By January 1988, only four private mills were servicing their short-term liabilities, a few had started to repay long-term loans, and about five were on schedule repaying the cash infusions made by the government to the mills when they were state owned. BTMC had also not been prompt in servicing loans when the same mills were under its control, but in that case nonpayment affected cash flows within the public sector rather than between the public and private sectors. This is an important difference if the economic value of a taka in public hands is different from that of a taka in private hands (Jones and others 1986 suggested that the opportunity cost of capital is higher in the public sector, but there is no evident reason for such an assumption in Bangladesh). Privatization may also have reduced the government's tax revenues because private companies were more prone than BTMC to evade taxes. Finally, privatization probably worsened BTMC's financial situation because privatized mills were more flexible than BTMC at seizing profitmaking opportunities. BTMC also suffered financially because it had to buy more than its due share of local cotton and barter cotton. The combined effect of all these factors on public finance was apparently negative in the 1982-86 period. Thereafter, it might have turned positive because of stepped up debt collection by the government and BTMC's return to loss making.

Privatization did not seem to have a major impact on other government objectives. It did not improve textile quality, cost, and production volume sufficiently to replace imports. The price and quality requirements of the booming garment export industry could not be met either, thus, privatization did not improve Bangladesh's trade balance. Nor did consumers get their cotton textiles much cheaper than before privatization, because local prices continued to be determined by the legal and illegal imports. On the plus side from a political standpoint, privatization did not produce major fallout for the government, because unions and the government protected the immediate interests of the urban workforce. Rural employment was not affected because the failure of the privatized mills to expand cloth production spared the hundreds of thousands of handloom weavers from stiff competition. Also, on the plus side, privatization in the textile sector initially sent a positive signal to the private sector. Later, however, the protracted controversy about debt restructuring and the government's inability to control labor leaders impaired the investment climate. The government may have also gained experience that was useful in subsequent privatizations (of which there were a few), although this was probably offset by the rotation of senior government officials every two or three years, and by later sales of state-owned enterprises on the stock exchange instead of their return to former owners. Besides, the government never carefully evaluated its experience with privatization in the textile sector.

Transaction and Restructuring Costs

Privatization usually involves considerable transaction costs, such as valuing the enterprises, preparing them for sale, selecting buyers, negotiating the terms of the sale, and winning support for the transaction from various stakeholders. Usually, it also involves complex restructuring, such as adapting firms to the new competitive environment and redesigning the regulatory framework. Most of these costs were minimized in the case under study. In the hurry to privatize, the pricing was simplified and the audit of each firm was postponed until it had been transferred. The decision to return the firms to their former owners eliminated the buyer selection step. Even after divestiture, the firms got little government support for debt restructuring or mill rehabilitation. Mills that remained under BTMC made little sustained effort to adjust to the new domestic competition. Martial law seemed to eliminate the need to win the support of stakeholders, at least initially. Finally, only few industrywide regulations were introduced that also applied to privatized mills. Only public mills continued to be subject to government control on procurement, pricing, and distribution.

This approach allowed the government to save short-term transaction and restructuring costs and to move forward rapidly with privatization, but it created costs down the road. A good example is the amount of fruitless negotiation that took place on the matter of the mills' debts. This, in turn, had severe consequences, including that it prevented modernization and expansion of the privatized mills and soured business-government relations in the textile industry. Another cost was that not all former owners or their heirs had the managerial and technical expertise and the financial resources to run mills they had taken over. Some were not even committed to running the mills as going concerns. Likewise, when martial law was finally lifted, opposition to privatization increased and President Ershad, who sought wide popular support for his rule, became more sensitive to opposition. This made it difficult for the government to resolve the controversy over the mills' debts, and to confront labor union leaders in their fight against dismissals and wage cuts and for their own control of the mills. It may have been the swiftness of the move that allowed Bangladesh to become one of a handful of developing countries that by 1988 had actually implemented a major program of privatization; however, this short-term advantage was at the expense of the industry's long-term efficiency.

Conclusions

Privatized mills outperformed public ones in static efficiency, albeit by a modest margin, in all but the procurement function. Their main strength relative to public companies was that their owner-managers were more concerned with profit maximization and avoided, through family-based management, formal control mechanisms that stifled initiative and flexibility. The main strength of the state-owned textile group was its overall scale, which family control did not permit in the private sector, but only in raw materials procurement and quality control did BTMC actually realize a cost advantage based on its size. Altogether, the privatization in the cotton spinning industry appeared to have produced an economic gain in static efficiency equal to approximately 6 percent (between 3 to 9 percent) of annual yarn cost, or about US$3.5 million per year (based on the value of yarn produced by privatized mills in 1985/86, and the average exchange rate of that period). From the private mill owners' perspective, the financial gain was more than twice as large as the economic gain, perhaps as high as 18 percent of annual yarn cost. The difference was due largely to the redistribution of income in favor of private mill owners as a result of privatization.

In terms of dynamic efficiency, the privatized enterprises seemed to enjoy little or no net advantage over those enterprises that remained state owned. The new owners invested little in technology, capacity, or human capital. The main barrier to their doing so was the failure to resolve the matter of the mills' debt. Other factors were the owners' focus on commercial matters, and their inability to expand because of a strong desire to keep control in the hands of family members.

Privatization changed income distribution primarily in favor of the new mill owners families at the expense of managers and workers. Moreover, private owners defaulted on the claims of public creditors, left some social tasks to the public enterprise, minimized their tax burden, and maximized profits at the expense of their inflexible public competitor. These transfers from the public sector largely offset the state's shedding of unprofitable enterprises. On the whole, the treasury seemed to benefit little or not at all from the privatization. The government's development objectives were not well served either, as privatization had hardly any impact on handloom weavers, garment exporters, and consumers.

All things considered, privatization did not turn out to be a leapfrogging strategy for industrial development. This was due in large measure to the common weaknesses of private enterprise in developing countries like Bangladesh, to deficiencies in the business environment, and to the privatization process itself. In a business environment where rampant violence, smuggling, corruption, phony accounting, and unchecked default on debt open opportunities for huge rents and pose severe threats to competitiveness, company owners seek an extraordinary degree of control over operations. The state sought to control its mill by rigid rules and minimal managerial autonomy. Private owners, by contrast, used family-based management. Thus, the latter achieved better control of their operations and enhanced their flexibility and concern for profits. At the same time, this family control severely limited the scale of private firms, and hindered intermill cooperation. Private mill owners had a short-term focus on commercial, financial, and political matters rather than on production, technology, and human resources. This orientation reflected their lack of industrial experience, but it also indicated that the main sources of profits in the industry lay in those areas rather than in improving internal operations and technology.

From the mill owners' view, the government did not live up to its initial commitment to the private sector. Increasingly concerned about the urban labor constituency, the government failed, for example, to protect private employers against strong-armed union pressure and interfered in the collective bargaining for wages. The lack of debt service and investment also fueled calls for government intervention, or even renationalization, which in turn alarmed investors. The government did not step up its reform of the banking sector sufficiently. More fundamentally, the government failed to strengthen the rights of creditors against defaulting debtors, of minority shareholders against phony accounting and business practices, and of mill owners against violence and the threat of eventual renationalization.

The privatization process also impaired efficiency gains in the textile industry. Anxious not to miss the political window of opportunity, the government simplified or skipped essential elements of the privatization process. For example, it deferred company audits and debt restructuring until after divestiture. Later, however, it sought to avoid the embarrassing and costly acknowledgment that the mills' liabilities had been inflated by inefficiencies and irregularities dating back to state ownership. Default on that debt barred the privatized mills from new loans, including international donor credit, and tainted their relations with government.

Another example was the decision to privatize in the seemingly easiest and fastest way, namely, to return companies to their former private owners without assessing their financial strength or managerial capabilities. This strategy placed several large mills in the hands of families that were managerially and financially weak. However, if privatization had been implemented at a slower pace, it may have become bogged down as martial law was lifted and political participation increased.

Thus, policymakers aiming for privatization in developing countries are faced with a dilemma. On the one hand, rapid privatization to ensure implementation jeopardizes longer-term economic gains; on the other hand, a slow and carefully thought out privatization program designed to maximize long-term economic impact jeopardizes the implementation of that policy. As a compromise, governments could scale down their divestiture programs to areas where *ex ante* assessments promise the strongest economic impact. Where the economic impact is less certain, governments might prefer to diversify into other methods of privatization or to attempt managerial reform within the public enterprise sector (Vuylsteke 1988). At least in the Bangladesh textile industry, privatization by itself did not seem to achieve major economic gains for the country. A shift in other public policies as well as growing confidence of the private sector in a predictable policy environment would be needed before the privatization program could be expected to reap large gains.

References

Ameen, H. H. M. 1987. "A Study of Divestment of Industries in Bangladesh." Dhaka, Bangladesh: Canadian International Development Agency. Processed.

Asian Development Bank. 1985. *Conference on Privatization Policies, Methods, and Procedures.* Manilla, Philippines.

Ayub, M. A., and S. Hegstad. 1986. *Public Industrial Enterprises— Determinants of Performance.* Washington, D.C.: World Bank.

Bangladesh Gazette, The 1982. "Notice of September 27, 1982." September 27.

Chishty, S. H. 1986. "Privatization in Developing Countries: The Experience of Bangladesh." Paper presented at the Conference on Privatization in Developing Countries, University of Manchester, U.K., December.

Chowdhury, T. E. 1987. "Privatization of State Enterprises in Bangladesh (1976-84)." Processed.

Commander, S., and T. Killick. 1986. "Privatization in Developing Countries: A Survey of the Issues." Paper presented at the Conference on Privatization in Developing Countries, University of Manchester, U.K., December.

Hemming, R., and A. Mansoor. 1986. "The Fiscal Impact of Privatization." Paper presented at the Conference on Privatization in Developing Countries, University of Manchester, U.K., December.

Humphrey, C. 1987. "Privatization in Bangladesh." Study submitted to the Center for Privatization. Washington, D.C. Processed.

Jones, L., P. Tandon, and I. Vogelsang. 1986. "The Economics of Divestiture: Ex Ante Valuation and Ex Post Evaluation." Cambridge, Massachusetts: Boston University. Processed.

Lorch, Klaus. 1987. "Efficiency Effects of Privatization—Ex Post Evaluation of Privatization in the Textile Industry of Bangladesh." Cambridge, Massachusetts. Processed.

_____. 1988. "The Privatization Transaction and its Longer-Term Effects: A Case Study of the Textile Industry in Bangladesh." Cambridge, Massachusetts: Harvard University, Kennedy School of Government. Processed.

Mallon, R. 1984. "Monitoring the Performance of the BTMC." Dhaka, Bangladesh: Trade and Industrial Policy Reform Programme. Processed.

Millward, R. 1986. "Measuring Sources of Inefficiency in the Performance of Private and Public Enterprises in LDCs." Paper presented at the Conference on Privatization in Developing Countries, University of Manchester, U.K., December.

Nankani, H. 1988. *Techniques of Privatization of State-Owned Enterprises,* vol. II, *Selected Country Case Studies.* Technical Paper No. 89. Washington, D.C.: World Bank.

Pack, H. 1987. *Productivity, Technology and Industrial Development—A Case Study in Textiles.* Washington, D.C.: World Bank.

People's Republic of Bangladesh. 1982. *New Industrial Policy.* Dhaka, Bangladesh: Ministry of Industries and Commerce.

_____. 1985. "Overview of Assistance Policies for the Textile Sector." Dhaka, Bangladesh: Trade and Industrial Reform Programme. Processed.

_____. 1986. "Overview of Industrial Project Appraisal." Dhaka, Bangladesh. Processed.

Sobhan, R., and A. Ahsan. 1984. *Disinvestment and Denationalization: Profile and Performance.* Research Report No. 38. Dhaka, Bangladesh: Bangladesh Institute of Development Studies.

Tariff Commission. 1987. *Report of the Committee on the Textile Sector.* Dhaka, Bangladesh.

Vermeulen, B., and R. Sethi. 1982. "Labor-Management Conflict Resolution in State-Owned Enterprises: A Comparison of Public- and Private-Sector Practices in India." In L. P. Jones, ed., *Public Enterprise in Less-Developed Countries.* Cambridge, U.K.: Cambridge University Press.

Vernon, Raymond, ed. 1988. *The Promise of Privatization: A Challenge for American Foreign Policy.* New York: The Council on Foreign Relations.

Vuylstcke, C. 1988. *Techniques of Privatization of State-Owned Enterprises,* vol. 1, *Methods and Implementation.* Technical Paper No. 88. Washington, D.C.: World Bank.

Wasow, B., A. Farouque, and O. Gani. 1984. "The Effects of Policy Choice on Choice of Technique in Textile Weaving." Dhaka, Bangladesh: Trade and Industrial Policy Reform Programme. Processed.

Yusuf, F. H. 1985. *Nationalization of Industries in Bangladesh.* Dhaka, Bangladesh: National Institute of Local Government.

7

PRIVATIZATION THROUGH LEASING: THE TOGO STEEL CASE

Ivan Bergeron

A government wanting to divest state-owned enterprises (SOEs) can theoretically choose among several courses of action: it can liquidate them, allow them to go into some sort of hibernation, or privatize their ownership through total or partial sales. It can also privatize the management of those enterprises by entering into management contracts with private parties or by leasing the enterprises' assets to those parties.Under the latter arrangement, the private partners undertake to run all or part of the enterprises, and lease the physical installations from the government for specified lengths of time in return for paying predetermined fees. The government retains ownership of the physical assets, thus leaving it free to pursue any of the other options when the leases expire. Thus, leasing is a form of privatization that permits a government to avoid making the drastic departure from the *status quo* entailed by liquidation or outright sale of an SOE, while leaving it free to pursue a wide range of options in the future, including divestiture, which might become attractive once an SOE has been turned around.

This chapter describes an actual leasing experience in Togo; one of the first of its kind in Sub-Saharan Africa. In 1984, the Lomé steel mill, a small smelting and rolling operation producing reinforcing bars, was leased to an American entrepreneur. The mill had been operating at a loss since its commissioning in 1979. The leasing venture turned out to be a commercial success for the private investor, and operations were subsequently expanded with a major diversification project. This study examines the Togo steel case with two questions of interest to policymakers:

1. Under what conditions is leasing to a private operator likely to be more attractive than either continued operation under state management (if this alternative is open) or outright liquidation?

2. How should the leasing agreement be structured so that it is sufficiently attractive to the private entrepreneur, while also safeguarding the country's interests?

Historical Background

Toward the mid-1970s, when Togo's economy was flourishing because of the high price of one of its major exports, phosphates, Togo became interested in establishing an iron and steel industry. Part of the rationale for doing so was the desire to exploit an iron ore deposit in northern Togo. However, due to its small size, poor yield, and distant location that deposit was never exploited. Instead, Togo accepted an offer made by a Swiss company, BBC, to construct a mini steel plant with an annual capacity of 20,000 tons of reinforcing bars. The proposed plant was to use local scrap iron as feedstock to produce ingots and rolled products. BBC's proposal was accompanied by a poorly prepared feasibility study that demonstrated the investment's economic viability. The study's shortcomings included an incorrect analysis of the scrap supply in Togo and adjoining countries, overoptimistic estimates of the local and regional market for reinforcing bars, and financial projections based on very unrealistic assumptions, such as full utilization of capacity at plant start-up. Nevertheless, the government accepted the report's conclusions and entered into an agreement with BBC.

A consortium of Austrian, Swedish, and Swiss companies was formed to supply the plant on a turnkey basis. In April 1976, the Togolese government signed a CFAF 13 billion contract with the consortium (approximately US$32.5 million).[1] A financing package of CFAF 9.5 billion was put together that same year in the form of medium-term loans

---

1. The CFA franc (CFAF) is pegged to the value of the French franc (F1 = CFAF50). The rate of exchange of the CFA franc in terms of U.S. dollars varied appreciably over the time period covered here. In 1984, at the time the leasing agreement was concluded, the rate was approximately CFAF400 to the U.S. dollar.

from Austrian, Swedish, and Swiss banks. The Togolese government funded the balance of CFAF 3.5 billion. The government set up a national iron and steel company, Société Nationale de Sidérurgie (SNS), to operate the plant. The mill was built in an industrial estate near Lomé and commenced operations in 1979.

The company's operating results were disastrous right from the start (table 7.1). Sales in 1980 were about one-fourth the original projections, and the operating results showed a net loss of CFAF 2,184 million instead of a projected net profit of CFAF 1,780 million. Total unit costs were more than six times BBC's projections, about three times the local selling price, and about six times the c.i.f. import price (CFAF 110-120,000 per ton). Direct costs alone were estimated at CFAF 177,600 per ton, which under the prevailing production conditions ruled out any prospect of improving profitability by raising production volume. Moreover, the constraints on local availability of scrap, ignored in the BBC study, forced the company to turn to ever more distant sources of supply, so that the price of the scrap increased with increasing production: the company estimated that at full capacity (20,000 tons), the cost of scrap per ton of steel produced would average CFAF 42,000 compared to the feasibility report's estimate of CFAF 13,200.

In 1980, the disappointing sales volume led the local authorities to grant SNS a monopoly on the import, production, and sale of reinforcing bars in the local market; a monopoly previously held by another state company. However, because Togo's domestic consumption of reinforcing bars did not exceed 6,000 tons, SNS had to develop export markets to utilize even 25 percent of its capacity. It did manage to export steel to Niger and Burkina Faso in 1980, but the amounts were small and the transactions were at a loss since the world price did not even cover SNS's variable production costs. Moreover, in those two countries Togolese steel was subject to import duties 8 percent higher than those applied to products of European origin. By the end of 1980, SNS's cumulative losses, after 18 months of operation, totaled CFAF 308 million before depreciation and financial costs, and CFAF 2.9 billion after depreciation and interest.

In 1981, a World Bank mission carried out the first diagnostic study of SNS. Among the main causes of poor performance it identified were (a) the lack of experience of SNS's management staff, especially in the areas of procurement, marketing, finance, and administration; (b) the small size

Table 7.1 SNS' Performance, 1979 and 1980

Category	Unit	1979 (6 months)	1980 Actual	1980 BBC projections[a]
Sales	Tons	1,100	5,450	20,000
Operating results				
Operating profit (loss)	CFAF millions	(314)	(1,400)	n.a.
Interest on external loans	CFAF millions	392	784	n.a.
Net profit (loss)	CFAF millions	(704)	(2,184)	1,780
Cash flow	CFAF millions	(186)	(1,111)	n.a.
Unit costs				
Direct costs and overhead	CFAF/ton	n.a.	240,000	n.a.
Depreciation	CFAF/ton	n.a.	200,000	n.a.
Financial charges	CFAF/ton	n.a.	143,850	n.a.
Total		n.a.	583,850	94,100

n.a. = not available

Numbers in parentheses indicate losses.

a. Based on projections contained in the feasibility report prepared by BBC in the mid-1970s.

Source: World Bank, 1981, *Report on State-Owned Companies in Togo* (Washington, D.C.).

of the local market, coupled with severe competition from European suppliers; (c) the inordinately high production costs, resulting largely from the high cost of imported raw materials; and (d) the inadequate financing, especially for working capital.

First Privatization Attempt

In mid-1980, the Togolese government and BBC started discussions with a view to rehabilitating SNS by setting up a new organizational and management structure. The negotiations took place sporadically over several months and finally collapsed in April 1981. The main elements of BBC's proposal were to set up a new company, Aciérie du Togo, S.A. (ATSA), jointly owned by BBC and the Togolese government. BBC would lease the steel works from SNS and manage the facility, using a team of nine expatriates. BBC would make a loan of SwF 9.4 million to ATSA, while SNS would continue to be responsible for its existing liabilities. BBC proposed that the plant be leased from SNS for a yearly rent, made up of a fixed sum of CFAF 50 million and a variable part equal to 75 percent of the gross operating profit.

According to the projected operating account of the new company, the project would generate a cumulative cash flow of CFAF 3.5 billion over 10 years, which would cover about 40 percent of the external loans contracted, equivalent to about 25 percent of total debt service. However, the projection optimistically assumed that the sales volume would rise from 5,250 tons per year in 1980 to 35,000 tons per year in 1985. A simple calculation showed that if sales in 1985 and beyond were 30,000 tons per year instead of 35,000 tons, the cumulative cash flow over ten years would fall to CFAF 837 million; and if sales were only 20,000 tons per year, the cumulative cash flow would actually be negative. Thus, the proposal was financially unsound, and the government's decision to reject it was understandable. An economic analysis using border prices to value inputs and outputs also indicated that value added would be negative even if BBC's optimistic sales projections were met.

At this juncture, the World Bank recommended that the plant be closed as soon as possible. One of the major preconditions of a World Bank structural adjustment loan in 1983 was the satisfactory resolution of the SNS problem by rehabilitation or privatization, if these alternatives were feasible, or by closure and liquidation. This pointed to the need for studies to explore the economic feasibility of rehabilitation and assess SNS's net worth in order to draw up a liquidation account in the event of closure or privatization.

In 1982, the government invited bids from specialist firms for a detailed technical and economic study of SNS. The terms of reference for this work included a technical assessment of the plant's operations and identification of possibilities for improvement, a study of scrap supply, a market study for the plant's products in Togo and the region, and an assessment of the company's organization. As one of the outputs of the study, the consultant was to recommend the most economical plan of action from among four alternatives: cease operations entirely and wind down the company, mothball the facilities until the economic situation warrants resumption of operations, close down the smelter while continuing to operate the rolling mill with imported billet, or rehabilitate the company if this could be done within a reasonable timeframe and with a decent chance of success.

The study was awarded to a reputable French firm, Hexatec, which estimated the Togolese demand for SNS's products at about 4,500 tons per year without plant modifications, and 6,000 tons if a rolling facility to produce small bars were added. Hexatec saw the potential export market as consisting of Burkina Faso, Niger, and Benin, which together could absorb 5,500 to 9,000 tons per year depending on whether or not plant modifications were made. Other countries of the region were found to offer little potential: Mali because of strong competition from European suppliers; Ghana and Nigeria in view of their own production capacity; and Cameroon, Côte d'Ivoire, Gabon, and Zaire because of the very low selling prices that would be required to match the competition. Even for the most promising countries, ex-works prices would have to be much lower than for the local market, where SNS enjoyed a high nominal rate of protection (projected by Hexatec to be on the order of 60 percent).

According to the consultant's study, scrap could be obtained from three sources, successively more distant and more expensive. Togo itself could provide some 3,000-4,000 tons per year at an average millgate price of CFAF 12,000 per ton; adjacent countries, from which the material could be trucked in, could supply 3,500-5,000 tons at CFAF 20,000 per ton; and other West African countries, from which sea transport had to be used, could supply scrap at CFAF 43,000 per ton. In comparison, the average delivered price of scrap in Europe was CFAF 25,000 per ton in 1983.

The most negative finding of the Hexatec study concerned unit manufacturing costs. Under conditions prevailing at the plant in 1983, Hexatec estimated the unit manufacturing cost at CFAF 183,000 per ton of finished product. By implementing a program of management and technical improvements, Hexatec calculated that the unit manufacturing cost could be decreased to CFAF 135,000-145,000 per ton depending upon the extent of rehabilitation. In comparison, unit manufacturing costs at similar plants in Europe, according to Hexatec, would not exceed CFAF 74,000. Thus, even with the reduction in unit costs that could be achieved by tightening operations—approximately 20 percent under the best scenario—the company would make no profit on export sales and only modest profits on local sales. Thus, Hexatec did not see any way SNS could fully absorb depreciation charges and debt servicing costs.

In view of the discouraging outlook presented by the Hexatec report, the government asked the consultant to study in greater depth the scenario of closing down the mill's smelter and operating the rolling mill alone with imported rather than locally made billets. Hexatec concluded that this option could work only if SNS's entire production were sold in the domestic market. Furthermore, Hexatec considered this scenario as involving a substantial long-term risk. If the world economy picked up, steel mills would be more interested in selling finished products than billets, and the company could find itself paying more for billets than for the finished bars.

Thus, the conclusion implied by the Hexatec study was that the government should close the SNS plant. The next logical step seemed to be the recruitment of another consultant to audit the company's books, ascertain the company's net worth, determine the plant's market value, and recommend the best liquidation procedure. At this juncture, as the Togolese government was pondering the Hexatec report, an American businessman with previous involvement in a mini steel mill similar to SNS in Central America, visited Togo and expressed an interest in taking over part of the plant's operation. By this time, as the audit report showed, SNS's cumulative losses since start-up totaled nearly CFAF 12 billion, the net book value of assets was negative CFAF 6.3 billion, and the market value of the company's physical assets was estimated at less than CFAF 1 billion. Thus, liquidation was an unsavory prospect, especially because of the mint condition of the plant, the quality of its equipment, and the CFAF 13 billion that the Togolese government had spent to build it.

The Ibcon Lease Proposal

In December 1983, the American entrepreneur's company, Ibcon S.A., submitted a proposal to the Togolese authorities to form a joint venture with the government that would lease the SNS mill and produce large diameter bars using imported billet and small bars using imported coils. The ingot casting operation was to be discontinued.

The proposal contained financial projections based on a production program of 6,000 tons per year, which matched Togo's domestic demand in 1982. On this basis, once stable operations were reached, net income was projected at 15 percent of sales after a modest lease payment to the government. The proposal also contemplated selling steel to a few large construction projects then in the planning stage, and projected the gradual development of about 4,000 tons per year of exports to Benin, Burkina Faso, and Niger. The plant would employ 65 people.

According to the Ibcon proposal, resumption of operations on this basis would require about CFAF 335 million of new investment, of which 35 percent would be financed through equity and the balance by a long term loan. Ibcon would own 40 percent of the equity, while the Togolese government and the International Finance Corporation (IFC) would each own 30 percent. IFC had expressed an interest in investing in the venture and in providing some long-term loans. The government's contribution would be in lieu of the lease payment for the first year of operation. The financial return on the operation, projected at 55 percent in the proposal, assumed that domestic sale prices would be approximately equal to import prices plus customs duty of 41 percent.

The unit manufacturing cost projected by Ibcon for the large reinforcing bars (rolled in the plant) was comparable to those in the Hexatec study. The concentration of sales in the local market, at protected prices, permitted an appreciable operating profit, whereas the Hexatec scenario also envisaged unprofitable foreign sales. Furthermore, the profit margin on small reinforcing bars (made from imported bar stock) was projected to be very high owing to the low processing expenses and the advantage conferred by tariff protection.

According to the terms set forth in the Ibcon proposal, a ten-year renewable lease for the plant would be concluded between the government and the new company, with both cancellation and renewal options. The proposed lease amount was set at the higher of either 20 percent of annual gross profit or CFAF 40 million (US$100,000). Ibcon proposed that the new company would sell all the unnecessary plant and inventory on behalf of the government at the best possible terms for an unspecified commission. A five-year, renewable management contract would be established between the new company and Ibcon S.A., whereby the latter would take full responsibility for managing the plant through an expatriate plant manager and senior company staff. In negotiating the final proposal, the government's goal was presumably to maximize the project's social benefits, while Ibcon's goal was presumably to maximize the return on its investment and minimize the risk involved.

As a foreign investor setting foot for the first time in Africa, Ibcon was believed to be quite concerned about the political, financial, and economic risks of doing business in Togo. Based on the projected operating account included in the investor's proposal, the government was able to determine how changes in various assumptions were likely to affect the project's economic and financial characteristics. For this purpose, the government's technical staff set up a spreadsheet model of the project. Four quantitative measures were of primary interest to policymakers: the economic rate of return to Togo, the impact of the agreement on the government's cash flow, the impact on the country's foreign exchange resources, and the financial rate of return earned by the foreign investor. Table 7.2 presents the results obtained along the four performance measures under various scenarios.

The net economic benefit was calculated as the difference between discounted sales proceeds and discounted input and factor costs over a ten-year period, with both inputs and outputs valued at border prices. The opportunity cost of using the assets, measured by the estimated liquidation value of the plant, was treated as a cost in year 0, revenues from the planned export of surplus scrap steel by Ibcon were accounted for in year 1, while the plant's salvage value was recognized as an inflow in year 10. Dividends, net of taxes, accruing to foreign shareholders were treated as

Table 7.2 Results of Evaluating Ibcon's Proposal Under Various Scenarios

Scenarios	Economic rate of return (%)	Impact on government cash flow (CFAF millions)[a]	Net foreign exchange outflow (CFAF millions)[b]	Financial rate of return to shareholders (%)
1. Base case, 6,000 tons/year, no exports[c]	Negative	–48.2	142.0	37.7
2. Base case, 10,000 tons/year, 2,500 tons exports	0.6	–26.6	107.6	45.8
3. Scenario 2, plus rent increased to 40% of gross margin	5.4	–9.0	89.5	34.0
4. Scenario 2, plus government share of equity increased to 49%	6.4	–11.2	92.0	34.4
5. Scenario 2, plus 10% import duty on coils	4.0	–12.9	94.7	38.7
6. Combination of 4 and 5	8.4	–0.8	82.6	28.9
7. Combination of 3, 4, and 5	10.7	9.7	72.0	21.4

a. Average annual cash flow to the government with the lease agreement minus the average annual cash flow to the government without the agreement. Thus, a negative sign indicates that the government's cash flow was worsened by the lease agreement.

b. Average annual net foreign exchange outflow with the lease agreement minus the average annual net foreign exchange outflow without the agreement. Thus, a positive sign indicates that the government's foreign exchange reserves would be worsened by the lease agreement.

c. Description of base case

Rent as percentage of gross margin	20.0
Government share of equity (%)	30.0
Tax on turnover (%)	10.0
Corporate tax on profits (%)	49.0
Tax on dividends (%)	25.0
Tax on salaries (%)	2.0
Import duties (%)	2.1

Source: Ministry of Planning and Administrative Reform, Togo.

Table 7.3 Ibcon's Proposal: Estimated Net Annual Economic Benefit After Stabilization of Operations

Category	Quantity (tons)	Price[a] (CFAF/ton)	Total revenues (CFAF millions)
Revenues:			
Large bars — domestic	5,600	147,800	827.7
Small bars — domestic	1,900	181,600	345.0
export	2,500	181,600	454.0
Total	10,000	--	1,626.7

	Foreign exchange (CFAF millions)	Local currency (CFAF millions)	Total (CFAF millions)
Costs:			
Large bars[b]			
Billets	512.1	56.9	569.0
Electricity, fuel, oxygen	48.6	20.8	69.4
Consumables	22.0	9.4	31.4
Spare parts	13.0	5.6	18.6
Management contract	39.2	16.8	56.0
Insurance	0	12.3	12.3
Direct labor/administrative salaries	0	32.5	32.5
Selling/General and administrative expenses	0	9.0	9.0

164

Audit expenses	0	1.1	1.1
Shrinkage	79.9	8.9	88.8
Subtotal	714.8	173.3	888.1
Small bars			
Coils	535.4	59.5	594.9
Transformation costs	5.3	21.1	26.4
Subtotal	540.7	80.6	621 3
Total costs	**1,255.5**	**253.9**	**1,509.4**
Revenues minus costs	371.2	(253.9)	117.3
Debt servicing	40.1	0	40.1
Dividend outflow net of tax	21.4	0	21.4
Net economic benefit	**309.7**	**(253.9)**	**56.0**

-- = not applicable

Note: Figures pertain to 1988, by which time the operations of the new company were expected to have stabilized. Figures in parentheses indicate losses.

a. Estimated border prices calculated on the basis of c.i.f. Lomé prices plus 20 percent handling and transport from port to plant, plus a 15 percent premium to reflect the advantages of local availability and quick delivery.

b. Estimated international prices used for all tradables; local taxes are excluded from input and factor costs; no shadow prices used for salaries and wages.

Source: Derived from: Ibcon S.A., Proposal to the Togo Government, (December 1983).

costs to the country. Debt servicing on foreign loans was handled the same way. The resulting costs and benefits for 1988, by which time operations were projected to have stabilized, are shown in table 7.3 for the base case, that is, the project as put forth in Ibcon's proposal. The project is seen to result in a small net economic surplus of CFAF 56 million in 1988. The numbers in table 7.3 provide some idea of the magnitude of individual revenue and cost categories that, in turn, yielded the economic rates of return presented in table 7.2.

The second performance indicator—impact on government cash flow—was defined as the incremental revenue obtained by the government with the project compared to without the project. In the latter case, government revenues would consist mainly of customs duties on imported reinforcing bars, while in the former case it would consist of rent, dividends, and tax receipts.

The third performance indicator—net foreign exchange impact of the project—was defined as the difference between the foreign exchange outflow with the project (capital goods and raw materials imports, interest on external loans, and after-tax dividends paid to foreign shareholders) and those without the project (finished product imports). Thus, a positive result on this measure would mean the project lowered Togo's foreign exchange reserves.

Table 7.2 shows that the project would generate a reasonable economic rate of return only if exports were realized, rents and import taxes were higher than assumed in Ibcon's proposal, and the government's equity stake was raised. Note that the economic return would not exceed 11 percent even in the most favorable scenario (no. 7). Government cash flow, as compared to the liquidation alternative, would at best be neutral (scenario 6) or slightly positive (scenario 7). In every scenario, the project's net impact on the balance of payments was likely to be negative: the manufacture of reinforcing bars from imported billet used more foreign exchange than direct importation of the finished product. However, the project's financial return after taxes was likely to be high in all the cases, ranging from a low of 21.4 percent to a high of 45.8 percent.

Thus, the government's first analysis seemed to suggest that the economic value of Ibcon's proposal, while not negligible, was likely to be small even if certain conditions were added to the original Ibcon proposal. However, Ibcon's proposal would save the government from the unpleasant task of closing a new, expensive industrial plant and laying off a few hundred employees. Among the government's other concerns was Ibcon's proposal to abandon smelting without a serious study of its profitability, especially since another mini mill expert had recently suggested to the government that smelting could be profitable. In addition, the government wanted to ensure that Ibcon did not sacrifice SNS's long-term interests in its pursuit of short-term profits. Specifically, the government was concerned that Ibcon might not bother to develop export markets, pursue diversification opportunities, and/or maintain the steel plant properly. These issues arose during the negotiations that followed Ibcon's proposal.

Negotiations with Ibcon

Negotiations between the Togolese government and Ibcon took place sporadically during a two-week period. On the matter of equity, the Togolese government said it preferred not to participate in the new company's capital, although it would welcome part of the capital being made available to private Togolese investors. Ibcon agreed to take care of the company's initial capital, with or without a contribution by the International Finance Corporation (with which no agreement was finally to materialize), and to make part of the capital available to Togolese investors after a few years. A second change to the original proposal was Ibcon's offer to include the collection, preparation, and export of steel scrap in the activities of the new company. The government accepted this after the computer model confirmed that it would improve the project's economic rate of return. Ibcon also agreed to explore diversification opportunities for the mill, including the possibility of recommissioning the arc furnace and resuming smelting if and when it appeared to be financially feasible. With that possibility in mind, the furnace and its ancillary equipment would be mothballed rather than dismantled and sold.

During discussions, the government expressed its concern about several issues, including the continued operation of the arc furnace, proper maintenance of the leased facilities, and a commitment by Ibcon to actively explore export possibilities. For its part, Ibcon expressed a strong preference that the government should participate in the venture's equity, and tried to obtain a lease, tax, and pricing package that would allow a financial return compatible with the venture's perceived risk. Tax provisions, in particular, were debated at length, with the Togolese government insisting that its cash flow with the lease arrangement should at least equal the import duties that it would have collected on finished products if the project were not implemented. The negotiations finally led to an agreement in principle between Ibcon and the Togolese government providing for the creation of a new company under Togolese law, the Société Togolaise de Sidérurgie (STS), whose capital would be subscribed entirely by Ibcon. STS was established in July 1984 and the final agreement was signed in October 1984.

The final agreement between STS and the Togolese government stated that the company would start operations by manufacturing reinforcing bars of 6-8 mm diameter from imported coil (that is, by simple straightening and cutting), while bars of 10 mm diameter and above would be made from imported billet or from other raw materials. The purchase, preparation, and export of the steel scrap held in inventory by SNS would also be STS's responsibility. STS would resume the use of the arc furnace and casting facilities when economic conditions warranted it. Ibcon would provide all new investments necessary to implement STS's manufacturing program, including working capital, without government guarantees. Furthermore, STS committed itself to explore promising diversification opportunities and new manufacturing operations that appeared financially viable.

For its part, the government offered STS several assurances. The legal guarantees included freedom for STS to exercise all the provisions of its statutes, including those relating to choice of shareholders and associates, with the understanding that STS would endeavor to sell up to 30 percent of its shares to Togolese private interests as soon as possible. The government's economic and financial guarantees dealt with import duties and taxes on competing finished products, which were to be kept at the levels prevailing at the time of signature for five years. At the end of this period the import tax and duty were to be reviewed by mutual agreement. Domestic selling prices were to be determined by a government-approved schedule, reviewed on a semi-annual basis, and indexed for automatic adjustment for direct operating costs outside the company's control (essentially, imported raw materials). Also, the government promised to make foreign exchange available for imported equipment, operating expenses, and the repatriation of profits and dividends. Finally, the government guaranteed that for the duration of the agreement STS would be exempt from import duties on equipment, spare parts, raw materials, and other inputs not available in Togo, including semifinished products such as coils. It also agreed to waive all export duties on the company's products.

The formula to be used for calculating the lease amount was as follows. The lease fee would be a fixed amount of CFAF 70 million for the first two years of operation; thereafter, and until year 6, the fee would be the higher of an increasing percentage of gross margin or a fixed amount, the latter also increasing annually. Starting in year 6 and to the end of the lease, it would be set at the higher of CFAF 80 million or 40 percent of gross operating income. The lease was to be valid for ten years, renewable by mutual agreement. Upon expiration of the lease agreement, all investments made by STS and inventories in excess of the initial level would be repurchased at book value by the government, which would retain a right to inspect all important investments made by STS after year 6.

Thus, the final agreement differed from Ibcon's original offer in three respects. First, the production program was altered so that 8 mm bars were no longer to be rolled from imported billet, but manufactured by straightening and cutting imported coils, and the collection, preparation, and export of steel scrap was added to the company's activities. Second, Ibcon was to be a majority shareholder of STS, with an initial holding of 100 percent that would be reduced to 70 percent following the issue of shares to Togolese investors. No longer was there any question of technical assistance fees or annual commission on gross profits payable to Ibcon. However, since Ibcon controlled STS, there was nothing to prevent transactions of this kind from taking place between the two companies. Finally, the amount of rent was increased significantly from 20 percent of gross operating profit (minimum CFAF 40 million) to 40 percent of gross operating profit (minimum CFAF 80 million) after five years of operation.

A Preliminary *Ex-Post* Evaluation

The draft agreement of March 1984, including the export of 6,000 tons of scrap a year, was projected to yield an economic rate of return of 6.3 percent (table 7.4). Compared to the alternative of liquidating the steel plant, it promised to yield a small net foreign exchange saving of CFAF 9.6 million and a worsening of the government's cash flow deficit by

Table 7.4 Evaluation of the Draft Agreement of March 1984 with Ibcon S. A.

Scenario	Economic rate of return (%)	Impact on government cash flow (CFAF million)[a]	Net foreign exchange outflow (CFAF million)[a]	Financial rate of return to shareholders (%)
Conditions as reflected in draft agreement of March 1984 (details in text)	6.3	−7.1	−9.6	21.8

a. Same definition as in table 7.2. Note that the final agreement, compared to Ibcon's original proposal (see table 7.2, base case) promised to improve both the government's cash flow position and the country's foreign exchange position. As this table shows, the final agreement was projected to *reduce* the country's foreign exchange outflows relative to the option of liqidating the steel plant.

CFAF 7.1 million. Even though these results appeared only marginally favorable to Togo, the project was deemed attractive for the intangible benefits it promised to yield. The World Bank officially concurred with this point of view. Subsequently, the final agreement was also appraised to measure the impact of altering the manufacturing program to produce 8 mm reinforcing bars from coil instead of billet. Due to the increase in exports projected as a result, the large contract subsequently obtained from a local construction project, and the diversification that had already begun (rolling of small shapes for the local market), the economic rate of return was of the same order of magnitude as for the draft agreement of March 1984, while government cash flow was better than projected earlier.

STS itself quickly turned a profit on its operations. For its first complete financial year (1985), the company realized a net profit, after lease payment and taxes, of CFAF 112 million on a turnover of CFAF 1.5 billion. That year, STS sold about 8,000 tons of reinforcing bars and exported 6,000 tons of prepared scrap. In 1986, it sold 11,000 tons of bars, of which about 3,000 tons were exported. By comparison, the projected sales in the Ibcon proposal were 6,900 tons for 1985 and 7,800 tons for 1986.

Several factors accounted for STS's financial success. In the first place, an energetic management team was able to develop markets rapidly through aggressive selling and good service, particularly with regard to delivery times. Another factor was effective control of production costs. A significant achievement in this regard was the decision to use second-hand railroad track steel rather than billets to produce bars. Railroad track steel was 30 percent cheaper than billets and was available in large quantities in many parts of the world, including Africa, and yielded a final product that was equivalent or superior in quality to bars produced from billets. STS's procurement of raw materials was also very effective, relying on flexibility, diversification of sources, and an aggressive search for opportunities. Finally, the government's pricing policy, based on a tariff protection rate of 41 percent, resulted in high profit margins in the domestic market. An analysis carried out in 1987 by the International Finance Corporation showed that the net margin (after depreciation) in the local market was 34 percent of sales for products made from rail stock and 21 percent of sales for products made from billet. In contrast, the net margins on exports were 9 percent of sales for products made from rail stock and -9 percent for products made from billets.

Ibcon also moved as promised to sell equity to local investors. In 1986, 35 percent of the company's equity was sold to private investors in the form of preferred stock, with 14 percent being subscribed by Togolese investors and the rest by other African investors. The shares had to be distributed through banks, since Togo had no stock exchange, and they were guaranteed to yield a minimum return of 10 percent.

From Togo's point of view, a surprising positive development was STS's early move into a new product line, pylon manufacturing. The project, undertaken in 1987, consisted of additional facilities to make pylons and structural beams from formed and welded reinforcing steel. The technology was obtained from a Danish firm, Ramboll & Hannemann (R&H), which was a world leader in the field with more than 35 years experience with the process. R&H prepared the feasibility report for the project and contributed toward the venture's incremental investment. R&H was also entitled to a royalty of 1 percent of sales. The capital cost of the project (CFAF 600 million or US$1.97 million) was financed through a combination of equity (31 percent of total cost) and long-term loans from the International Finance Corporation (CFAF 260 million) and the Danish Industrialization Fund for Developing Countries (CFAF 152 million).

The new product fit in nicely with STS's operations by allowing existing manufacturing assets to be more fully utilized. It gave Togo access to a superior technology while also advancing the country's technological expertise. While delivering roughly the same performance as traditional concrete and welded angle-iron structures, pylons made of reinforced steel were cheaper to manufacture (10 to 20 percent less) and transport (25 percent less) and are also more durable. Moreover, the new product could use STS's existing marketing, distribution, and transportation systems, both within Togo and in neighboring countries. Over a period of four years, annual sales were expected to grow to about 1,500 tons of pylons and 350 tons of structures, with roughly half the volume coming from export markets.

The pylons project probably raised the economic returns to Togo from the lease arrangement with Ibcon. Pylons manufacturing added more value than the making of reinforcing bars because it used facilities and labor more intensively. It added to STS's employment and to the taxes the firm paid. One study conducted in 1987 estimated the marginal economic return to Togo from the lease arrangement with Ibcon, including the pylons manufacturing project, at between 11.0 to 14.5 percent depending on the exact assumptions made. This range is significantly higher than the range of returns projected when the original agreement with Ibcon was signed.

Apart from the benefits reflected in the economic return calculations, policy makers in Togo were pleased with the intangible gains from the Ibcon agreement. For one thing, jobs were preserved by the agreement: although the workforce was reduced from over 200 to 120, all jobs might have been lost without the agreement. Most of the workers employed by STS were former employees of SNS, and they received higher salaries than before, better training, and more responsibility. Second, by continuing to operate the plant, the government avoided the political embarrassment of shutting down a brand new facility erected at considerable cost. Third, the sale of stock in STS in 1986 broadened share ownership by Togolese people; a development viewed with satisfaction by government policymakers as well as international agencies. Finally, the agreement with Ibcon had a positive impact on international donors, who hailed the agreement, and on the international investment community in general. The manner and speed with which Togo had negotiated an agreement with a foreign company was believed to have signaled to others that Togo was an attractive country in which to do business. Not only did the government allow Ibcon to reap attractive returns, it also freely allowed the repatriation of profits as per the agreement. Soon after the Ibcon agreement was signed, Togo concluded other lease agreements with foreigners. Thus, the STS venture was believed to have paved the way for privatization on a bigger scale in Togo.

Conclusions

This chapter began with two policy questions: (a) Under what conditions is leasing a troubled SOE to the private sector likely to be preferable to the alternatives of continued state operation, outright privatization, or liquidation? (b) How should the leasing agreement be structured so that it is simultaneously attractive to the private party as well as to the country? The Togo case sheds light on both questions.

On the first question, the Togo case shows that leasing can bring new skills to the organization—technical and managerial—that allow the available assets to be utilized more fully. Leasing may also be the means for providing an SOE with greater managerial autonomy, although as the Togo case shows, leasing may not be an inexpensive method for achieving that objective. At the same time, leasing may be preferable to outright privatization—that is, selling 100 percent of the SOE's equity to the private sector—because it keeps several options open for the government down the road. If the SOE's performance improves under private management, the SOE can be sold later for a more attractive price than when it is in deep waters. Alternatively, the government might decide to keep the firm under state ownership after it has been turned around. Finally, leasing may be preferable to liquidation for several reasons. Among the principal advantages is that some, if not all, jobs can be preserved, and the government can also avoid the political costs associated with closure and layoffs. Another advantage is that the government can postpone the embarassingly big write-off that will accompany liquidation of the company. Such a write-off is also likely to be required under outright privatization because the troubled SOE could probably be sold for only a fraction of its book value.

The Togo case further shows that international agencies such as the World Bank may look favorably upon a lease agreement, which is likely to be seen as a form of privatization, even if it is less dramatic than outright sale to the private sector. In many developing countries, governments are torn between keeping SOEs alive and satisfying external or internal demands for improving their financial performance. Under these conditions, leasing may be an option that satisfies several groups, including politicians, employees, private entrepreneurs, and international agencies. Finally, in the SNS case, the government saw the lease arrangement as generating other advantages, especially the creation of a climate in Togo that made other, larger privatization moves possible. The successful deal with Ibcon was also believed to have earned Togo the reputation of being one of the more progressive Sub-Saharan countries when it came to reforming the SOE sector.

On the second policy question, the Togo case highlights the difficulty of framing an agreement that is sufficiently attractive to the private party, and yet does not give away the store from the country's standpoint. Given the political and economic uncertainties entailed in lease arrangements with SOEs in developing countries, private entrepreneurs are likely to seek high and quick returns on their investment. They are likely to demand attractive prices, protection from imports, and special privileges with regard to taxes and duties or government regulations; to offer very low fees or rents for the use of an SOE's expensive assets; and to ask that these matters be guaranteed to some extent via formal agreements. At the same time, they are likely to tolerate little interference from the government in the running of the business. For its part, the government is likely to seek assurances that the private entrepreneur will not run down the firm's assets during the lease period or neglect noncommercial objectives important to the country.

The process of negotiation can therefore be complex and difficult. The challenge before governments is to give away enough to the private entrepreneur to keep the entrepreneur's interest in the agreement, but not so much that the alternatives of liquidation or continued state management become more attractive from the country's point of view. In the SNS case, the odds appear high in hindsight that Ibcon might have accepted a less generous package of tariffs, pricing, import duty on coils, or lease payments than it did in March 1984. Also, the government might have put in place stronger incentives for Ibcon to promote exports or diversification. As things turned out, the last two objectives seem to have been fairly well achieved with no other incentive than the prospect of increased profits. Yet the Togo case points to need for governments to be extremely careful in handing out protection or monopoly rents to private investors.

One possible way to avoid conceding too many benefits to the private party is to structure lease agreements so that they contain a mechanism to review the agreement within a reasonable period of time. In the Togo case, the pricing policy was to be reviewed after five years, although the lease itself had a ten-year duration. At that time, the government could use the venture's actual experience (and profitability) in the previous five years to renegotiate the pricing formula so that the extent of protection might be lowered and a greater part of the benefits passed to Togolese consumers. Another interesting element of the SNS lease agreement was the requirement that about a third of the company's equity be sold to local shareholders over a specified period of time. This, too, ensured that if the venture turned out to be a financial success, at least some part of the surplus would go to people in Togo rather than all of it go to the foreign investor.

PART II

CONTROLLING
STATE-OWNED ENTERPRISES

8

PERFORMANCE EVALUATION FOR STATE-OWNED ENTERPRISES

Leroy P. Jones

Public enterprise inefficiency imposes great costs in terms of foregone social welfare. For example, improving the real operating efficiency of the public enterprise sector by only 5 percent without changing prices or making new investment would (Jones 1980a, 1981a,b):

- in Egypt, free resources amounting to about 5 percent of GDP, which is equivalent to 75 percent of all government direct taxes, or enough to triple government expenditures on education;

- in Pakistan, free resources amounting to 1 percent of GDP, which is equivalent to 50 percent of direct taxes, or enough to increase government expenditures on education by 50 percent;

- in the Republic of Korea, free resources amounting to 1.7 percent of GDP, or over one billion dollars in 1981;

- in the People's Republic of China, free resources worth US$11 billion, which would fund a 150 percent increase in government expenditures on education, health, culture, and science.

The magnitudes of these potential gains may surprise some readers, but the existence of inefficiencies will shock no one. Critics and defenders of public enterprise will, of course, differ in their analysis of the problem. Economists writing in the Austrian, property rights, Chicago, and related

An earlier version of this paper was presented at a November 1981 conference in Islamabad sponsored by the United Nations and Pakistan's Ministry of Production. Support from these organizations and Boston University's Public Enterprise Program is gratefully acknowledged.

179

traditions, stress that the root of the problem lies in the separation of ownership from control. That is, managers are unlikely to make the difficult decisions needed to improve efficiency if they do not share in the resulting benefits. Their solution is to marry ownership and control through privatization on the capitalist model. This chapter is sympathetic to this conservative analysis of the source of the problem, but suggests an alternative solution, namely, the introduction of a signaling system to guide and motivate managers to act in the interests of society as a whole.

Such a signaling system has three major components. The first is a performance evaluation system, in which national goals are translated into explicit enterprise objectives and quantified in a performance criterion. The second is a performance information system, which monitors actual achievements. The third is an incentive system, in which the welfare of managers and workers is linked to national welfare by a pecuniary or nonpecuniary bonus system based on achievement of particular target values.

This chapter discusses the components of a signaling system in detail. A basic indicator of efficiency is first derived and then modified to account for some of the exogenous factors beyond the control of management. Given a criterion (a metric) that is broadly applicable across enterprises, it remains necessary to establish criterion values (standards), that demarcate "good" from "bad" performance and that vary according to the specific circumstances of individual enterprises. The next step is to extend the system to allow for noncommercial objectives and dynamic effects (innovation and growth).

The initial focus on static operational efficiency is justified by the argument that its improvement takes first priority. That is, an enterprise that is not using its existing resources efficiently is not a likely candidate for new resources and is unlikely to have the ability to make a maximum contribution to noncommercial objectives. Nonetheless, it remains essential to incorporate indicators of noncommercial and dynamic performance. Performance evaluation is not confined to providing a bottom line judgment, but also involves diagnosis to understand the sources of problems and achievements. Thus, diagnostic indicators are also discussed.

Performance evaluation of public enterprises is not a simple matter and a workable system cannot be imposed arbitrarily or overnight. Rather, it must be the product of an evolutionary process involving both enterprise managers and government supervisors. Accordingly, a phased system of implementation is proposed.

The Importance of Performance Evaluation

Internationally, many of the problems of the public enterprise sector are traceable to inadequacies in performance evaluation. This is not surprising. The goals of public enterprises are difficult to specify due to the problems of multiple objectives (including commercial versus noncommercial) and plural principals (different organizational units having different perceptions of what the goals should be). If goals cannot be specified, then "good" performance cannot be distinguished from "bad," managers cannot be rewarded on the basis of performance, and inefficiency can result.

What if the goal area were eliminated in a soccer football league and no alternative means of keeping score were substituted? What would be the effect on the quality of play? Initially, players might continue to exhibit their old skills through professional pride or force of habit. Eventually, however, new forms of behavior would emerge. Selfish show-boating might yield rewards in crowd applause without its old penalty of reduced teamwork and scoring. Movement without the ball would cease as the old costs of being out of position would have been eliminated. Being out of condition would incur few penalties and practice might become perfunctory or canceled altogether. Coaches would have little reason not to indulge their whims and play their favorites regardless of their skills. Better players would yearn for recognition and the satisfaction of playing to win, and would move to other leagues and be replaced by weaker players. At best the game would become quite different—akin to a Sunday afternoon game of frisbee at the beach—pleasant and occasionally incorporating some spectacular moves, but with marginal appeal to competitive, goal-oriented individuals. In terms of efficiency, one can imagine the results if a member of this league were to play a competitive game with a conventional team.

While the situation of public enterprises is by no means as bleak as this little analogy might suggest, it remains true that organizations without meaningful quantifiable objectives have great difficulties in controlling efficiency. Compare government agencies and private enterprises in this respect. The outputs of government departments are generally difficult or impossible to quantify: how do you measure the performance of the ministries of finance or defense? For private enterprises, however, long-term profits and growth provide quite reasonable first approximations to performance. The relative difficulty of measuring performance is a major explanation of the widespread view of governments as inefficient.

Public enterprise is a hybrid, sharing characteristics of public governmental institutions and private enterprise. Like government, some of its goals (noncommercial, for short) are difficult to quantify; like a private enterprise, some of its objectives (commercial, for short) are readily quantifiable. If "poor" commercial performance can be readily explained away in terms of "noncommercial" objectives, and if no effort is made to distinguish between legitimate reasons for poor commercial performance (for example, government pricing policies) and illegitimate reasons (for example, incompetence leading to high costs), then even the quantifiable objectives lose their power to guide, motivate, evaluate, and control. In effect, the enterprise then becomes just like a government agency rather than a hybrid. The public enterprise manager plays a game without a score.

For some public enterprises this is perhaps inevitable. In a regional development bank the noncommercial objectives may so outweigh the commercial ones that quantification is not feasible. For most public enterprises, however, the bulk of their services to society come through their commercial activities and systematic performance evaluation becomes feasible.

In short, most public enterprises are evaluated like a public institution, which is to say, not at all, and if they are to be made more efficient, they must be made more like private enterprises, with quantified performance indicators to serve as a first approximation to performance. *This is not to say that they are to be evaluated like private enterprises, but rather, that like private enterprises, they must be evaluated.*

Autonomy and Decentralization

Performance evaluation is critical in its own right, but its importance is compounded because it is a precondition for reform of the autonomy structure as a whole. When asked how to improve their efficiency, many public enterprise managers respond: "Give us clear objectives, then give us the autonomy to pursue those objectives, and judge us by the results." They are right in linking the signaling system to autonomy, because without clear objectives and an incentive system, autonomy cannot be delegated.

To illustrate, consider the determination of the level of working capital. In a private enterprise, the shareholders and the board of directors almost invariably delegate the power to set the level of working capital to the chief executive officer (CEO). The assumption is that the CEO will keep as much working capital as necessary for efficient operation, but no more, since the funds could otherwise be used to generate income directly (in economists' jargon, the CEO will acquire working capital only up to the point where its marginal cost equals its marginal revenue product). The reason why this is a safe assumption is that the manager is judged and rewarded on the basis of profit, which will rise or fall (in part) according to the correctness of decisions on the level of working capital. The board can therefore exercise its control function by examining outcomes (profit) rather than the process by which the outcome is generated.

If, however, the CEO has little or no reason to be concerned with raising the profit of the firm, then the manager might not make the correct decision on the level of working capital. The CEO might divert funds from more productive uses by keeping levels of inventory and cash far beyond the level necessitated by prudent management, thus reducing risk and avoiding difficult decisions. After all, keeping all your funds in a checking account is easier than constantly shuttling them between short- and long-term interest-bearing accounts. Similarly, maintaining high levels of input inventories is much easier than managing a "just-in-time" delivery system. In such situations, the shareholder cannot wholly delegate the working capital decision.

In the case of public enterprises there are two reasons for government involvement in the working capital decision. The first is macroeconomic control of the aggregate level of credit. This, however, could be better accomplished by setting an overall credit ceiling to be allocated by price rationing. The second is that this effective delegation using market mechanisms would fail, however, if the government feared that managers would take "too much" regardless of the price. As a result, various representatives of the government—often high level—find themselves trying to decide exactly what constitutes legitimate working capital levels for individual firms. The difficulties are that the process is time consuming, the ministries often lack the information and the business expertise to know just what levels are "reasonable," and scarce ministerial talent could be better used elsewhere. In sum, by any standard of modern management, the working capital decision should be delegated to the enterprise, but given the signaling system's inadequacies, it often cannot be.

The foregoing is merely one illustration of two general propositions. The first is that a policy of increasing reliance on market forces—"getting the price right"—is bound to fail unless accompanied by measures to ensure that enterprises are motivated to respond to the signals those prices provide. The second is that when principals cannot control outcomes, they must control processes. Delegation of operational process decisions to an agent presupposes effective control of outcomes. This in turn requires that desirable outcomes be quantified, and that some incentive mechanism exists to ensure that managers care about the outcome. In sum, if more decisions are to be delegated to the enterprise, then the signaling system must be reformed to ensure that those decisions are made in the public interest. If autonomy is to be efficiently and permanently delegated to the enterprise, then accountability must be ensured by a signaling system that specifies and rewards socially desirable behavior.

Lessons from International Experience

Although the need for a signaling system is logical, international experience demonstrates the obstacles to implementing such a system. Space does not permit a detailed examination of this experience, but only a summary of its lessons.

Internationally, the evolution of public enterprise signaling systems follows a surprisingly predictable pattern. In the first phase, no explicit system exists. This may be for reasons of ideology ("from each according to his ability; to each according to his need") or bureaucratic precedence ("civil servants don't get bonuses; why should managers?"). In the USSR, for example, this phase lasted from 1917 to about 1932, when the second phase was entered with bonuses paid, but according to very unsophisticated performance criteria (Nove 1969).

At the beginning of phase two, success is typically measured by some simple partial indicator, such as quantity of production (Kornai 1959). This leads to abuses, because managers are not motivated to provide quality products or to reduce costs. Over time, additional indicators are added to reflect these other considerations and a system of multiple indicators evolves. These can become quite elaborate, and are often superficially appealing, but generally suffer from a basic structural flaw.

This can be seen from a simple example. Assume that success is measured by three indicators: output, profit, and labor productivity (value of output per worker). Further assume that from one year to the next, an enterprise changes in only two ways: the real value of its output increases and the real value of raw materials consumed rises by an equal amount. From the nation's point of view, the enterprise is doing neither better nor worse. There is more of one good (the output), but less of another (the input), and the two changes precisely offset one another in terms of welfare. However, two of the three indicators increase, and the enterprise is rewarded. The problem is that the increase in output is credited three times (it raises all three indicators), while the increase in costs is debited only once (only profit falls). Because of this asymmetric counting of costs and benefits, rewarding the enterprise for actions that make society worse off is quite easy.

The lesson of phase two is that performance criteria must meet the fundamental principal of performance evaluation, namely, that *all benefits and all costs must be counted once and only once.* Partial indicators fail because they ignore some benefits or some costs. Most multiple indicator systems fail because they weight benefits and various costs components asymmetrically.

Phase three occurs with a shift to a criterion that meets the fundamental principle. Only a small class of indicators meet this criterion. One is profitability (variable benefits less variable costs over fixed costs). Another is the French global productivity of factors. In the USSR, an attempt at entering phase three was made with the 1965 reforms (Liberman 1966) announced by Kosygin in a speech including the following:

> "The size of profits characterizes, to a considerable extent, the contribution made by an enterprise to the country's net income, which is used for the expansion of production and the improvement of the people's well-being" (Kosygin 1965).

In this view, what is wrong in a capitalist society is not the concept of profit, but who receives it. The main point of this review of international experience is that there is no simple alternative to profitability as the basis of a performance evaluation system for public enterprises. To heed this lesson, however, is no guarantee of success, as much more needs to be done to achieve the transition to phase three. The remainder of this chapter suggests some of the necessary considerations.

Objectives and Performance Criterion

A performance criterion is simply a quantifiable expression of the enterprise's objectives. Even though public enterprises have many objectives, multiple criteria are not necessary. Multiple objectives can be handled by aggregation if they are individually quantifiable and if everyone can agree on the relative weights to be assigned to each. The simplest private company has multiple objectives in the form of maximizing benefits and minimizing costs for each of its various outputs. A composite performance indicator can be created by applying positive weights (prices) to each of the benefits (outputs) of operation and negative weights to each of the costs (inputs) and adding them up. The result is a single indicator called profit, that is constructed by weighted addition of multiple subsidiary indicators.

The problem with constructing a performance criterion for a public enterprise is not that its objectives are multiple, but that some of the objectives are difficult or impossible to quantify, and that agreement cannot be reached on the tradeoffs (relative weights or prices) to be used in aggregation. In dealing with these problems, it is useful to think in terms of two sets of objectives: commercial and noncommercial. Commercial objectives are similar to those of private firms and are reflected (albeit imperfectly, as will be explained below) in commercial accounting procedures. Noncommercial objectives concern the external effects of enterprise operations, (for example, the benefits of opening up a backward area or the costs of pollution), which are not reflected in private accounting procedures. Noncommercial objectives are particularly troublesome because they are typically difficult to quantify (for example, the benefits of opening up backward areas) and/or difficult to put weights on (for instance, the degree of pollution can be measured in terms of various particulate counts, but it is not easy to convert this to dollars and cents).

Fortunately, for purposes of performance evaluation, the problem of noncommercial objectives can be substantially reduced by recognizing that many noncommercial objectives are existential rather than operational. That is, they are achieved by the very existence of the enterprise and do not alter operational goals. They affect investment decisions, but not operating decisions. Project evaluation criteria are altered, but not performance evaluation criteria. For example, the decision to build an integrated steel mill might be influenced by such noncommercial objectives as the desire for national autonomy in a strategic material. Nonetheless, once the plant has been built, the noncommercial objective has been achieved (so long as steel is produced) and the remaining operational objectives are only commercial: to produce as much steel as possible at minimum cost. Similarly, a plant may be located in a backward region partly to achieve the noncommercial objective of regional equity, but once it is built, this objective has been achieved and strictly commercial considerations dominate.

In both of the foregoing cases, of course, the enterprises will presumably be less successful commercially than enterprises built without reference to noncommercial objectives. Assuming for the moment that profit captures commercial objectives, this is equivalent to saying that the enterprise will be expected to earn a lower commercial rate of return. Nonetheless, the operational goal is still to maximize that rate of return (or minimize the loss). The level of profit that represents "good" performance will be lower, but profit remains the criterion.

This last example leads to the important methodological distinction between a general performance criterion and a particular criterion value (or target). The first step in performance evaluation is to select a criterion, say profitability, which allows firms to be ranked on a continuum. As many noncommercial objectives are existential, they can be ignored in constructing an operational criterion for dealing with commercial objectives. The second step is to select a criterion value, for instance, 10 percent, which differentiates "good" from "bad" performance. Criterion values will be discussed later.

Enterprise Performance Criterion: Public Profit

Assume an enterprise has no noncommercial operating objectives. This does not mean that standard private accounting profit serves as a performance criterion. Publicly relevant profit is quite different from privately relevant profit for two reasons: first, publicly relevant accounting categories are different from privately relevant categories; second, publicly relevant prices differ from privately relevant prices (Sen 1970).

Accounting differences occur because private costs are often public benefits and vice versa. As one example, consider corporate income taxes. These are a private cost and a private manager should be rewarded for reducing taxes in favor of increasing dividends and/or retaining earnings. For a pure public enterprise, however, taxes are not a cost but merely one way in which the benefits are distributed to the government shareholder. A public manager should be neither rewarded nor penalized for reducing taxes while increasing dividends, retained earnings, or the depreciation allowance. This is not to say that the distribution of the enterprise's disposable surplus is irrelevant; important financial and motivational implications exist (Gillis, Jenkins, and Lessard 1983; Jones 1980). Rather, the purpose of performance evaluation is to encourage the maximization of the socially relevant profit. Determining the distribution of that surplus is a separate question. Taxes are a privately relevant cost, but not a publicly relevant cost. Therefore, public performance should be measured before taxes and private performance after.

As a second example of the divergence between public and private relevance, consider a situation in which a manager takes advantage of multiple interest rates to borrow from one government bank at, say, 6 percent, while depositing in another government bank at, say, 12 percent. The shareholders of a private firm should certainly reward a manager for such interest arbitrage activity, but from the standpoint of a government shareholder, such behavior should be neither rewarded nor penalized.[1] This sort of arbitrage constitutes a private benefit but a public transfer.

A third illustration is given by a large South American public manufacturing firm that moved from large losses to significant profits in a single year. However, investigation revealed that this was due largely to:

- the conversion of government debt to equity on the balance sheet, thus reducing interest payments;
- the government making other interest payments directly to foreign lenders on behalf of the company;
- the enterprise capitalizing interest payments on construction in progress.

---

1.   Recall the assumption that both banks are wholly public. If they are foreign, then the conclusion is reversed, and if they are wholly or partially held by private domestic parties, the conclusion might be modified.

The first two actions made the company better off, but the government and its banks worse off by an identical amount, and the third action made no one better off in any real sense. Even though the nation as a whole was no better off, private profit rose for all three reasons.

These are but three of many examples of differences between publicly and privately relevant accounting categories. All arise because the private manager is charged with looking out for the interests of only one economic actor (the shareholder), while the public manager should be concerned with the interests of all domestic actors. The performance indicator that reflects this broad interest will be called "public profit." It is defined as single-period variable social benefits less variable social costs; that is, the difference in the value to society between what the enterprise takes out of the economy (costs) and what it puts back in (benefits) in any one period. More precisely, this is the quasi-rent generated by the fixed capital owned and operated by the enterprise, or:

Production

- Intermediate Inputs
- Employee Wages and Other Benefits
- Rental Payments
- Opportunity Cost of Working Capital.

Alternatively and equivalently, in terms of a standard profit and loss statement, public profit is:

Sales

± Inventory Charges
- Manufacturing Costs
- Administrative and Selling Costs
- Total Employee Costs
+ Depreciation and Amortization Allowances
- Opportunity Cost of Working Capital.

The second source of divergence between public and private performance criteria lies in the relevant prices (Jenkins and Lahouel 1981). Often, an enterprise is forced to sell its output in a price-controlled market where the price to the enterprise is less than what society is willing to pay; or it is allowed to acquire imported inputs at a preferential exchange rate below the real value of the foreign exchange to society. In both cases, the actual price received or paid is the relevant price for shareholder evaluation of the private enterprise, since these are the prices that determine private returns. However, from the viewpoint of a government shareholder as custodian of all national resources, the relevant price is that which reflects economic scarcity. In principle, the solution is simple: revalue the accounts using shadow prices, just as economists usually do for project evaluation.

In practice, shadow pricing is unlikely to occur. Shadow prices are complex and controversial at best, and a government would have to have great faith in economists to fire a powerful retired general, politician, or bureaucrat based on whether the shadow multiplier for unskilled labor was, say, 0.1 or 0.7. My own feeling is that the best solution of actually making market prices reflect social scarcity is more likely to become reality than the second-best solution of using shadow prices to evaluate performance. If neither solution is adopted, how can public enterprises be evaluated?

Fortunately, there is a practical way out of the dilemma. Later on the chapter argues that prices are generally beyond management's control and that the best available standard for evaluating enterprise 'A' in year 't' is provided by the same enterprise in year 't–1'. Thus, for control purposes, managers should be evaluated based on the trend in public profit at constant prices.

If this conclusion is accepted, then the solution to the shadow pricing dilemma follows directly from the empirical observation that while the levels of public profits will differ when evaluated at shadow as opposed to market prices, the trends will generally be similar. Consider the simplest possible case of an enterprise with only one output and no inputs. The trend in public profit would then be a quantity index of outputs that differs by only a monotonic transformation when evaluated at shadow rather than market prices. In this extreme case the two trends are identical. Introduction of multiple outputs and inputs eliminates this simple identity because of the usual index number problem. Nonetheless, the empirical evidence supports the assumption that the resulting differences will generally be minor. In sum, the trend of public profit at constant market prices can provide a useful and practical approximation to the theoretically ideal, but practically unobtainable, trend at constant shadow prices. The logic is similar to that used when looking at the trend in real GNP per capita as a measure of the trend in national welfare. The approximation can be further improved if major differences between market and shadow prices are captured through the introduction of a "social adjustment account," which will be explained later.

Management Performance Criterion

Many factors that determine enterprise performance are beyond managers' control. The quantity of capital a manager has to work with and its quality (technology) and age affect relative performance, but were determined in previous periods, usually by someone other than the current manager. The government or world or domestic market forces outside management's control usually set prices. Decisions such as hiring workers or procurement procedures affect performance, but in a public enterprise may be circumscribed by government policy. For such reasons, a clear distinction must be made between enterprise performance and managerial performance. There are four steps in the process:

- The first step is to make a standard adjustment for two readily quantifiable exogenous factors: price changes and the quantity of capital. Simply divide public profit by the quantity of fixed capital and convert to constant prices. The resulting indicator—public profitability at constant prices—is greatly superior to public profit (though still imperfect) as a measure of managerial performance and should be routinely computed as part of a performance evaluation system for all enterprises.

- For some enterprises, a second step of industry-specific quantitative corrections can be taken. Engineering data on the effects of scale, vintage, and technology can sometimes be used to generate adjustment factors for the quality of capital. Low capacity utilization due to shortages of inputs or inadequate demand can sometimes be corrected for by an "as if" expansion factor.

- The third step is to recognize that often one of the best ways to correct for a wide variety of enterprise-specific exogenous factors is to divide by the same enterprise's achievements in previous years. That is, by focusing on the trend in performance, one controls for the quality of capital and, to some extent, for the nature of output and input markets.

- The fourth step is to have a review meeting during which managers are allowed to "explain" their level of performance. Even after a superb job of measuring performance, nonquantified factors that affect the result will remain. The aim of quantification is not to replace the final judgment of superiors, but to aid it. The evaluation exercise quantifies, as much as possible, and thus reduces the scope for discussion, but does not eliminate the need for individual judgments to account for special circumstances.

All these steps (except the first) can be alternatively (and probably better) treated by incorporation into the criterion value specification, since they are necessarily industry- or enterprise-specific.

Setting Enterprise-Specific Criterion Values

Given the choice of any performance criterion, be it private profit, public profit, labor productivity, capacity utilization, miles per gallon, seconds per hundred yards, or anything else as appropriate for evaluating a particular endeavor, then the still more difficult task remains of selecting a particular criterion value. While the criterion establishes a scale, the criterion value establishes the points on the scale that distinguish bad from average from good performance. Consider sprinters. The natural performance criterion is seconds per hundred yards. The criterion remains valid for men, women, children, senior citizens, and those in wheelchairs; what differs is the standard (criterion value) that distinguish meritorious performance. The same is true for public enterprises. Public profitability is an appropriate indicator for a manufacturing company whether it is located in a major port or in a remote and backward province; but whereas a 5 percent performance might be good in the region that is far from the source of imported raw materials, it might be bad in the port where transport costs for raw materials are negligible.

The function of the criterion value, then, is to allow for the plethora of enterprise-specific constraints that affect a particular unit's ability to generate public profit. As the number of such factors is large, this is no simple task. The sources of information that can assist in setting criterion values include:

- comparison with similar firms elsewhere;
- comparisons with the same firm's performance in previous years;

- professional judgments by third parties;

- professional judgments at the ministry level;

- professional judgments at the enterprise level.

If many similar units are operating in similar circumstances, then the problem is mechanical. Simply collect data on relevant variables for a sufficiently large number of units, estimate a regression plane (preferably of the "outer-bound" form), and individual unit performance is measured as a deviation from that norm (plane). If the number of observations is large relative to the number of discriminatory variables, this is a practical approach. Consider the following example. The city of Cambridge holds a rowing race and encourages participation by people of all ages. The organizers collect historical data on rowing time and age, run a regression, estimate the effect of age on time, generate a correction factor in seconds per year, adjust participants' actual times to yield age-corrected times, and give awards based on this corrected time. This allows 70-year-olds to compete against 20-year-olds.

The difficulty with this approach for public enterprises is that the number of similar enterprises is usually small. A country may have one integrated steel mill and only two oil refineries. It may have four public fertilizer plants, but their technology may be sufficiently different to preclude direct comparisons.

The number of observations can be increased by international comparisons, but now the number of control variables increases geometrically. One country may have a sister plant of apparently identical size and technology in another country. Knowledge of its performance is of course useful in forming a judgment as to the first plant's performance, but there is no way to run a definitive regression because of differing national conditions. Similarly, in evaluating cement and fertilizer plants, knowing that the international standard for operating days is 330 and that many developing countries achieve these figures is essential. However, other exogenous factors (notably, the availability, quality, and price of energy) differ, making global comparisons difficult. The point is that while comparisons with other domestic or foreign plants can serve as useful partial aids to judgment in setting criterion values, they are in themselves insufficient.

How then can one find a "similar" enterprise as a basis for comparison? In the entire world, the enterprise most similar to enterprise 'A' this year is generally enterprise 'A' last year. This leads to the use of last year's performance as the starting point for a criterion value against which to judge this year's performance. The focus is on the trend in performance rather than the level. While this is a step in the right direction, it is not a final solution for two reasons. First, even for a single enterprise things change from year to year. Most important, prices change. As already noted, this can (and should) be treated mechanically by shifting to constant price evaluations. However, other changes (for example, in demand conditions or the availability of inputs) also affect performance and cannot be treated so simply. Second, the room for improvement varies from unit to unit. In a plant that has historically been poorly run, a 20 percent improvement in the indicator might require the same level of managerial effort and skill as that required to produce a 2 percent improvement in the indicator of a plant that has always been well run.

In sum, intertemporal and interenterprise comparisons are essential when setting criterion values, but in the end, a subjective professional judgment is required. Third-party evaluations can sometimes be used for this purpose. For a new firm, the project proposal provides some standards. One can also commission detailed internal evaluations by consultants, but this is expensive and should probably be confined to weaker firms. In most cases, the ultimate target will have to be arrived at through negotiation between the enterprise and the government.

The Disclosure Bonus and Criterion Values

The people with the best information about what is feasible for a particular enterprise are the managers of that enterprise. Unfortunately, their judgment is likely to be biased because a low target is in their interest. A manager negotiating a performance target with the ministry naturally stresses all the difficulties and tries to achieve the lowest possible target so as to increase the ease of its accomplishment. The resulting process of negotiation between enterprise and ministry, well known in Eastern Europe, will normally result in a target that is below the enterprise's real potential.

To induce managers to reveal their best estimate of the enterprise's potential, a "disclosure bonus" system can be used. Briefly, the process is as follows:

1. the ministry uses its best judgment to set a target criterion value and an associated target bonus level;

2. the enterprise is then free to adjust the target criterion value, and if it does so, the bonus is adjusted in the same direction by an amount calculated according to an adjustment formula;

3. the actual enterprise bonus may be above or below the adjusted target bonus depending on whether actual performance is above or below the adjusted target criterion value.

The system is described in more detail in figure 8.1.

The purpose of the disclosure bonus is to induce managers to give their best estimate of enterprise potential at the beginning of the period, and to do their best during the period, regardless of their original estimate.

In a single period case with no uncertainty, this is accomplished as suggested by the examples in figure 8.1, and proven elsewhere (Weitzman 1976). The danger of a ratchet effect remains (this year's performance alters next year's proposed target/bonus relationship), but this can be reduced by setting targets several years in advance. This is not feasible for price-dependent criterion values, but may be feasible for constant-price criteria. Uncertainty is an unavoidable problem. The disclosure bonus is thus not a panacea, but it does provide a useful aid in determining criterion values.

Allowing for Noncommercial Objectives: Social Adjustment Accounting

How are operational noncommercial objectives to be dealt with? The central proposition is that they must either be dealt with explicitly or ignored altogether. Otherwise, the entire signaling system breaks down, and with it, the basis for a sensible autonomy structure. If managers are allowed to get away with arguing that their poor commercial performance is due to pursuit of vague, unquantified, noncommercial objectives, then distinguishing between legitimate and illegitimate reasons for losing money becomes impossible. In this situation, holding managers accountable for

Figure 8.1 The Disclosure Bonus

I.   The Scheme

A. *Variables*

B $\equiv$ Bonus
T $\equiv$ Target (any criterion, say profitability)
α $\equiv$ Overfulfillment factor
τ $\equiv$ Underfulfillment factor
ß $\equiv$ Bonus adjustment factor
G $\equiv$ Superscript for planning value set by government
E $\equiv$ Superscript for planning value set by enterprise
A $\equiv$ Superscript for value actually achieved

B. *Process*

1. Government announces α, ß, t subject to constraints that:
   $$0 < \alpha < \beta < \tau < 1.$$
2. Government assigns preliminary B^G and T^G.
3. Enterprise chooses own T^E, which automatically yields a new bonus according to the formula:
   $$B^E = B^G + \beta\,(T^E - T^G).$$
4. At the end of the period, the actual bonus is either:
   $$B^A = B^E + \alpha\,(T^A - T^E) \quad \text{if overfulfillment, or}$$
   $$B^A = B^E + \tau\,(T^A - T^E) \quad \text{if underfulfillment.}$$

II.   Example

A. Purpose: to give a heuristic demonstration that under this scheme, it is in managers' best interests to both:

1. tell the truth (i.e., to reveal the T^E they thing best represents enterprise potential); and
2. do their best (i.e., to maximize T^A regardless of what they predicted at the beginning of the year).

This assumes perfect knowledge (by managers) and no ratchet effect.

Figure 8.1 The Disclosure Bonus (cont'd)

B. Parameters

1. Let $\alpha = .30$; $\beta = .60$; $\tau = .90$.
2. Assume:

T*	=	100	(the actual technologically possible maximum)
T^{t-1}	=	80	(last year's accomplishment)
T^G	=	90	(government thinks enterprise can do 10 better than last year)
B^G	=	5	(bonus for doing 10 better)

C. Alternative Strategies and Associated Payoffs

	Bonus
1. Do nothing (accept $T^G = 90 = T^E$ and actually produce $T^A = 90$).	5
2. Do not negotiate but do best (accept $T^G = 90 = T^E$ but produce $T^A = 100$).	8
3. Negotiate downward but overachieve (set $T^E = 85$, but produce $T^A = 100$).	6-1/2
4. Brag and do best (set $T^E = 110$, but produce $T^A = 100$).	8
5. Tell the truth and do best ($T^E = 100$ and produce $T^A = 100$).	11

achievement of either commercial or noncommercial objectives also becomes impossible, and delegating autonomy is therefore undesirable.

If we accept this proposition, then the question is how to quantify the achievement of noncommercial objectives and incorporate it into the performance evaluation system. This is not a simple task and few countries have dealt with the problem successfully.

One straightforward solution is to eliminate the problem by simply denying the validity of noncommercial objectives in public enterprises. Any worthwhile noncommercial responsibilities are to be hived-off to separate public institutions, leaving public enterprises free to operate according to strictly commercial principles. Some observers simply despair of ever imposing effective commercial discipline on an enterprise that has recourse to noncommercial objectives as an excuse for poor commercial performance. The separation of commercial and noncommercial objectives is not uncommon in practice, for example, it is explicit in Chile and implicit in much of the public enterprise sector of the Republic of Korea.

Ignoring operational noncommercial objectives (or transferring them to another agency) may well be a step in the right direction compared to the common nihilistic practice of recognizing both objectives, but holding managers accountable for neither. However, a further step is possible. This involves quantifying the costs and/or benefits of meeting noncommercial objectives and entering them explicitly into the enterprise accounts, a process I will call social adjustment accounting.

One variant of social adjustment accounting is reflected in the French "program contract" system. The basic principle is that the enterprise should pursue only commercial objectives unless specifically instructed to the contrary by the government. In such a case, a bargain is struck as to the incremental costs incurred in meeting the stated objectives, and the enterprise is compensated by this amount. The obvious advantage of this system is that it allows pursuit of legitimate noncommercial objectives, but controls illegitimate pursuits by subjecting them to an open discussion of costs (and thus of the tradeoffs) involved.

One technical feature of this particular variant should be noted: costs are measured rather than benefits. In principle, of course, the ideal solution would be to base compensation on the benefits, allowing the enterprise to earn a social profit on the difference between benefits and costs, and permitting decentralized, nonbargained decisionmaking. The problem with this is obviously that most noncommercial benefits are difficult or impossible to measure. One does not attempt to measure the benefits of having a military unit of a particular sort: rather one measures the costs and asks only whether the (unmeasured) benefits are greater than the costs, not how much greater. Alternatively, and more commonly, one compares the costs of different methods of achieving a particular sets of benefits. Similarly, when assessing the benefits of keeping open a factory in a backward area, focusing on costs is a practical second-best alternative to measuring both benefits and costs.

The second variant is similar to the first in that it is based on a negotiated agreement about the costs of meeting legitimate, noncommercial objectives. It differs in that the compensation is not actually paid. Instead, the expenditure is entered not as a cost above the public profit line, but as a transfer below the line. That is, the expenditure is treated as a dividend paid in kind to the government. The quantum of public profit is not affected by the noncommercial activity, but some of that profit is distributed in kind rather than as taxes, dividends, or retained earnings.

Managers would naturally prefer the compensated to the uncompensated variant, because of the financial impact on retained earnings. Nonetheless, assuming the firm is financially viable, the uncompensated version is simply a form of internal cross-subsidization that avoids the unnecessary circular step of transferring funds up to the center as taxes and dividends, only to be returned as subsidies. The important point is that in both variants, a conscious decision is made about which noncommercial objectives are worth the cost and which are not.

Social adjustment accounting can also be used to deal with incorrect prices on major inputs and outputs. If fertilizer is sold ex-factory at low prices as a result of a conscious government decision to subsidize farmers and/or wage goods, then the enterprise can be compensated by a per unit subsidy. Similarly, if the factory is receiving underpriced natural gas or electricity, then a per unit tax can be levied to make the firm's price approximate real economic value. This is, of course, a cumbersome second-best alternative to simply setting the right price in the first place, but in some situations it may be the only politically or bureaucratically feasible way to ensure that managers receive correct signals as to economic scarcity. If so, then it is desirable that the tax/subsidy combinations should be actually compensated, but they could also be uncompensated (via the below-the-line distribution method) if financial viability is not threatened. In the latter case the output subsidy would be credited to sales, the input debited under manufacturing costs, and the net effect entered *per contra* as a social dividend (levy), implicitly paid (received) in kind. Public profit would then reflect the real economic surplus generated by the enterprise and managers could be rewarded according to their real contribution to society, independently of whether or not the right prices were actually paid.

The ultimate variant of social adjustment accounting is to create an entire set of shadow accounts altering each and every accounting entry by a multiplier reflecting the divergence between market and economic prices. While such an exercise is theoretically ideal and has major utility in research, it is unlikely to be feasible as an actual control device. In which case, the social adjustment account is a practical means of capturing the most important benefits of the theoretical ideal.

Any remaining noncommercial benefits that are deemed critical can be evaluated in qualitative terms and entered into the system as supplementary indicators.

Allowing for Dynamic Effects

A major weakness of any single-period performance indicator, be it private or public profit, labor, or total productivity, is that it ignores future effects. We can think of an enterprise as a living organism: many current decisions impose costs in the present that are associated with offsetting benefits in the future. Deferring maintenance can increase output and reduce costs this year at the expense of lower output and higher costs next year. Current expenditures on research, training, and planning increase costs in the present, but generate benefits in the future. Single-period indicators capture only one side of the benefit/cost calculations for decisions that have an impact on more than one period. Performance indicators that only consider current flows can thus lead managers to neglect the future by devoting inadequate attention to innovation, planning, consumer goodwill, and maintenance.

This problem is often more acute in public enterprises. Private enterprises are less likely to sacrifice the future to the present for several reasons. In owner-operated firms the self-interest of the decisionmaker will lead him or her to value the future. When ownership is divorced from control, long managerial tenure and deferred managerial compensation (stock options) can tie decisionmaker interest to future effects. Finally, the value of shares traded on the stock market is heavily determined by investor perception of future effects. For public enterprises in developing countries, however, management is divorced from capital, tenure is typically brief, there is no deferred compensation, and shares are either not traded at all or traded in an imperfect market where government-imposed dividend policies dominate as a determinant of value. Accordingly, performance evaluation systems for public enterprises must explicitly incorporate indicators of future effects if innovation, planning, maintenance, and so on, are to be encouraged (for an example of the negative impact of single-period performance on evaluation see Berliner 1976).

What is needed are answers to such questions as the following:

- Is preventive maintenance adequate?
- How rapid is implementation of investment projects?
- Does the company have a coherent and up-to-date corporate plan?
- Is the company devoting adequate attention to research and development?
- Are training and motivation of personnel adequate for the company's future needs?

Answering such questions will necessarily be a subjective process. One approach is to use a five-point rating scale from inadequate to superior. Initially, most companies might be rated at the mid-point level of adequate, with attention devoted to identifying a few of the best and worst performers.

The set of relevant questions, and the weight attached to each, will vary from company to company. Many companies will have no ongoing investment projects, but for those that do, the rate of progress will be an important indicator of performance.

An Indicator System

Three sorts of performance indicators are necessary:

1. the primary indicator (public profitability) covers static operational efficiency plus any noncommercial or dynamic effects that can be valued in monetary terms;
2. supplementary indicators cover dynamic effects and noncommercial effects that can only be rated, but not monetized;
3. diagnostic indicators are used to explain movements in the primary indicator (for example, capacity utilization, inventory turnover).

Diagnostic indicators must not be given independent weight in the evaluation process or this will result in multiple counting. They are important, however, in explaining performance trends and identifying causal factors. Supplementary indicators, however, must be given independent weight. They do not duplicate the primary indicator, since they only cover factors left out of the primary indicator because monetary quantification is not feasible.

An example of the use of diagnostic indicators is given in table 8.1. The last column gives changes in values between 1990 and 1991. Overall, it shows that the company's contribution to the nation (public profit) declined by 0.46 billion pesos. Reading up the column we see that this was due primarily to increases in the cost of working capital (0.36 billion pesos), and secondarily to an increase in wages (0.08 billion pesos). There was also a major decline in production (–1.24 billion pesos) but this was almost exactly offset by reduced consumption of intermediate inputs (–1.23 billion pesos) so that the net change in value-added (or gross national product) was negligible (–0.01 billion).

Table 8.1 Sources of Changes in Public Profits
(billions of pesos)

Variable	-----Profit change due to changes in-----				
	Quantities	+	*Prices*	=	*Values*
Production	–1.68		0.44		–1.24
- Intermediate inputs	–1.76		0.53		–1.23
= Value added	0.09		–0.10		–0.01
- Wages and benefits	–0.01		0.08		0.08
- Rentals	0.06		–0.06		–0.00
- Opportunity cost of working capital	–0.04		0.40		0.36
= Public profits	0.07		–0.52		–0.46

Note: Billion = 1,000 million.

We next ask whether these changes were due principally to price or to quantity changes. This is particularly important since price movements are largely outside the control of management, who can only affect quantities. The first two columns of the table allow this question to be answered by decomposing the value change into its price and quantity components. Starting at the top of the table, we observe that while output prices rose (0.44 billion), input prices rose even more (0.53 billion) so that the net effect on value added was unfavorable (–0.10 billion). At this level, prices on average moved against the firm, more than offsetting the nominal decline in value. In quantity terms, therefore, value added actually increased (by 0.9 billion). This is equivalent to saying that the enterprise's contribution to real GDP rose by 0.09 billion, but that this was more than offset by unfavorable price movements, so that the contribution to nominal GDP actually declined slightly (by 0.01 billion).

Moving down the table, we see that the major sources of decline in public profits—namely, increasing costs of working capital and labor—were entirely due to price effects. The real quantities of both inputs actually declined slightly during 1991, but price increases more than offset these savings.

Overall then, the decline in public profits (–0.46 billion) is more than explained by unfavorable price movements that on balance cost the company 0.52 billion pesos. Looking only at the effect of quantities—the variables under management's control—the company actually contributed 0.07 billion pesos more to the economy in 1991.

Implementing a Signaling System

Performance evaluation is not a simple task in private enterprises, and it is even more complicated in public enterprises. In addition to appreciation of the technical analytic issues discussed above, it requires a high-level political/administrative decision that a signaling system should be implemented, a willingness to pay performance based bonuses, an information system for monitoring performance, and a communication system in which the process and its results are discussed and modified in meetings between representatives of the enterprises and the government. A system unilaterally and suddenly imposed from above without the operating units' input, cooperation, and appreciation is likely to fail.

The message of this chapter is, therefore, emphatically not that performance evaluation is a simple task. Rather, its goal was to suggest how to avoid common errors. Privatization is one way to improve efficiency by linking it to management interests. Performance evaluation is another.

References

Berliner, Joseph. 1976. *The Innovation Decision in Soviet Industry.* Cambridge, Massachusetts: MIT Press.

Gillis, Malcolm, Glenn Jenkins, and Donald Lessard. 1983. "Public Enterprise Finance in Developing Countries: Towards a Synthesis." In Leroy Jones with Richard Mallon, Edward Mason, Paul Rosenstein-Rodan, and Raymond Vernon, eds., *Public Enterprise in Developing Countries.* New York: Cambridge University Press.

Jenkins, Glenn, and Mohamed Lahouel. 1981. "Evaluation of Performance of Industrial Public Enterprises: Criteria and Policies." Paper presented at UNIDO Expert Group Meeting on the Changing Role and Function of the Public Industrial Sector in Development, Vienna, October.

Jones, Leroy P. 1980a. *Comments on Development of a Performance Evaluation System for the Korean Public Enterprise Sector.* Seoul: Korea Development Institute.

—————. 1980b. "Determinants of the Debt/Equity Ratios in Public Enterprises." Paper presented at United Nations Conference on Investment Decisionmaking in Public Enterprises, International Center for Public Enterprises, Ljubljana, Yugoslavia, October.

—————. 1981a. "Efficiency of Public Manufacturing Enterprises in Pakistan." Report for Pakistan Ministry of Production and the World Bank. Washington, D.C.: World Bank.

—————. 1981b. "Improving the Operational Efficiency of Public Industrial Enterprises in Egypt." Report for USAID Washington, D.C.

Kornai, Janos. 1959. *Overcentralization in Economic Administration.* Oxford, U.K.: Oxford University Press.

Kosygin, A. 1965. "On Improving Industrial Management, Perfecting Planning and Enhancing Economic Incentives in Industrial Production." *Izvestia.* September 28. Reprinted in Myron Sharp, ed. 1966. *Planning, Profits and Incentives in the USSR,* vol. 1. White Plains: International Arts and Sciences Press.

Liberman, E.G. 1956. "Plans, Profits and Bonuses." In Myron Sharp, ed., *Planning, Profits and Incentives in the USSR,* vol. 1, pp. 79-87. White Plains: International Arts and Sciences Press. Also in *Pravda,* September 9, 1965.

Nove, Alec. 1969. "Microeconomic Problems." In *The Soviet Economy,* pp. 171-181. New York: Praeger.

Sen, Amartya. 1970. "Profit Maximization." Lecture delivered at Kerala University, Trivandrum, March 31.

Weitzman, M.L. 1976. "The New Soviet Incentive Model." *The Bell Journal of Economics* 7 (Spring):251-257.

9

CONTROLLING STATE-OWNED ENTERPRISES

Ravi Ramamurti

It is not unusual in the public policy arena to find that by the time an idea—even a good one—has been implemented, the intent or concept underlying that idea has been lost sight of, and reality is a far cry from the motivating vision. So it is with state-owned enterprises (SOEs), which were created in large numbers in many developing countries during the past three or four decades with high hopes that they would play a role that neither the government nor the private sector could play. Policymakers in most developing countries today would agree—at least privately—that SOEs have not lived up to that expectation.

Why has this state of affairs come about, and what can be done about it? These are the central questions this chapter addresses. It argues that state-owned enterprises have failed to deliver the expected results, not necessarily because the concept was poor, but because governments did not implement it well. To be sure, good reasons for this existed, but even today policymakers do not fully understand or appreciate those reasons. Therefore, there is a risk that the SOE concept will continue to be implemented poorly or that it will be rejected prematurely as an instrument of public policy.

State-owned enterprises often spearhead economic change in developing countries; thus it should come as no surprise that their actual

Adapted from "Controlling State-Owned Enterprises," *Public Enterprise*, vol. 7, no. 2 (February 1987), pp. 99-117. Research leading to this article was conducted while the author was a United Nations consultant to the Government of Bangladesh. Useful discussions with Tony Bennett, Leroy Jones, Richard Mallon, and Haroonur Rashid are gratefully acknowledged.

behavior and results reflect many of the frustrations and tribulations of development itself. Assuming that all those problems will disappear simply by handing SOEs over to the private sector is naive. After all, in developing countries the real choice is between an imperfect public sector and an imperfect private sector, not between an imperfect public sector and a perfect private sector. Therefore, for the public sector (just as for the private sector), searching for ways to make it less imperfect is essential.

Doing the Right Things versus Doing Things Right

Before turning to possible measures to improve the performance of state-owned enterprises, recalling the logic underlying their creation is useful. In most countries, the SOE, a hybrid institution, was created with the expectation that it would apply the strengths of the private sector to the pursuit of socially relevant goals. A widely held belief is that private firms do things right—that is, efficiently, quickly, and innovatively—even if they do not always do the right things. Governments, however, often do the right things, such as providing housing, education, or health services, but do not always do them right. The SOE, to put it simply, was expected to do the right things and also to do things right. Managerial autonomy was the method to ensure that SOEs did things right and managerial accountability the method to ensure that they did the right things.

Difficulties arose, however, in operationalizing these ideas. For the most part, governments relied on legal devices to ensure that the SOE concept would work as intended. For instance, they often "ensured" managerial autonomy by making SOEs legally distinct from the state, by placing them under an independent board of directors, excluding their employees from civil service rules and privileges, and allowing them to operate bank accounts and retain surpluses. Government involvement was restricted by law to setting objectives or policies and staying out of operational matters. Similarly, they "ensured" accountability by stipulating in the statutes or articles of association that SOEs should promote the "public interest," follow government directives on goals and policies, and be subject to government or legislative audits.

Unfortunately, making the SOE concept work took more than laws or regulations. New administrative systems, institutions, and personnel were necessary to coordinate government-SOE relations, but most developing countries created SOEs faster than they could develop those aids.

Therefore, in the early years, they often borrowed readily available management systems from the private sector or the government, and used readily available institutions and personnel to manage SOEs. These were not always appropriate for the hybrid institution. A few examples will illustrate this point.

In most countries, state-owned enterprises were not expected to maximize profits, although profit was often one of their goals. Yet, the accounting system used in SOEs, generally borrowed from the private sector, was designed to measure just that and governments often judged SOEs based on their financial profit. Even if government officials were aware of the limitations of profit as a performance measure for SOEs, there was often no alternative, composite measure they could rely on. Many others simply did not recognize its limitations. (For an empirical confirmation of these assertions in one developing country, see Ramamurti 1987). Consequently, governments were not well equipped to ensure that SOEs were "doing the right things."

Turning to the other half of the SOE concept (the expectation that they would do things right), once again the methods readily available were not always suitable for SOEs. Systems for planning, budgeting, monitoring, performance evaluation, financial control, and personnel management in SOEs were often modeled after those in government. Furthermore, government controllers dealing with SOEs tended to think of them as extensions of the government apparatus and focused on issues they were used to controlling in government itself, such as headcount, perquisites, and discretionary expenses. Government controllers who tried to go beyond these issues to more fundamental ones were constrained by a shortage of time and supporting staff. Thus in practice, doing things right often amounted to following proper procedures rather than accomplishing goals efficiently and creatively.

When government control took this form, at least five dysfunctional consequences followed. First, frequent intervention consumed a lot of time, and the time of senior policymakers is one of the scarcest resources in most developing countries. Second, it demotivated managers and reduced operational efficiency. Third, managers could not be held accountable for results, since outsiders made so many internal decisions. Fourth, managerial effort was often directed at finding ways to get around government controls, which in turn magnified the mutual suspicion between managers and government controllers. Finally, and perhaps most importantly, controllers and managers were so distracted by minor issues that fundamental questions about objectives and strategy often remained unaddressed.

To sum up, governments have found implementing both halves of the SOE concept difficult. Consequently, some SOEs have neither done the right things nor done things right. Disappointed with such results, many countries have privatized SOEs in recent years, but none have come close to liquidating the SOE sector. The fundamental problem of controlling SOEs remains; it has merely grown a little smaller in some countries.

Eliminating SOEs (through privatization or liquidation) is certainly one solution to the problem of controlling SOEs, and it may represent a socially desirable choice under certain conditions. But when that is not the case, governments must seek other solutions, which they can invent only through a process of creative and planned experimentation. It was experimentation of this sort that produced many of the management systems and tools that are commonplace in the private sector today. A classic example is the multidivisional structure with its attendant administrative systems that was invented over 50 years ago to manage companies with increasing product and market diversity (see, for instance, Chandler 1962; Galbraith and Kazanjian 1986, pp. 13-45). Likewise, new management systems and processes appropriate to SOEs must be developed, tested, and applied. Otherwise, governments risk rejecting a potentially valuable tool without having applied it properly.

Quantity and Quality of Control

Any organization, including an SOE, can be thought of as a black box into which certain inputs go and from which certain outputs emerge. A good control system will focus on the organization's outputs and specify the inputs required to produce those outputs efficiently. This approach, often called management by objectives or management by results, requires few interventions, but takes a lot of skill to execute. (One of the earliest proponents of this approach was Drucker [1954, pp. 121-136]; see also Humble [1970]).

An alternative approach is to probe the black box and control the individual processes through which inputs are converted into outputs. This results in many interventions, but it allows the controller to focus on those processes with which he or she is most familiar. Most governments are not organized to control by results and therefore try to make up for it by controlling a variety of internal processes. The result is a high quantity but low quality of government control (Jones 1985).

The important point in all this is that if governments can find a way to raise the quality of control while lowering the quantity of control, they can raise both managerial autonomy and managerial accountability. More accountability implies less autonomy only if accountability focuses on internal processes, not if it focuses on results. In other words, governments do not have to strike a balance between managerial autonomy and managerial accountability, as the SOE literature so often recommends. If, indeed, governments do not have to choose between managerial autonomy and managerial accountability, why do so few governments succeed in raising the quality of control and lowering the quantity of control? The reason is that it is far easier to lower (or raise) the quantity of control than it is to raise the quality of control.

Managerial autonomy in such areas as pricing, financing investments, diversifying, or divesting can be raised (or lowered) almost with a stroke of the pen, through an executive order or even a new law, for instance. Not surprisingly, governments—and international agencies such as the World Bank and the IMF—that are trying to improve the performance of SOEs look for quick reforms in the quantity of control, hoping perhaps that this alone will solve the problem.

Unfortunately, managerial autonomy without managerial accountability is an undesirable and unstable situation: undesirable, because it overlooks one half of the SOE concept (doing the right things), and unstable, because it can result in managerial abuses, which almost surely will lead a future administration to cut back on managerial autonomy. The result will be the familiar "autonomy pendulum" observed in many countries.

The above discussion is summed up in figure 9.1. The two dimensions of the matrix shown are (a) the quantity of government control, measured by the extent to which the internal processes of state-owned enterprises are controlled, and (b) the quality of government control, measured by the extent to which SOEs are controlled by results. The matrix indicates the degree of strategic autonomy and operational autonomy enjoyed by managers in each cell. Strategic autonomy refers to autonomy in matters

Figure 9.1 Quantity and Quality of Government Control

		Quantity of control (extent to which internal processes of SOEs are controlled)	
		LOW	HIGH
	LOW	**Cell 1** Strategic autonomy = HIGH Operational autonomy = HIGH	**Cell 2** Strategic autonomy = HIGH Operational autonomy = LOW
Quality of control (extent to which SOEs are controlled by results)	HIGH	**Cell 3*** Strategic autonomy = LOW Operational autonomy = HIGH	**Cell 4** Strategic autonomy = LOW Operational autonomy = LOW

* Desired position.

such as objectives, strategies, and investment. Operational autonomy refers to autonomy in day-to-day matters, such as production, marketing, and personnel management.

In terms of these definitions, the SOE concept implies that managers ought to have low strategic autonomy and high operational autonomy (cell 3), that is, governments should be actively involved in setting objectives, strategy, and policy while giving managers considerable freedom in implementing approved programs. However, in reality, as discussed earlier, most governments find themselves in exactly the opposite situation, that is, in cell 2, where SOEs enjoy more strategic autonomy and less operational autonomy than they should. While governments invariably have the final say on strategic matters, they are not organized to give direction independently in these areas in cells 1 and 2. Therefore, managers can enjoy considerable autonomy in practice on strategic matters. This does not imply that all managers will exercise that autonomy; sometimes both managers and government controllers may abdicate that autonomy to the environment and allow the SOE to drift along without a clear purpose.

Let us now consider possible movements away from cell 2. A shift to cell 4 is not easy because it requires an improvement in the quality of control, and it is not particularly desirable since it too ignores one half of the SOE concept; perhaps, therefore, it is uncommon. Movement from cell 2 to cell 1 is relatively easy, but cell 1 is not a stable equilibrium, often generating a swing right back to cell 2 (producing the autonomy pendulum). Although cell 2 is not a satisfactory state of affairs, it is a more stable combination than cell 1, which is probably why more countries are found in cell 2 than in cell 1. Movement from cell 2 to cell 3 is what countries really need but find difficult to implement for reasons that will be discussed.

Barriers to Improved Control

The conclusion up to this point is not only that autonomy and accountability *can* be increased simultaneously, but that they *should* be increased simultaneously. This turns our attention to the crucial question: Why do governments find raising the quality of control difficult? The reason is that in trying to do so they run into a variety of technical and organizational barriers.

TECHNICAL BARRIERS. There are at least three types of technical barriers:

- *Finding the "ideal" performance criterion.* Profitability (at market price) is widely regarded as a reasonable measure of the performance of private firms, at least from the viewpoint of their shareholders. Economists have long pointed out the limitations of that criterion for state-owned enterprises, which leads to the question: if not profit, then what? One theoretical answer is to substitute economic profitability or national profitability for commercial profitability. Jones (Chapter 8) proposes another answer, a measure called "public profitability," which is less satisfactory theoretically, but more easily applied in practice. Yet another answer is to combine an SOE's multiple objectives into a composite performance measure using weights that reflect the relative importance of those objectives. While all these "answers" create technical complexities, and none is entirely practical or theoretically valid, these are not reasons to give up efforts to control SOEs by results.

- *Distinguishing management performance from SOE performance.* Governments are often at a loss how to separate the contribution of managers to a state-owned enterprise's performance from all other contributing factors. Since it is managers who must be controlled—and not abstract things called SOEs—the distinction is important. Specific examples of this problem, such as changes in prices, aggregate demand, or degree of competition, are discussed later. Fortunately, the private sector has faced this generic problem for years, and various practical methods are available for making the separation, at least in critical areas. Unfortunately, not all these methods can be used in SOEs, because SOEs often do not operate in competitive markets. Nevertheless, most governments could make the separation much better than they are currently doing.

- *Balancing short-term and long-term goals.* Managers of all firms, public or private, can usually improve short-term results at the expense of long-term results. Some method is necessary to ensure that SOEs are making the correct tradeoffs in this regard. This, too, creates complex technical problems, but, again, the private sector has faced them for years. The solution in the private sector is called "strategic planning" or "long-range planning," which ensures that short-term goals are consistent with long-term objectives and strategies. There are no overwhelming technical reasons why the same approach cannot be used at the government-SOE interface, although the organizational barriers discussed in the next section can make it difficult to do so.

ORGANIZATIONAL BARRIERS. Organizational barriers arise for three kinds of reasons, and are much more difficult to overcome than the technical barriers.

- *Encountering asymmetry in expertise and information.* State-owned enterprises invariably have more expertise and knowledge of their enterprises than the government trying to control them. Without a good understanding of the technical relationship between inputs and outputs and the markets in which the organization operates, setting "good" targets is difficult, that is, targets that focus managers' attention on the right criteria, and then require them to achieve difficult yet attainable results of those criteria. Government controllers also have to depend on SOEs for information to do the controlling. Here, they face the problem that the information supplied may be either distorted or selective because SOEs know how the controlling authority will use the information.

To be sure, problems of information asymmetry and information impactedness are common in most principal-agent relationships, but they tend to be particularly great in the government-SOE relationship. It is more the exception than the rule that a government controller has worked in the very industry or industries in which an SOE is operating. The practice of rotating civil servants at regular intervals across an amazing range of assignments prevents them from building expertise in any field. These points are even more true for the civil servant's boss, the minister. Few developing countries have information or support systems that help compensate for these problems.

- *Conflicting values.* Even if all relevant facts are known (which is seldom the case), there is an element of subjectivity in choosing among alternative goals or strategies. In small, owner managed firms, owner managers make decisions based on their personal values. The task is more complex in large, professionally managed firms, but is routinely tackled in most of them through the organizational hierarchy, culminating with the chief executive officer or the board or directors. In the government-SOE structure, however, it is often not clear who the boss or the real principal is. Is it the most senior civil servant in the administrative ministry, the minister in charge of that ministry, the chairman of the board, the prime minister, or the head of state (see Aharoni 1981; Ramamurti 1986b; Vernon 1984)? Although the prime minister or head of state could always have the final say, that person is very busy doing many things and is far removed from the problem.

  In practice, of course, many individuals in the government-SOE hierarchy are involved in any decisionmaking process. All of them bring a particular viewpoint to the issues at hand depending on their roles and personal values. The multiplicity and range of goals governments pursue complicate the problem. Furthermore, in the government-SOE context, individuals with three quite different "cultures" are forced to work together: professional managers, bureaucrats, and politicians. The three groups tend to differ in how they would trade off short-term results for long-term results. For these kinds of reasons, for ministers and bureaucrats to provide SOEs with a clear set of goals and targets can be difficult.

- *Coordinating a loosely coupled organization.* Finally, government is one of the most loosely coupled organizations one can find. It is large and sprawling, but not very tightly integrated. Even heads of state sometimes have difficulty coordinating decisionmaking across this organization, let alone individual ministries or government agencies. Controlling SOEs by results will demand time bound, coordinated activities and decisions, which may be difficult to orchestrate given the loose coupling.

Conclusion

Any serious proposal for improving the quality of government control over state-owned enterprises must address the problems discussed here. Local or foreign experts can help solve the technical problems, but overcoming the organizational barriers will call for the creation of new centers of expertise and information in government, new "integrating devices," and new "integrating departments" to run those integrating devices (see Galbraith 1973, pp. 46-54, 89-107). Therefore, the quality of control cannot be raised easily or quickly, although most countries need to embark on the task quickly. Unfortunately, no short cut, quick fix, or painless remedy exists. The only alternative is to abandon the attempt to control SOEs by results (or to do so very poorly) and to revert to controlling their internal processes.

An Outline of the Performance Contracting System

This part of the chapter presents the outline of a system called here the performance contracting system, which tries to deal with the technical and organizational barriers discussed earlier. In rudimentary form, this system was tested with generally positive results in Bangladesh during 1985-86. While it is not a panacea for the problems of the SOE sector, and introducing it effectively is no easy task, it represents the kind of constructive and creative experimentation that is necessary if governments are ever to realize the promise of the SOE concept. The proposed system is intended for application only to the largest SOEs in any country, because it is both time intensive and skill intensive. In most countries, the 10 or 12 largest SOEs invariably account for 70 to 80 percent of the total sales and assets of all SOEs. For smaller SOEs, a less cumbersome and comprehensive system than the one described below would make more sense.

Basic Principles

Any system of management by results requires that goals and targets be agreed upon through discussion at the beginning of the year. Accordingly, that is the first area that must be addressed.

PRINCIPLE No. 1. Performance criteria and targets should be derived from a well-thought-out and approved three- to five-year plan designed to improve performance.

Having no planning and control system is better than having one that motivates SOEs toward the wrong goals. Therefore, performance criteria must not be selected arbitrarily but derived from a carefully worked out plan. That plan must look at least three to five years into the future, not just into the forthcoming year as is commonly the case in government. Furthermore, the plan must focus on improving performance, regardless of how well an SOE is already doing: financial profitability should not be taken to mean that performance is good when it is actually only satisfactory, and heavy losses should not inevitably lead to the conclusion that an SOE is beyond repair. Finally, the plan should be explicit and approved by the government, rather than be implicit or known only to managers.

PRINCIPLE No. 2. The performance improvement plan must be consistent with national goals and not merely enterprise goals.

State-owned enterprises can be useful instruments for promoting national goals to which the market pays little attention. To ensure this, however, the government must formulate strategies and policies for the sector in which any SOE operates. These strategies should be used to evaluate or guide the performance improvement plans drawn up by SOEs.

Principle No. 2 also implies that the government measures all costs and benefits at economic rather than market prices. One way to do this is to actually measure economic profitability on a continuing basis and motivate managers to strive for the highest levels of economic profitability. Unfortunately, measuring economic profitability is cumbersome, complex, and controversial, and both managers and bureaucrats, not to speak of politicians, have difficulty comprehending it. Therefore, this is not a practical solution.

An alternative approach is to use "public profitability" using the minimum amount of theoretical compromises, as proposed by Jones (1981). Jones suggests two kinds of adjustments to private profitability: first, definitional adjustments to exclude those accounting heads that are irrelevant from a national point of view (such as interest, taxes, and subsidies); and second, price adjustments and social accounting adjustments to reflect differences in the valuation of costs and benefits at market and economic prices. Practically speaking, the first adjustment is easy to implement (except in the case of subsidies, unless one limits this to explicit subsidies), but the second is not. In Pakistan and the Republic of Korea, where the concept was applied, the second kind of adjustment was not made. Without the second kind of adjustment, calling the resulting measure public profitability is misleading. Therefore, in the performance contracting system the measure is referred to as return on total assets before interest, taxes, and subsidies at market prices.

It is possible, however, to do better than that using a different approach. Even if costs and benefits are not measured at economic prices regularly, they can be measured this way at least periodically by government specialists who watch out for specific areas where economic profitability deviates from private profitability.

Figure 9.2 sets out a simple 2 x 2 matrix presenting four possible relationships between economic and private profitability. Cells 1 and 4 pose no problems since the two measures are in agreement, but in the other cells there is a conflict. In cell 2, what is good for the country is bad for the enterprise. The solution is to include an explicit criterion into the set of performance criteria that will require the SOE to achieve a minimum amount with regard to that criterion. In cell 3, what is bad for the country is good for the SOE. Here the solution is to prevent the SOE from achieving more than a specified level with regard to a suitably defined criterion. Thus, through the inclusion of constraints of the "no less than" and "no more than" variety on carefully selected criteria, steering SOEs in the correct direction should be possible.

Figure 9.2 National Interest versus State-Owned Enterprise's Interests

Is it good for the country?

		YES	NO
Is it good for the SOE?	**YES**	**Cell 1** No conflict	**Cell 2** Government should DISCOURAGE SOE from pursuing natural tendencies.
	NO	**Cell 3*** Government should ENCOURAGE/FORCE SOE to go against its natural tendencies.	**Cell 4** No conflict

For example, enterprise A might prefer to buy an input from abroad rather than from another public enterprise, B, because B's prices are higher. However, at economic prices, the country may be better off if A purchased from B (an example of a cell 3 situation). In that case, one of the performance criteria for A would be the amount or proportion of its needs of the input that it purchased from B. This kind of constrained maximization of return on total assets before interest, taxes, and subsidies is envisaged in the performance contracting system.

Each dimension should have a third possibility, namely, neutral, which falls between the Yes and the No. Many important issues would fall in the neutral category from the government's point of view, for example, a transfer payment, such as a subsidy from the treasury to a state-owned enterprise, which would neither raise nor lower national welfare, but would affect the SOEs' cash flow. However, the performance contracting system will not be concerned with resolving issues of this type.

While there is no doubt a great deal of potential for conflict between governments and SOEs (cells 2 and 3), the enormous potential for improvements that fall in cell 1 (non-zero sum) should not be underestimated. An important example of the latter would be elimination of waste, for which there is usually considerable potential in SOEs.

Consistent with the above line of reasoning, SOEs will be expected to focus on improvements in real performance rather than improvements in financial performance brought about by special tax breaks, protection, price hikes, or subsidies. However, they may be left free to pursue such demands through channels other than the contracting system.

PRINCIPLE No. 3. Any potential for improving the performance of SOEs by improving coordination between SOEs or ministries should be examined and exploited as part of the performance contracting process.

This principle is merely a corollary of the more general principle that the government should be concerned not just with improving the performance of individual SOEs, but of the whole public sector, which includes the complete network of SOEs. The government has the obligation of managing the interdependencies between SOEs or ministries well (marketing, technological, human resource, and financial). In most countries, such interdependence tends to be high, but the government's management of those relationships tends to be poor.

PRINCIPLE No. 4. The multiple performance criteria derived from the previous steps should be combined into a single, composite measure using an explicit set of weights.

This principle is essential to obtain a sense of the overall performance of an SOE and to compare it with the performance of other SOEs. The weights used should reflect the importance of different elements of the long-term strategy agreed upon.

PRINCIPLE No. 5. Performance criteria should encompass only areas within the control of SOE management, and targets for those criteria should be adjusted (or "flexed") when major factors outside the control of managers change.

As discussed earlier, governments often judge managers of SOEs by the performance of their enterprises, which depends among other things, on factors outside their control. One of the most common examples of this is changes in input and output prices, which materially affect profitability, but are often determined by government policy or set by the market. As a result, managers can show dramatic improvement in profits the year the government allows them to raise prices on outputs, even if the SOE's resources are being used inefficiently. Conversely, no amount of cost cutting may make up for the decline in profit resulting from a rise in input prices when the government will not allow output prices to rise in proportion. Managers of SOEs typically spend an inordinate amount of time and effort trying to persuade the government to raise output prices, and neglect more difficult (and possibly unpleasant) measures for improving real performance. To correct this, financial targets should be set at constant prices for SOEs facing price controls.

Apart from prices, other uncontrollable factors that vary from case to case may confound managerial performance. Examples include uncontrollable and unpredictable—but foreseeable—changes in input markets (for example, availability of raw materials in an agriculture-based industry) or output markets (for example, cyclical or lumpy demand).

A practical problem in operationalizing this principle, however, is that many factors are likely to fall into the gray area of semicontrollable factors. As a rule, no more than two or three factors—all clearly outside management control and all clearly having a major impact on results—should be conceded as uncontrollable factors. There are two reasons for this. First, good managers should be able to "manage" many semicontrollable factors. Second, the task of setting targets increases exponentially in complexity as more uncontrollable factors are recognized in the target-setting process.

The top management of a private, diversified firm do not usually make such adjustments for uncontrollable factors while setting targets for constituent divisions, because they can often compare those divisions with other private firms competing in the same industry under similar environmental circumstances. However, this is usually not true for SOEs, which tend to be one-of-a-kind firms.

PRINCIPLE No. 6. Once performance targets have been set according to the principles outlined earlier, managers should be left free to manage, subject to government policies and guidelines and good monitoring/management information systems. At the end of the year, the SOEs' performance should be judged systematically against the targets negotiated at the beginning of the year.

Allowing managers to enjoy operational autonomy is as important as constraining their strategic autonomy. Once targets have been set, managers should be left free to manage, subject only to prescribed policies and periodic monitoring. The need to link the evaluation process with targets requires no explanation. The methodology for evaluation should be clear to the SOEs. As a rule, targets should not be changed because some of the original assumptions turned out to be wrong, although the evaluation process should recognize the favorable or unfavorable impact of those changes on performance.

PRINCIPLE No. 7. To the extent possible, SOE employees should receive a bonus or reward linked to their actual performance so that personal goals become congruent with organizational goals.

The link between performance and rewards is essential to give teeth to the whole process, but it must be introduced carefully because of its implications for employee relations and SOE finances. Establishing such a link will make delivering results easier for top management of SOEs. Ideally, the scheme should cover all employees, managers and workers, although the contracting system need not be the only basis for granting rewards. Depending on the national context, provision could also be made for negative rewards (demotion, firing, transfer, withholding of increments, and so on).

The Planning and Control Cycle

The principles presented above are captured in the cycle of planning and control activities shown in figure 9.3. The first two steps of the cycle—preparing a performance improvement plan and drawing up the performance contract—are planning activities that must be carried out prior to the start of the financial year. They are the most difficult steps in the process, taking up perhaps 70 percent of the total effort all parties expend in the entire cycle. If they are done well, the remaining steps should be easy to execute. The third step—monitoring performance—is carried out during the financial year on a quarterly basis through the management information system (MIS), supplemented by a mid-year review meeting and at other times as necessary. This step should take about 10 percent of the total effort. The fourth step—evaluating performance—commences shortly after the end of the financial year, and is likely to pose technical problems and generate some conflicts. It may demand up to 20 percent of the total effort expended in the planning and control cycle. The last step—rewarding performance—is relatively straightforward if the evaluation has been completed and the reward system is well defined.

Figure 9.3 Performance Contracting Cycle

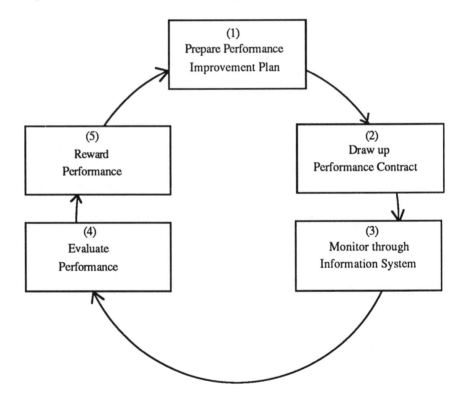

Who Should Do What

No planning or control system is fully specified until the organizational setup for its execution is specified and responsibility for carrying out various steps is assigned. However, this assignment will vary from country to country depending on the government structure and how SOEs have been spread across ministries. In some countries, SOEs fall under a separate ministry, while in others they are spread out among sectoral ministries. In some countries, finance and planning are under the same ministries, while in others they are separate. In smaller countries, ministers are actively involved in managing SOEs (by being members of the board of directors), while they are less actively involved in large countries. Some countries have an active legislature, while others do not. Finally, some countries already have an SOE bureau or its equivalent, while others do not, and those that do may differ on where this bureau is located. For all these reasons, the process has to be tailor-made to the national context. Despite these differences, some general principles apply.

PRINCIPLE NO. 8. A small group must be created at some central location to become the nucleus of the government's expertise and information base relating to SOEs. This group must be primarily responsible for orchestrating the performance contracting system.

Governments can never hope to match SOEs in their expertise or access to relevant information for planning and control, but they must try to reduce the gap by assigning primary responsibility for this to some group located in a central ministry, such as planning, finance, or cabinet affairs. This group should also be concerned with other policy matters relating to SOEs. If at all possible, it should enjoy greater flexibility in recruitment and operations than the typical government department. Among other things, for instance, it should be able to hire consultants at short notice to assist in specific areas so that all the necessary expertise does not have to reside within the group itself. In addition, this group must be made responsible for running the contracting system on schedule. Finally, this group could also maintain an information system on SOEs and produce periodic reports on functional aspects or the overall performance of SOEs.

PRINCIPLE NO. 9. Preparatory work on strategic planning and contracting should be done by a working level, interministerial task force for which the state enterprise bureau serves as a technical secretariat.

The contracting process invariably requires the participation of officials from several ministries, including the supervising ministry, finance, and planning. If an SOE has critical dependencies on SOEs under other ministries, those SOEs and their supervising ministries would also have to be involved. Officials from all these organizations must participate if the contract is to be taken seriously. Officials selected must be at a level where they can spare the time required. Much of the spade work for meetings would have to be done by the SOE concerned and the state enterprise bureau, while the task force meetings should be used to educate members on key issues and obtain views. This process will invariably be slow and generate conflict, but it is the only meaningful way to generate some clarity about goals and priorities. Ideally, a representative of the state enterprise bureau should chair the task force.

The composition of task forces should be tailor-made to each SOE, although some members may be common to several task forces.

PRINCIPLE No. 10. Debate and discussion in the task force must be integrated with decisionmaking at higher levels of government (at the bureaucratic and political levels).

The analyses and recommendations emerging within the task force must find their way up to the decisionmaking levels through a hierarchy of interministerial committees. Probably two committees will be necessary above the task force: one consisting of the most senior bureaucrats and another consisting of ministers. This is essential to give teeth to the whole process and to ensure that goals and targets are consistent with political priorities. The higher committees would meet at fewer intervals than the working task force and would provide the latter with broad directives and guidelines.

What the System Will Not Solve

At the risk of stating the obvious, the performance contracting system is not a panacea for the public sector's problems. For instance, if the party in power is not seriously interested in improving the performance of state-owned enterprises, introducing such a system or running it well will be difficult. The system will almost certainly not produce perfect goal clarity for SOEs, although it might reduce goal confusion. It will not prevent abrupt shifts in goals and priorities if the ruling party changes. It will not eliminate political interference, although it will reduce the likelihood that such interference will go unnoticed. It will not solve the accountability problem caused by frequent changes in chief executives, bureaucrats, or ministers, although it will provide all concerned with a record of their predecessors' commitments. Finally, if government is not equipped with the right kind of staff for contracting, the system will probably do more harm than good by wasting the time of managers and civil servants who are already hard pressed for time.

Application in One Developing Country

During 1985-86, the performance contracting system was applied on an experimental but serious basis in Bangladesh as part of an ongoing project funded by the United Nations. Two problematic state-owned enterprises were selected for the purpose, one a process industry and the other an engineering industry. The exercise was carried out through a hierarchy of interministerial committees, with most of the work being done by the lowest level team, which consisted of representatives of the SOEs, their parent companies, supervising ministries, and the ministries of planning and finance. At a later stage, representatives of two other SOEs that vitally affected the performance of the focal SOEs (in one case as a supplier of raw materials and in the other as a purchaser of outputs) were included in the lowest level task force. The SOEs themselves did much of the spade work with support from an "expert" group in the ministry of finance.

The various steps discussed in the previous sections were followed in the course of about five months to draw up the performance contracts. The lowest level task force met three to four times for each contract, and presented the resulting contracts for discussion and approval by higher level committees. Four months later, one of the two contracts had been worked out in full and successfully negotiated, while the other was close to completion.

The experience showed that the performance contracting system was workable in a developing country context, although it took considerable effort to mobilize everyone's support and involvement. The task force proved to be a valuable device for education, consensus building, information sharing, and coordination. By and large, a collaborative and constructive relationship emerged between the SOEs and government representatives; one that was quite different from the usual mudslinging and mutual suspicion prevalent in the past. Besides isolating meaningful areas for managerial evaluation and forcing everyone to look beyond the short term or narrow financial results, the exercise promoted better coordination across SOEs in critical areas. Managers, in particular, found the exercise useful and helpful.

The Ministry of Finance convened a high level interministerial meeting at which the trial exercises and the resulting contracts were presented and discussed. Many managers and bureaucrats involved in the exercises were present and expressed support for the approach. Senior officials decided to extend the system to cover the ten largest SOEs, which accounted for more than 80 percent of the sales and employment and 75 percent of the assets of all Bangladesh's nonfinancial SOEs. The *ad hoc* institutional mechanisms used in the trial exercises were to be replaced with official committees working under the supervision of a ministerial committee. The experts group in the finance ministry was to be strengthened and was expected to serve as the engine driving the performance contracting system. The experiment's success hinged on the exceptional perseverance and boldness of the local civil servant who headed this project. Such leadership, as well as broader political support for reform, is vital when introducing any new administrative system that deviates from traditional decisionmaking methods.

International Comparisons

We turn finally to a comparison of the performance contracting system with two other innovative methods for controlling state-owned enterprises: the program contract system used in France and Senegal, and the signaling system used in Pakistan and the Republic of Korea. (See also Brown 1982; Cadic 1979; Hartman and Nawab 1985; Jones 1981; Language Services n.d.; Mallon 1983; Park 1985; Ramamurti 1986a.)

Comparison with the Program Contract System, France

As concerns similarities, the following features are present in both the performance contracting and program contract systems:

- Performance criteria and targets are derived from a long-term plan or strategy negotiated between SOEs and relevant government ministries. Therefore, both result in multiparty agreements and both have a multiyear time horizon. Most program contracts have a four- or five-year time horizon, whereas targets may be specified for no more than three years at a time in the performance contracting system.

- Contracts are drawn up selectively, that is, only for some SOEs, although the selection criteria are explicit in the performance contracting system but not explicit in the French system.

With regard to the differences between the systems, these can be categorized by features found in one system but absent in the other. The following features are present in the program contract system but absent in the performance contracting system:

- In the program contract system, the contracts are more like legal agreements than in the performance contracting system. The government makes formal commitments to supply funds, allow price increases, or permit specified contractions or expansions in products or services. This feature is not present in the performance contracting system for two reasons. First, holding a government to commitments over a three- or four-year period is hard. Government budgets are firmed up one year at a time, and changes in ministers or the party in power could make past commitments obsolete. In addition, a contract containing firm commitment over a three- or four-year period is much too rigid for the uncertain world all firms operate in. Not surprisingly, most of the first generation contracts drawn up in France in the late 1960s and early 1970s collapsed because they contained commitments that were very unrealistic in the post-oil crisis era from the viewpoints of both the government and the SOEs involved. Second, at least in the introductory stage, requiring the government to make firm commitments can produce resistance from civil servants and ministers, who prefer to extract commitments from SOEs but not make any themselves, especially when those commitments have financial implications.

- The government commitments in the program contract system also includes greater managerial autonomy in areas such as pricing, investment, borrowing, and changes in product or market scope. The performance contracting system provides for a similar redefinition of autonomy, but only to the extent that an SOE has distinctive problems that require special adjustment. Systemic changes in managerial autonomy in the usual areas of procurement, personnel, or financing are excluded on the grounds that these should not be changed on a case by case basis. However, SOEs are encouraged to draw the government's attention to adjustments in managerial autonomy demanded by industry specific factors.

- Finally, the program contract system envisages financial compensation to SOEs for "public service obligations," while such compensation was not initially envisaged in the performance contracting system. Financial compensation for such government imposed obligations is useful if (a) SOEs are judged on the basis of financial profitability; and (b) the economy has few price distortions, so that after adjusting for public service obligations, financial results are a good measure of an SOE's real, economic performance. In developing countries, condition (b) seldom holds, and if a good control system is used, condition (a) will not hold either. To be sure, many SOE managers talk about their public service obligations, but most grudgingly also agree that their firms enjoy explicit and implicit subsidies. Seldom do they have careful calculations to support the view that, all things considered, their firms deserve net compensation from the government. Even a well-trained economist would have a hard time making the necessary calculations, since in a highly regulated economy, measuring the magnitude of implicit subsidies is hazardous and controversial.

The following are among the important features present in the performance contracting system but absent in the program contract system:

- The performance contracting system is intended to be a system, that is, a set of activities to be carried out on a regular and systematic basis, whereas program contracts were drawn up in France irregularly, one set in the late 1960s and early 1970s, and another in the early 1980s.

- Program contracts take far more time to draw up than performance contracts: one to two years for the former versus six months for the latter. The program contract's legal nature, comprehensiveness, and requirement for government commitments tend to delay the process considerably. In contrast, the philosophy of the performance contracting system is that all issues need not be resolved at once; some can wait until a following cycle.

- The performance contracting system envisages that economic costs and benefits should guide the government's choices on strategy, whereas such calculation is not done explicitly in the program contract system. Again, if one assumes that price distortions are limited and that the government compensates SOEs for losses created by its directives, economic cost-benefit analysis may not be necessary.

- The performance contracting system provides an integrated performance measure using explicit weights for individual criteria. Program contracts specify several criteria and targets, but no procedure for evaluating overall performance on the basis of those measures.

- The performance contracting system requires a systematic evaluation of all "A" category SOEs every year through a prespecified procedure. The program contract system provides for monitoring of the contract, but not for a systematic evaluation at the end of each year.

- The performance contracting system recognizes the need to link rewards with actual performance, although the link was weak in the initial contracts. The program contract system, however, has no link between results and rewards. Of course, the question of such a link arises only if results are judged systematically in the first place, a condition that was not satisfied by the French contracts.

Comparison with the Signaling System, Pakistan, Republic of Korea

We turn next to the similarities and differences between the performance contracting system and the signaling system, which was first applied in Pakistan, and then, with modifications, in the Republic of Korea. Regarding the similarities between the two systems:

- Both systems are systematic, that is, intended for application year after year according to some calendar of activities.

- Both systems generate composite measures of performance by requiring the government to specify weights for various performance criteria. Indeed, the signaling system served as the model for the performance contracting system in this matter.

- Both systems envisage that actual performance should be evaluated systematically at the end of the year and the results made public.

Turning to the differences between the two systems, the following features are present in the signaling system, but absent in the performance contracting system:

- The link between results and rewards is much stronger in Pakistan and Korea. A bonus of up to three months' salary is paid in both countries, although in Pakistan only executives are covered by the scheme and workers receive bonuses according to pre-existing criteria based on production, sales, and profits.

- In the signaling system all SOEs are subject to the same target setting and evaluation approach, whereas in the performance contracting system comprehensive goals and targets are drawn up for only the most important SOEs, with less sophisticated approaches used for the large numbers of less important SOEs.

The following features are present in the performance contracting system but absent in the signaling system:

- An important difference between the two systems is that in the performance contracting system, criteria and targets are derived from a medium-term strategy for improving performance. The signaling system, however, is mainly concerned with operational efficiency, that is, with getting more out of the existing resources, assuming that products, technology, markets, and government policies are more or less constant.

- The signaling system has a one-year time horizon, compared to the three- to five-year time horizon of the performance contracting system.

- The signaling system sets many quantitative targets through trend analysis, especially in Korea, whereas the performance contracting system derives them from a medium-term strategy.

- Performance improvement through improved inter-SOE or interministerial coordination of policies and decisions is explicitly emphasized in the performance contracting system.

- Members of the SOE-government hierarchy are actively involved in finalizing the medium-term performance improvement plan, selecting criteria and targets, and evaluating performance, whereas in Korea some of these functions are performed by a part-time task force of professors, certified public accountants, and other outside experts.

The collective impact of the differences is that the performance contracting system is procedurally and technically more complex than the signaling system. However, the gain is a more meaningful set of targets and an improved understanding of issues and plans among managers and government officials.

Conclusion

The performance contracting system is one of a handful of innovative methods for controlling state-owned enterprises that has actually been tested in a country. A historical look at SOEs around the world over the last three or four decades reveals the striking absence of such experimentation. None of these innovative methods was easy to implement and none is entirely satisfactory, but they all go some way toward making the SOE what it was intended to be: an institution that does the right things and does things right.

References

Aharoni, Y. 1981. "State-Owned Enterprises: An Agent Without a Principal." In L.P. Jones, ed., *Public Enterprises in Less Developed Countries*. Cambridge, U.K.: Cambridge University Press.

Brown, J.C. 1982. "The World Bank and the Parapublic Sector in Senegal." Washington, D.C.: World Bank. Processed.

Cadic, J.Y. 1979. "The Program Contract: An Attempt to Rationalize the Management of Public Enterprise." *Doctrine* (December 20). Translated from the French by the Language Services Division, World Bank, October 1981.

Chandler, A.D. 1962. *Strategy and Structure*. Cambridge, Massachusetts: MIT Press.

Drucker, P.F. 1954. *The Practice of Management*. New York: Harper.

Galbraith, J. 1973. *Designing Complex Organizations*. Reading, Massachusetts: Addison Wesley.

Galbraith, J., and R.K. Kazanjian. 1986. *Strategy Implementation: Structure, Systems and Process*. St. Paul, Minnesota: West Publishing.

Hartman, A., and S.A. Nawab. 1985. "Evaluating Public Manufacturing Enterprises in Pakistan." *Finance and Development* (September): 27-30.

Humble, John W. 1970. *Management by Objectives in Action*. New York: McGraw-Hill.

Jones, L.P. 1981. "Toward a Peformance Evaluation Methodology for Public Enterprises: With Special Reference to Pakistan." Paper presented at the International Symposium on Economic Performance of Public Enterprises, Islamabad, Pakistan, November 1981. Processed.

Language Services. n.d. Translations of program contracts between the French government and SNCF, and between the Republic of Senegal and Sonatra, Air Senegal, Sotrac, and RCFS. Washington, D.C.: World Bank.

Mallon, R.D. 1983. "Performance Contracts with State-Owned Enterprises." Processed.

Park, Y.C. 1985. "Reform of Public Enterprise Sector in Korea—with Special Reference to Performance Evaluation of Government-Invested Enterprise." Washington, D.C.: World Bank, West Africa Projects Department, Public Sector Management Division. Processed.

Ramamurti, R. 1986a. *Observations on the South Korean System for Performance Evaluation of Public Enterprises*. Working Paper No. 86-33. Boston, Massachusetts: Northeastern University.

————. 1986b. "Strategic Planning in Government-Dependent Organizations." *Long Range Planning* 19(3):62-71.

————. 1987. "Performance Evaluation of State-Owned Enterprises in Theory and Practice." *Management Science* 33(7): 876-893.

Vernon, R. 1984. "Linking Managers with Ministers: Dilemmas of the State-Owned Enterprise." *Journal of Policy Analysis and Management* 4(1): 39-55.

10

EVALUATING THE PERFORMANCE OF STATE-OWNED ENTERPRISES IN PAKISTAN

Mary Shirley

This chapter provides an assessment of Pakistan's performance evaluation system for its industrial state-owned enterprises (SOEs). This assessment aims to describe it to officials of other countries interested in replicating the system and suggests ways in which it might be adapted to circumstances different from those in Pakistan. The chapter begins with a brief history and description of the system, followed by an assessment of its day-to-day workings, its impact on performance and management, and its impact on government policy. It concludes with policy suggestions for other developing countries.

Brief History and Description of the System[1]

From independence in 1947 to 1971, the private sector carried out most economic activity in Pakistan; the public sector supported development largely by providing basic infrastructure. The state's presence in the manufacturing sector began in 1950 with the establishment of the Pakistan Industrial Development Corporation to create enterprises that presumably were to be transferred to the private sector at some future date. From 1972 to 1977, as the government progressively nationalized the industrial and financial sectors, the number of SOEs increased from 22 to 55. The nationalized industries included iron, steel, basic metals, heavy engineering, motor vehicles, chemicals, petrochemicals, and cement.

For a more detailed version of this chapter, including a complete statistical appendix on the Pakistani SOEs, see Shirley (1989).

1. This section draws heavily on Leroy Jones and Istaqbal Mehdi (1985a).

After 1977, the government adopted a different strategy that emphasized the importance of market forces in economic development. Sustained growth was to be achieved on the basis of greater private sector participation and more diversified and export-oriented production. Accordingly, the government privatized some public corporations, reestablished fiscal control, and acted to restore private sector confidence. The Sixth Plan (1984-88) aimed to expand the role of market forces through increased private sector participation, deregulation, appropriate input and output pricing, and opening up the economy to competition from abroad. During the first three years of the plan, progress was achieved in a number of areas. For example, the government liberalized investment approvals; deregulated the prices of cement, edible oils, and nitrogenous fertilizer; rationalized natural gas prices for both producers and consumers; opened up Basmati rice, edible oil, and fertilizer production to the private sector; and adopted a more flexible exchange rate policy. As part of this same effort the government reviewed the public manufacturing sector, which resulted in two reports (the Uqaili and Beg reports). Based on the reports' recommendations, the government reorganized the industrial SOE sector.

In 1988, the Ministry of Production had under its supervision 66 industrial SOEs grouped into eight holding corporations and a new steel project (table 10.1). The Ministry of Production was responsible for monitoring SOEs to ensure that they were managed efficiently. (The Ministry of Industry set sectorwide policies and had no direct administrative responsibility for industrial SOEs.) The Ministry of Production formulated long-term policies for public sector enterprises in consultation with the corporations, coordinated among corporations and enterprises, set objectives, evaluated performance, and appointed senior executives. A special unit, the Experts Advisory Cell (EAC), was created in 1980 to assist the ministry in planning, monitoring, and performance evaluation. The cell was financed by a levy on the SOEs and its staff were not part of the civil service.

The Signaling System

The concept of a performance evaluation system for public enterprises was introduced at a symposium sponsored by the Government of Pakistan and the United Nations in Islamabad in November 1981 (see chapter 2 for

Table 10.1 Pakistan: The Holding Corporations of the Ministry of Production

Holding corporation	Acronym	No. of subsidiaries in 1986	Net sales 1985/86 (Rs million)	Pretax profit (loss) in 1985/86 (Rs million)	No. of employees, June 30, 1986
Federal Chemical and Ceramics Corp.	FCCCL	14	1,679	14	7,549
National Fertilizer Corp.	NFC	6	4,391	646	5,442
Pakistan Auto Corporation	PACO	12	4,709	157	7,469
Pakistan Industrial Development Corp.	PIDC	10	473	–182	5,733
State Cement Corporation	SCCP	13	4,599	766	12,510
State Engineering Corp.	SEC	10	2,217	–23	14,683
State Petroleum Refining and Petrochemical Corp.	PERAC	3	8,227	112	1,229
Textile Machinery Corp. Ltd.	TMC	2	36	–26	483
Total		70	26,330	1,463	55,098

Note: Does not include Pakistan Steel Mills Corporation.
Source: Experts Advisory Cell annual reports.

a description of the basic concepts introduced at that time and the principles underlying the system). The government decided to proceed with the system and signed a contract with a consulting firm (Institute for Development Research, Boston) in December 1981 to implement the system.

The system was supposed to have three components:

1. performance evaluation system to specify socially desirable performance;

2. public enterprise performance information system to measure economic performance accurately;

3. an incentive system to reward managers and staff on the basis of actual versus targeted performance.

The EAC was given the main responsibility for developing and implementing the performance evaluation system.

The performance evaluation system consisted of four key steps: the selection of general performance evaluation criteria, the selection of specific units to measure enterprise performance, the assignment of weights to evaluation criteria, and the negotiation of criterion values to differentiate good from bad performance. These criterion values were to provide the basis for evaluating performance at the end of the year and rewarding employees.

Performance Evaluation Criteria

The original proposal for the system asserted that performance evaluation of state-owned firms in Pakistan ought to differ from that of private firms because (a) SOEs should be rewarded for maximizing the benefits to society as a whole and not just to the equity holders of the firm; (b) SOEs generally have noncommercial as well as commercial objectives; and (c) many factors that determine enterprise performance, such as quantity and quality of the stock of capital employed or location, were beyond the control of public managers.

Accordingly, the criterion that Jones calls "public profits at constant prices" was to be used to evaluate the SOEs. Where necessary, public profits would be adjusted to take into account the costs of any noncommercial, social objectives that might affect performance trends. However, since such costs were not likely to fluctuate much from year to year at constant prices, it was felt that this complication could be safely ignored, at least in the start-up phase.[2] The original design also called for supplemental indicators to take into account dynamic considerations, such as expenditures for research and development, maintenance, training, introduction of new products, and so on. Otherwise, SOEs might tend to neglect activities that have short-term costs but offer long-term benefits. Other qualitative indicators measuring such factors as project implementation were also proposed. However, these had not been implemented in Pakistan by 1988 and, as discussed later, there was some evidence that SOEs were sacrificing the long-term health of their companies for short-term profits.

The original design of the system was substantially changed to win the Ministry of Finance's agreement to the bonus system. The ministry agreed to allow bonuses to be paid only if the primary performance evaluation criterion was private profits after taxes. One reason for this was the ministry's reluctance to permit bonuses to be paid to staff of SOEs that showed private losses, but registered an improvement in public profits at constant prices. (This was possible since many of the enterprises faced price distortions.) The ministry also worried about the public relations impact (officials envisioned such headlines as "Public Sector Loses Money; Managers Rewarded"). Another concern was that workers in money-losing SOEs would have to be paid bonuses when their managers got bonuses, but workers in profitable SOEs would be unlikely to forego bonuses even if their managers were not rewarded. (This could happen if the trend in constant priced profits was downwards.) A third reason, which was not explicitly voiced by the ministry, may have been MOF's understandable concern that the SOE's maximize private profits, since that would reduce fiscal pressures on the government. Finally, the ministry was concerned that noneconomists, including the managers of SOEs, would find the concept of public profitability hard to grasp.

In 1988, the system was evaluating SOEs principally on the basis of private financial profits after tax at current prices. The EAC had added some other indicators to measure physical production or energy

---

2. The more common costs stemming from social objectives (besides price controls) are associated with remote locations (to promote regional development) or redundant workers (to increase employment), and these usually do not markedly affect the year to year trends in efficiency.

consumption, and it tried to adjust profits for companies facing cost plus pricing. When more than one criterion was used, the EAC assigned weights that reflected the importance government attached to each one.

Setting Targets

Targets were based on budgetary proposals presented by the enterprises according to a format provided by the EAC. The EAC analyzed the proposals based on each enterprise's initial objectives, designed capacity, past performance, anticipated constraints during the evaluation period, and its projected macroeconomic environment. It also looked at the actual results for the past year and the budgeted and expected results for the current year. Based on these considerations, the EAC attempted to set optimum targets, prepared a draft summary of possible targets, and invited the individual managing directors for discussions. The EAC focused on how to increase production and sales while minimizing costs. For each proposed criterion, the EAC prepared five targets, representing the range from highest to lowest performance. The C target was usually based on the enterprise's budgeted figure. B was usually 5 percent higher and A was 10 percent higher than C; D was 5 percent lower and E was anything less than D.

Targets were officially agreed in a contract between the EAC and the managing directors, subject to the approval of the Ministry of Production. After signing the contract, the enterprise management was, in principle, left on its own to make all efforts necessary to achieve the targets.

Evaluation

Once it received the audited accounts, the EAC calculated a composite performance score for each enterprise by multiplying the assigned target weight by the grade obtained and then aggregating the resulting scores. At this time or earlier, the managing director could try to convince the EAC that unforeseen and uncontrollable circumstances (for example, power outages) warranted a change in the enterprise's targets.

Incentive System

The incentive system consisted of bonuses based on the enterprise's achievement of the targets. Depending on the enterprise's grade, the management and all nonunionized staff received the following rewards:

Grade	Description	Amount of Bonus
Grade A	Excellent	3 months base salary
Grade B	Very good	2 months base salary
Grade C	Good	1 month base salary
Grade D	Poor	15 days base salary
Grade E	Unacceptable	Nil

Only profitable SOEs received a bonus. The original proposal was to reward managers of loss-making firms who reduced the losses by a targeted amount, but the Ministry of Finance worried about having to finance bonuses. As a result, all SOE targets had to show profits. Furthermore, the EAC set a cut-off point for most SOEs equivalent to the C target (which was usually equivalent to the firm's budget), and SOEs with profits that fell below that point were not usually rewarded. In addition some chronic money losers whose viability was questionable were at times excluded or dropped from the system.

Table 10.2 presents the grade distribution for SOEs covered by the system in the first three years of operation. One might expect grades to follow a normal distribution with the mean at the C grade. The actual distribution was single-tailed in 1983/84 with over 40 percent of the SOEs in E grade and roughly equal shares in the other grades. In 1984/85 and 1985/86, the distributions become increasingly bimodal with 35 percent in A and 40 percent in E in 1985/86. These results reflect weaknesses in the criteria used and imperfect information. One problem was that loss-making companies were automatically assigned E, which inflated the bottom grade[3] Another might have been that EAC generalists, who had limited knowledge of the workings of the SOEs or of industry standards in other countries, dominated the negotiations.

---

3.   However, the distributions are still skewed if loss-making companies are excluded. Thirty-five percent received E in 1983/84, much more than in other grades. The next year was bimodal: 34 percent in E and 29 percent in A. The period 1985/86 became single-tailed toward the top: 46 percent in A versus 20 percent in C and 23 percent in E.

Table 10.2 Distribution of Final Grades by Year
(*percentage of total for each year*)

Year	A	B	C	D	E	Total
	---	---	--- Grade	---	---	---
1983/84	17.07	9.76	19.51	12.20	41.46	100.00
1984/85	21.43	16.07	8.93	5.36	48.21	100.00
1985/86[a]	35.56	8.89	15.56	0	40.00	100.00

a. Considers preliminary results for 45 units under the eight holding corporations and excludes 6 units with pending documents.
Source: EAC.

Impact on Performance

To judge the system's impact on performance, quantitative measures and qualitative evidence were gathered by the author through a field visit in 1988. Both managers of SOEs and officials in supervising ministries were interviewed. The quantitative assessment relied principally on a detailed analysis of a sample of 12 enterprises chosen from six large corporations. Table 10.3 presents background information on these companies. The original intention was to compare enterprises inside and outside the system. Unfortunately, the SOEs outside the system under the Ministry of Production were smaller and tended to be the worst performers. Without this control group, we were unable to isolate the system's impact from other influences on SOE performance. However, we did examine other plausible factors that could explain changes in performance and attempted to assess their contribution relative to that of the signaling system.

In judging the sample enterprises, we looked at their performance in terms of the main target indicator—private profits after tax—and in terms of public profits at constant prices. Public profits in constant prices measures net real benefits, that is, changes in efficiency. It is equivalent to a quantum index of outputs minus a quantum index of inputs and gives a trend similar to the trend in total factor productivity. This enabled us to isolate the influence of pricing on results and to judge whether any efficiency gain had occurred in addition to any financial improvements.

Table 10.3 Background Information on Sample Enterprises

Corporation	Enterprise	Main product	Total assets as of June 30, 1986 (Rs millions)	Employment as of June 30, 1986	Net profit (loss) in 1985/86 (Rs millions)
FCCCL	Sind Alkalis	Soda ash	219.00	750	3.74
FCCCL	Ravi Rayon	Acetate rayon yarn	319.25	1,075	8.58
NFC	Lyallpur Chemical and Fertilizer	Single super phosphate	108.88	548	3.34
NFC	Pak Saudi Fertilizer	Urea	1,968.67	897	56.78
SCCP	Javedan Cement	Ordinary cement	552.88	1,124	93.71
SCCP	Zeal Pak Cement	Ordinary cement	494.05	1,988	116.89
SCCP	Gharibwal Cement	Ordinary cement	289.65	954	168.45
SEC	Heavy Mechanical Complex	Cement plants and sugar plants	1,162.97	3,102	3.06
SEC	Pakistan Engineering	Machine tools, HSD and SSD engines, electric motors, spares	638.85	4,431	-41.70
SEC	Pakistan Machine Tool Factory	Machine tool units, transmission group, tractor components	905.41	2,580	4.31
PACO	Millat Tractor	Tractors group	654.76	1,029	9.53
PERAC	National Refinery	Lube I and fuel, Lube II	3,753.07	841	120.00

Source: EAC annual reports.

Thus we were trying to answer two questions: did the system have an impact on private financial profits (its explicit target) and did it have an impact on efficiency (its underlying goal)?

Quantitative Evidence

We begin with the quantitative evidence on private profits at current prices and public profits at constant prices:

PRIVATE PROFITS AT CURRENT PRICES. Incentives were awarded principally on the basis of private profits after taxes at current prices. On the basis of that indicator, SOE performance generally improved between 1982/83 and 1985/86. Thirty-three SOEs were in the system for its entire three years of operation, of which 19 (or about 58 percent) improved their private profits after tax, from losses of Rs 100 million in 1982/83 to profits of Rs 617 million in 1985/86. Fourteen showed a deterioration from profits of Rs 445 million to profits of only Rs 67 million. As shown in table 10.4, the

Table 10.4 Trend in Profits of Pakistani SOEs, 1982/83 to 1985/86 (*Rs millions*)

Category	1982/83	1983/84	1984/85	1985/86
Total profits of 33 SOEs participating in system for three years	344.14	467.16	937.81	684.00
Of which: Total profits of 19 SOEs with profit improvement	100.75	221.08	717.45	616.74
Total profits of 14 SOEs with profit deterioration	444.89	246.08	220.36	67.32

Source: EAC.

total profits of the 33 SOEs in the system almost doubled in the three-year period.

The sample enterprises showed a similar trend. Of the 12 enterprises, 5 improved their profits after tax from the system's introduction in 1983/84 to 1984/85 and 7 showed an improvement up to 1985/86 (based on unaudited data for 1985/86).[4] Further, sample enterprises with a grade of C or better increased from six in 1982/83 to seven in 1984/85 and to nine in 1985/86.

PUBLIC PROFITS AT CONSTANT PRICES. Of course, if the aim is to improve efficiency, in most cases looking at public profits at constant prices is more meaningful. Data on public profits at constant prices were available for sample SOEs for 1980/81 through 1984/85, which covered only the first two years of the system's operation. Table 10.5 summarizes how the companies performed on the two indicators: private profits after tax and public profits at constant prices. Graphs 10.1–10.12 show the trend in public profitability at current and constant prices for the sample enterprises between 1980/81 and 1984/85.

In 7 of the 12 sample SOEs, public profits at constant prices increased above the 1982/83 level in the first two years of the system's operation. These seven included four for which the increase was also an improvement over past performance (borne out by comparing the increase in real value added with a trend line based on data for the previous five years). These SOEs were Sind Alkalis, Lyallpur Chemicals, Pakistan Machine Tool Factory, and National Refinery. All four also improved private profits after tax. The other three enterprises in this group improved efficiency over 1982/83, but were still below their past trends (Pak Saudi, Javedan Cement, and Millat Tractors).

Four of the enterprises shown in table 10.5 showed opposite trends in private profits and public profits at constant prices. This occurred either because of administered prices, or because private profit contained items such as nonoperating income that did not move in parallel with efficiency gains.

---

4. The five enterprises were Lyallpur Chemicals, Javendan Cement, Zeal Pak Cement, Pakistan Machine Tool Factory, and National Refinery. The seven included these five plus Sind Alkalis and Gharibwal Cement.

Table 10.5 Trend in Performance of Sample SOEs after Introduction of Signaling System
(*base year = 1982/83*)

Public profits at constant prices	*Private profits after tax at current prices*
SOEs showing an upward trend	*SOEs showing an upward trend*
Sind Alkalis	Sind Alkalis[2]
Lyallpur Chemicals	Lyallpur Chemicals
Pakistan Machine Tool Factory[1]	Pakistan Machine Tool Factory
National Refinery	National Refinery
Javedan Cement[3]	Javedan Cement
Pak Saudi Fertilizer[1, 3]	Zeal Pakistan Cement
Millat Tractors[3]	Gharibwal Cement[2]
SOEs showing a downward trend	*SOEs showing a downward trend*
Gharibwal Cement	Pak Saudi Fertilizer
Zeal Pak Cement	Millat Tractors
Heavy Mechanical Complex	Heavy Mechanical Complex
Pakistan Engineering	Pakistan Engineering
Ravi Rayon	Ravi Rayon

1. Improvement in 1984/85 only.

2. Improvement in 1985/86 only.

3. Improvement was below the trend established in the five years immediately preceding the introduction of the signaling system. In all other cases, the improvement was above the trend line.

Graph 10.1 Sind Alkalis: Public Profitability

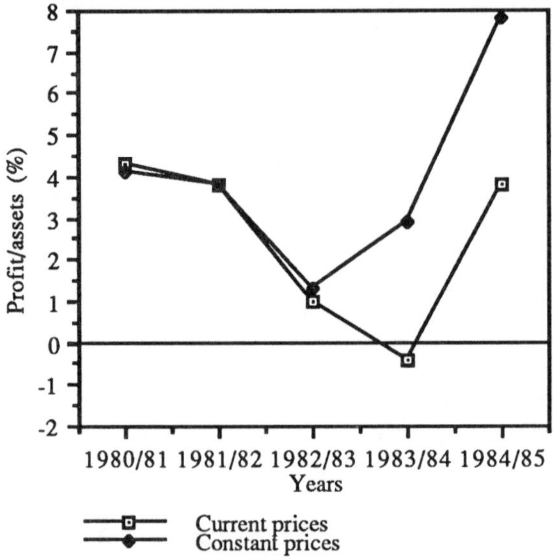

Graph 10.2 Pak Saudi: Public Profitability

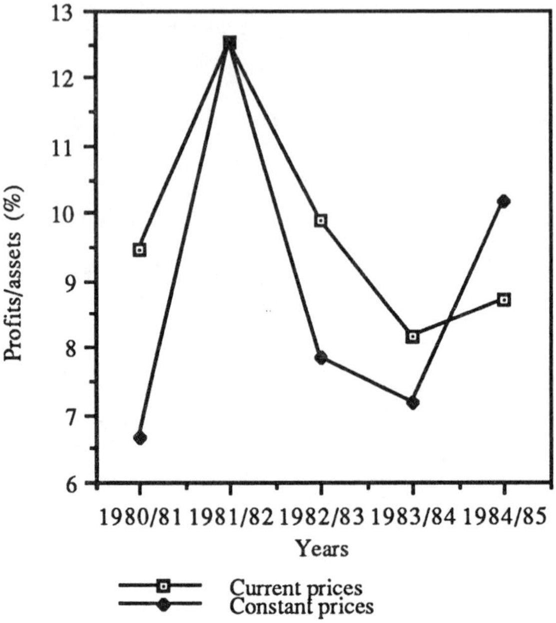

Graph 10.3 Ravi Rayon: Public Profitability

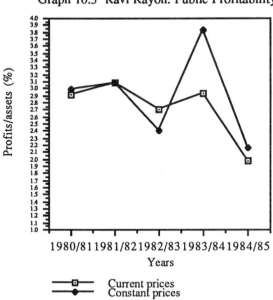

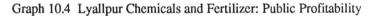

Graph 10.4 Lyallpur Chemicals and Fertilizer: Public Profitability

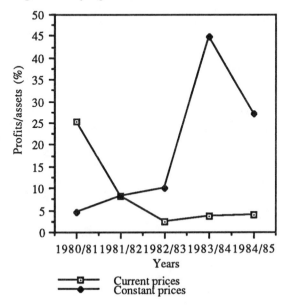

Graph 10.5 Javedan Cement: Public Profitability

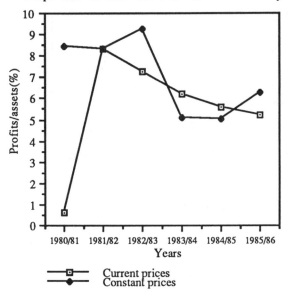

Graph 10.6 Gharibwal Cement: Public Profitability

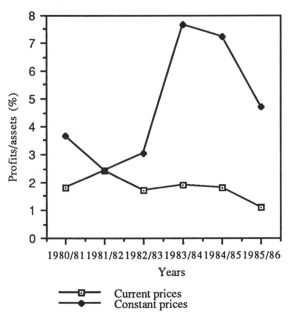

Graph 10.7 Zeal Pak Cement: Public Profitability

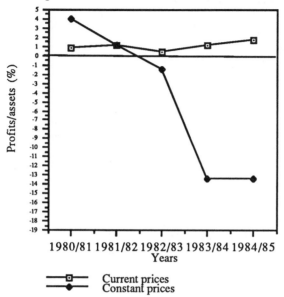

Graph 10.8 Millat Tractors: Public Profitability

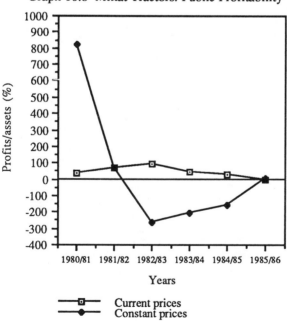

Graph 10.9 Heavy Mechanical: Public Profitability

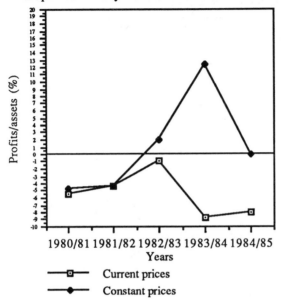

Graph 10.10 Pakistan Machine Tools: Public Profitability

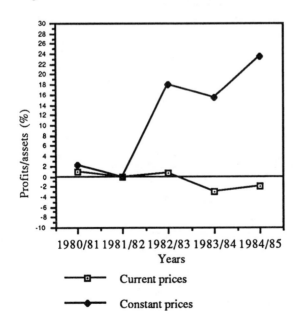

Graph 10.11 Pakistan Engineering: Public Profitability

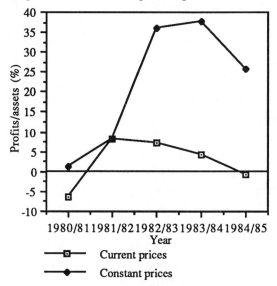

Graph 10.12 National Refinery: Public Profitability

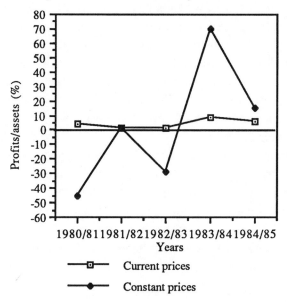

Public profitability is defined as public profits (at current or constant prices) divided by fixed operating assets.

We can examine the divergence caused by the different definitions of public and private profits by comparing the two sets of profits at current prices. For most of the sample companies public profit is higher than private profit, principally because the definition of public profits does not view interest and depreciation charges as costs. Since most managers had little or no influence over the initial investment decisions, private profit penalized some managers for factors they could not control. For example, if the high capital charges resulting from the government's past investment decisions made it impossible for managers to earn a passing grade, then the system would provide no incentive for those people to improve factors they could control.

At the same time, private profit would fail to motivate managers to use wisely factors that they could control by not measuring those items, notably, working capital, and the inclusion of nonoperating income might allow an enterprise to achieve its targets thanks to windfall income that had little or nothing to do with efficiency. For example, in 1984/85, 3 of the 12 sample SOEs had public profits at current prices that were lower than private profits; public profits were actually negative in all three cases. In two cases (Pakistan Engineering and Pakistan Machine Tool Factory), this was due to the opportunity cost of working capital, which exceeded profits before interest and depreciation. Pakistan Engineering went from an E to a C grade, despite a large build-up in accounts receivable, thanks to government debt relief in the form of other financial income. The extreme example of the distortions that can be caused by using private profits as a target occurred in the case of Heavy Mechanical Complex, which made the A grade in 1984/85 only because of other income (principally, interest on deferred credits on overseas sales).

In most of the sample firms, the difference between public and private profits was in the level of profits, not the trend. With the exception of Pakistan Engineering, the trends in public profits at current prices and private profits did not diverge dramatically. The trends in current and constant priced profits did differ sharply for most companies, showing that prices were the main reason why some firms registered an improvement (or deterioration) in one measure but not the other in table 10.5.

Explanation for Changes in Performance

As already mentioned, since establishing a clear causality between the performance changes and the signaling system is impossible, we tried to consider other explanations of performance to see if they left room for the system as a factor. The main explanations included (a) changes in prices; (b) changes in markets; (c) changes in the macroeconomic environment; and (d) changes in management. Explanations we rejected because they did not fit with the circumstances were a drop or rise in labor unrest (no significant change occurred); an improvement or deterioration in the supply of inputs such as electricity, water, and transport (SOEs experiencing these problems saw little change); and technological changes (no significant changes occurred in the technology used in the sample enterprises during this period). Changes in liquidity was another explanation we considered and rejected. Levels of liquidity were low in most of the sample firms and showed little improvement during 1983/84 or 1984/85.

Additions to capacity were also not significant during this period. The government's policy was to curb new investment in the SOEs. Only two SOEs showed any major increase in fixed operating assets at constant prices from 1982/83 to 1984/85: Millat Tractors and National Refinery. Assets of the other SOEs rose by only 2.7 percent on average during this period. In the event, capacity change was corrected for by including fixed operating assets in the denominator of public profitability. (Millat Tractors and National Refinery showed a deterioration in public profitability in both current and constant prices in the years when fixed operating assets increased more than profits.)

CHANGES IN PRICES. The government set the prices of four of the corporations under the Ministry of Production: those concerned with cement, fertilizer, petroleum, and automobile production. As a result, the level of public profits at constant prices diverged widely from public profits at current prices for most of the sample SOEs. In six cases, the SOEs showed opposite trends in these two measures. In two of these cases, the price effect was positive: increases in administered prices explained why Gharibwal and Zeal Pak Cement could improve their financial profits even though efficiency deteriorated. Prices had the opposite effect on Pak Saudi Fertilizer and Millat Tractors, which showed modest improvements in efficiency that were canceled by adverse price effects. In 1983/84, Heavy Metal Complex also improved its constant priced profits while its current priced profits declined. In this case, it was because the company's market for higher priced products such as turnkey cement plants deteriorated, and it had to shift into lower value items such as galvanized steel structures.

Pricing policies clearly affected the extent to which achieving private profit targets required SOEs to improve efficiency. For the two years for which constant priced figures are available (1983/84 and 1984/85), the grade that sample companies would probably have received based on their public profits at constant prices differed from the actual grade awarded (based on private profits) in 14 out of 24 cases. For example, Lyallpur Chemicals made a C in 1983/84 on its private profits target, but would probably have been an A company at constant prices. The following year it was an A company, but would probably have made a C at constant prices.

The EAC has made some effort to reflect changes in administered prices while setting targets for SOEs. For example, it calculated the achievements of two sectors with administered prices, cement and fertilizer, on the basis of the budgeted price that was used to determine the original target, even though the actual price given to the company was higher. This, however, only corrected for the pricing problem on the output side, not the input side. The EAC also added some nonfinancial targets in these cases, such as physical production or energy consumption targets, but these did not appear to improve the system's capacity to measure efficiency. For example, Zeal Pak Cement earned a C grade in 1983/84 on a combined target of private profitability (40 percent) and volume of production (60 percent); it earned an A grade in 1984/85 on a target of profitability (60 percent), production volume (30 percent), and productivity (10 percent). In contrast, Zeal Pak's efficiency (public profitability at constant prices) fell sharply in 1983/84 (a 3 percent increase in output was offset by a 60% increase in inputs at constant prices) and stayed about the same in 1985/86.

CHANGES IN MARKETS. Competition could explain an improvement in profits and efficiency if the SOEs reacted to competitive pressures by working harder to cut costs, expand production, improve quality, and so on to retain or expand their markets. If, in contrast, the SOEs could not or would not respond, the result would be a deterioration in performance. Competition increased in Pakistan during the period under review, thanks to trade liberalization, easier private entry into previously public activities, and the earmarking of credit for the private sector. Competition had a favorable impact on some public firms that were striving hard to improve efficiency and retain their market (Petro Carbon, which was not part of the sample, is an example). However, competitive pressure did not seem to be the main explanation for the efficiency improvements in the sample firms. Some of these firms, such as Heavy Metal Complex and Pakistan Engineering, faced competition even before the period under examination. Others, such as the fertilizer plants and the refinery, faced no change in competition, but nonetheless showed efficiency gains. In most cases where SOEs faced increased competition, the result during the short period under examination was a deterioration in efficiency.

An example is cement. Pakland Cement, a private cement plant, began operations in 1982/83 and immediately established new standards of quality control, marketing, and timely delivery. Pakland's nearest state-owned competitor, Javedan Cement, improved its efficiency in the period under review, but was still below its past trends. The other two cement plants in the sample, however, showed declines in efficiency. The public cement plants had a long history of operating in segmented markets and they may have required more time to react to competition by improving efficiency. Moreover, for competition to have a positive impact on efficiency, SOE management had to have the capacity, autonomy, and capital to respond. This was often not the case; autonomy, in particular, seemed to have been insufficient. In addition, liberalization shifted demand in ways that made responding difficult or impossible for some SOEs. An example of this was Ravi Rayon, a poor performer in both current and constant prices. This company had been having trouble with competition from a substitute, polyester, and its problem worsened with liberalized imports of viscose, a direct substitute for rayon.

In sum, increased competition was not a major factor explaining the improvements in efficiency, but it was a reason for the deterioration in results in some cases. To explain improvements in performance we must look elsewhere for answers.

CHANGES IN THE MACROECONOMIC ENVIRONMENT. Changes in the macroeconomic environment could explain part of the trend in performance. The first year of operation of the signaling system, 1983/84, was not a buoyant one for the economy: GDP grew by 4.4 percent in real terms, which was well below the average of about 7 percent in the 1970s and early 1980s. GDP grew by 8.8 percent in the second year of the system, 1984/85. The trends in public profits, however, were not strongly correlated with movements in GDP. Only three SOEs (Pak Saudi Fertilizer, Javedan Cement, and Pakistan Machine Tools) showed a slack growth in constant priced profits in 1983/84 and an acceleration in 1984/85.

However, the easing of import restrictions, reflected in a 22 percent real growth in imports in 1983/84 and 7.1 percent in 1984/85, may have been a more important explanation. For those SOEs that were supply, not demand, constrained, greater access to imports could have made a real difference to their output. This explanation does not suffice, however, because most SOEs lacked the capital to take advantage of import opportunities.

CHANGES IN MANAGEMENT. In several of the sample companies, much of the improvement in performance can be explained by management changes. This was especially true for the four companies that showed efficiency gains above their past trends. For instance, much of Sind Alkalis' improved performance was probably due to a change in the management team at the start of the period. Sind Alkalis increased its soda ash capacity utilization from 38 percent to 90 percent, improved productivity sharply, increased the volume of production by 140 percent, and reduced its gas consumption. Lyallpur Chemicals and Fertilizer was already above rated capacity and managed to increase utilization still further while curbing raw material and fuel consumption. Pakistan Machine Tools also improved capacity use somewhat, coped with stagnant demand by shifting production, and registered a sharp increase in productivity. The National Refinery, which was always a good performer, increased its inventory turnover and kept energy consumption in check.

In other cases, the same managers strove harder to curb costs and expand output. An important reason for this was the general "hardening" of the environment for SOEs during this period, of which the signaling system was only one component. Top authorities were reacting to performance indicators (many of which were being calculated well before the signaling system was introduced) with new seriousness and demanding explanations. They were firing managers for mismanagement, curbing subsidies and easy access to credit, and sharply curtailing SOE investment funds. The installation of the signaling system was itself part of this trend. Separating these environmental changes from the performance system to judge to what extent the harder environment by itself was responsible for the efficiency gains was difficult. The signaling system alone, without these environmental changes, is unlikely to have been sufficient to create the efficiency improvements.

CONCLUSION. The argument that the efficiency improvements were partly due to the system could not be ruled out since none of the other explanations fully explained the efficiency improvement. However, it was not fully persuasive because the targeting system was not really measuring efficiency and the system was operating under a number of constraints on its capacity to affect change. Nevertheless, the system may have influenced efficiency even though it was not measuring it effectively. Managers motivated to increase profits, particularly public enterprise managers, had only so many ways to react. Most of the sample enterprises were not in a position to change prices or to increase transfers. Increasing the quantity of output or reducing the quantity of inputs may have been one of the few ways they could improve their private profits. Such a reaction may have been especially likely in the initial years of the performance evaluation system, when managers were less likely to be cynical about the flaws in the indicators or to have figured out ways to achieve targets without improving efficiency.

An important feature of the system was that it was part of the general policy changes mentioned earlier. The qualitative evidence described below suggests that the system provided managers with an added incentive to respond to these changes as well as a tool to rally and motivate staff. In sum, despite its flaws, the system seems to have had a positive impact on efficiency, an impact that was intimately linked to other changes in the SOEs' managerial environment.

Qualitative Evidence

Most managers and government officials interviewed felt that the system had a positive impact on performance. They attributed this not only to the targets and bonuses, but also to a number of other, parallel features of the system: the systematic gathering and processing of information on performance, the serious discussions of performance in the negotiations and review meetings, and the resulting better understanding of the enterprises in the ministry of production.

All the managers interviewed cited the targeting and bonus system as a positive factor, provided it was properly handled, including those critical of the system and those not receiving bonuses. Managers that had received bonuses maintained that their staff were very aware of the targets and knew what they and their departments had to do on a daily or monthly basis to achieve the A target. Since the C target was the same as the budget for most companies and the A and B targets were typically 5 and 10 percent above that level, for the SOEs to convert their budgets into targets was fairly simple. Judging from the enterprises visited, Pakistan's SOEs had thorough management information systems. They monitored budget achievement and other indicators on a quarterly, monthly, weekly, and daily basis for each work unit. Under such circumstances, it is plausible that staff members knew what the targets meant for their units and where they stood in relation to their goals during the year.

Even companies that had not achieved their targets in the past seemed to be influenced by the signaling system. One such company, Petro Carbon, for example, was attempting to compete against imports of carbon black in a limited market. Petro Carbon was a small-scale, inefficient producer that had accumulated Rs 75 million in losses over seven years. Nevertheless, thanks to aggressive management and the motivation to receive the bonus, the company converted its Rs 9.0 million loss in 1984/85 to a Rs 7.5 million profit in 1985/86, brought down average production costs from Rs 16,000 per ton to Rs 9,000 per ton, and expected to earn an A grade the following year.

For many years, the Ministry of Production had produced a great deal of information on industrial SOEs. The difference introduced by the signaling system was that the information centered around a few key indicators that were being monitored. This allowed decisionmakers to focus on achievements plus a few explanatory variables and helped them make sense of a flood of data. Furthermore, it used a weighted comprehensive indicator (private profitability) that reduced the distortions caused by partial indicators. In addition, information arrived in a more timely fashion. Before the signaling system, the Ministry of Production used to receive audited reports one or two years after the end of a fiscal year. After the signaling system, they arrived on average within five to seven months because incentive payments were linked to the audited accounts and results. Furthermore, the follow-up to auditors' comments was more serious. If, for example, the auditors' report stated that they were "unable to verify inventories," the ministry sent a team to investigate and, in extreme cases, fired the manager. Finally, the analysis of the improvement in efficiency and its probable causes would not have been possible before the installation of the signaling system.

Another important change was that targets were negotiated rather than set from above, and that the targets were now linked to a tangible reward, the bonus. Both of these factors caused managers to treat targets more seriously. Targeting was more rational and realistic and managers understood the reasons for the target and, with some exceptions, accepted the targets. The main exceptions were the money-losing firms that did not have a chance of achieving a profit target. Several of these refused to sign the agreement.

All enterprises met regularly (at least twice a year) with the secretary of the Ministry of Production, the heads of their corporations, and other managing directors in their respective corporations. The EAC prepared an agenda that was circulated beforehand. These meetings always began by following up on issues raised during the previous meetings. In particular, the secretary reported on any commitment he had undertaken (usually with regard to negotiations with other ministries) and the managing directors of the holding corporations reported on any responsibilities or improvements in performance that they had pledged to achieve in the previous meeting. The discussions centered around a comparison of budgeted and actual performance provided by the EAC. After the meeting, the EAC prepared minutes. Managers regarded these performance review meetings as effective devices for motivating them to do better and for informing the secretary of their situation and problems. It also helped them understand their standing compared to other SOEs in their corporations.

Constraints on the System's Impact on Efficiency

Besides the fact that targets were an imperfect reflection of efficiency, the following factors may have constrained the system's impact on public enterprise efficiency:

- the rewards were not sufficiently large or distributed in such a manner as to motivate performance improvements;
- the managers lacked sufficient autonomy to change performance;
- the managers were not competent to respond to rewards with changes in performance;
- some public enterprises were excluded from the system;
- the macroeconomic environment was not conducive to performance improvements.

To some extent all these constraints operated in Pakistan during the period under review.

FAILURE TO MOTIVATE EFFICIENCY IMPROVEMENTS. Most managers consulted thought that the size of the bonus was sufficient to motivate their staff. Nonunionized staff had not received bonuses in recent years and the managers saw the prospect of a bonus as an inducement. Not surprisingly, if the firm had once received a bonus, the motivation to keep or increase the bonus the following year was stronger than if the firm had never received a bonus. In contrast, a senior staff member of one money-losing firm was not even aware of the existence of the signaling system. Lower level staff of one SOE that made the A grade only because of nonoperating income were also not aware of the target.

The way the bonuses were distributed may have reduced the impact of the incentive system. First, all nonunionized staff of an A grade firm received three months of salary across the board. Some managers rewarded a lower bonus or none at all to a few individuals that received below average merit ratings (all firms studied had some sort of individual performance evaluation system); others did not realize that they could reduce the award. However, managers could not raise the award for an above average individual, nor could they distinguish between units or departments on the basis of their performance. The original proposal was that managers be given complete discretion in awarding bonuses, but this was dropped in the face of opposition from the Ministry of Production, corporations, and some managers. Second, unionized staff received a bonus (the level was decided by the government) regardless of whether the firm had achieved its target, and with no differentiation among workers on the basis of merit. Typically, the bonus for unionized workers was a higher multiple than the bonus awarded to nonunionized staff (seven to ten months). In 1988, the Ministry of Production was considering linking workers' bonuses to their enterprises performance through the collective bargaining process. Third, the bonus under the system was usually awarded six months after the end of the fiscal year, which may have reduced its impact as an incentive.

LACK OF MANAGEMENT AUTONOMY TO AFFECT EFFICIENCY. Among the main constraints on management's capacity to increase operating efficiency were their inability to fire workers, contract services, drop products, fix compensation levels, obtain inputs from their choice of source, and obtain the foreign exchange required for importing capital goods, technology, and raw materials. Some of these constraints were due to the power of unionized labor in Pakistan. The Ministry of Production had taken steps to decentralize some personnel decisions to the corporations and enterprises, such as disciplinary firings, promotions, and compensation decisions in collective bargaining agreements. Reductions in the work force, however, were virtually impossible; therefore managers could not cut costs by laying off workers and closing lines or plants.

Managers also had limited flexibility in controlling compensation. Individual managers could be faulted for a tendency to give in to labor demands in collective bargaining—a common trait in public enterprise management where there is cost plus pricing, easy access to subsidies, or cheap credit—but this tendency also reflected a long history of union power in the public sector. The government enforced bonus system for unionized workers further reduced managerial control over labor costs. Because of this, increases in the wage bill bore little relationship to productivity increases. This situation appeared to deteriorate during the period under review; with one exception (Sind Alkalis), all the sample enterprises showed faster increases in average labor costs than in productivity during 1983/84–1984/85, while the opposite was true for most of the sample firms between 1980/81–1981/82. A similar trend seemed to hold throughout the Ministry of Production, as shown in table 10.6. However, by 1988 the ministry had become concerned about rising labor costs and had begun to stress measures to cut costs. Managers were being asked to bargain for reasonable wage levels and to reduce overtime, bonuses, and the like.

Table 10.6 Comparison of Labor Costs and Productivity Increases for Industrial Enterprises under Ministry of Production
(*percentage change*)

Category	1982-83 versus 1981-82	1983-84 versus 1982-83	1984-85 versus 1983-84
Manpower	−1.1	10.6	0.2
Average labor costs	14.8	7.5	13.9
Production[1]	18.6	9.4	5.9
Productivity	19.8	−0.1	6.7

1. At constant 1977-78 prices.

Source: EAC.

Procurement procedures also reduced management's flexibility in cutting costs or seeking new technology. For example, Heavy Metals Complex, which produced heavy equipment, including turnkey sugar and cement plants, had to consult its corporation for all purchases over about US$12,000. If the item was a capital good, Heavy Metals had to go for competitive bidding. Raw materials purchases over about US$118,000 also had to go for competitive bidding. This required an advertisement, 45 days for submission of bids, and 40 days for study and selection. The firm was expected to accept the lowest bid. A ministerial committee had to approve purchases over US$600,000 and a high-level cabinet committee had to approve purchases over US$3 million. Some of these approvals could take two years. Thus, even if managers felt motivated to seek out lower cost inputs or to develop new methods of operation or product lines, they had to deal with a lengthy procedure that could stifle initiative or force the firm to miss opportunities.

Some of the firms were also constrained in their choice of markets, products, and suppliers. Not surprisingly, import substituting enterprises like National Refinery had to satisfy domestic demand before exporting. The Pak Suzuki automobile company was required to produce a certain number of its lowest priced passenger cars and to purchase a portion of its inputs from another state enterprise. Judging whether this was a constraint was difficult, since most managers were not aggressively seeking new markets or changing their product mixes. Years of operating in a controlled environment seemed to have made them complacent even in the face of rising competition.

Government imposed social welfare objectives placed another burden on SOEs that reduced management's flexibility to cut costs. For example, Pakistan Machine Tools was required to train five people for every one person they intended to hire. Plants located in remote areas at government behest had to provide education, housing, health services, and transportation to employees as well as bear added transport costs.

The operations of the financial system were another constraint on management. Credit and foreign exchange ceilings were allocated as part of the budgetary process through negotiations, first between the corporations and the ministries of Production and Finance, and then between the corporations and the companies. There was no reason to believe that these ceilings tended to favor the more efficient firms, especially since price distortions made judging efficiency hard. A related constraint was that SOE managers could not get coverage for their foreign exchange purchases, even though Pakistani private enterprises have this facility.

Finally, management was constrained by the inherited capital stock. Management could still improve operating efficiency within that constraint, but the task could be considerably harder when the plant was grossly undersized or oversized or the equipment was antiquated and worn out.

LACK OF MANAGEMENT COMPETENCE. A danger in many developing countries is that SOE managers lack the competency to understand the efficiency target or to improve efficiency in the face of the target. Pakistan was fortunate in having SOE managers who seemed generally skilled and competent. Nevertheless, these managers and their staff were accustomed to operating in a protected environment without the pressures for efficiency that the signaling system set out to provide. As the system was trying to motivate managers on the basis of public profitability, they needed to be educated about the rationale of the profit adjustments. Some may also have needed training and assistance in areas that had not been very important in the past, such as cost cutting, marketing, and planning. Deregulation and the pressures for efficiency from the EAC created new incentives for managers to acquire these skills.

EXCLUSION OF SOME PEs FROM THE SYSTEM. In 1985/86, the incentive system was applied to 51 of the 70 enterprises under the Ministry of Production. The enterprises excluded were mostly small in terms of assets, employment, and revenues (most of the small firms under the Pakistan Industrial Development Corporation were excluded). In 1987-88, all the ministry's firms were nominally under the system, but in reality the coverage was incomplete because loss-making enterprises were effectively excluded. Managers of loss-making enterprises tended to become demoralized if they felt targets were not realistic and to ignore the system. Six enterprises made losses through the three years of the system and were, in effect, excluded. Thus overall, only 45 of the 70 SOEs under the Ministry of Production in 1985/86 were really covered by the system.

MACROECONOMIC ENVIRONMENT. Finally, several exogenous factors appeared to have constrained efficiency gains by the SOEs. Depressed demand, shortages of inputs, weaknesses in the infrastructure, and other constraints of this sort made effecting changes difficult for managers. For example, many of the SOEs suffered because of power shortages during this period; Millat Tractors faced a drop in demand because the Agricultural Development Bank provided inadequate funds for farmers to buy tractors; and Pakistan Engineering suffered when the electricity company canceled an order for transmission towers. Despite such problems, most of the sample firms were able to improve their efficiency.

PERVERSE EFFECTS ON PERFORMANCE. Performance evaluation systems can motivate short-term improvements in profitability and yet have a perverse effect on long-term performance. The design of the Pakistani system took into account the fact that if the targets were solely based on short-run measures, firms would tend to sacrifice expenditures with short-run costs and only long-run benefits. This tendency could have been a problem in Pakistan, where the average tenure of an SOE manager was about three years. Nevertheless, it was quite rightly decided to begin with a simpler system based on short-run targets only and to add targets for items like maintenance, training, investments, and R&D as the system matured and the short-run targeting system was working well. The Ministry of

Production was actually in the process of introducing corporate planning for all SOEs in 1988, and a qualitative measure of corporate planning was to be included in the targets in future years.

Some evidence indicated that the lack of longer-term targets might have had an adverse impact on performance. For example, one of the sample firms (Gharibwal Cement) achieved a B grade partly because it did not carry out its budgeted repair and maintenance program and hence worked 316 days instead of 300 days a year. Several managers also worried that their targets were based on full or more-than-full capacity operation without enough provision for preventive maintenance. EAC made an effort to ensure that the targets were realistic and made provisions for preventive maintenance. It was also willing to change targets if unforeseeable and unpreventable problems cropped up. At the time of the evaluation, EAC checked that SOEs had adhered to their agreed maintenance schedules.

Impact of the System on Government Policy

The signaling system gets its name from the notion that it would signal to managers the behavior that government desired, and likewise signal to government the effects that policy was having on SOE performance. The first set of signals was the system's primary purpose, but the second set could be even more important if government policy was the primary determinant of performance.

Impact on the Regulatory Environment

In theory, the system signaled the need for regulatory reform through the adjustments that had to be made in the targets to take account of government imposed costs, lack of managerial autonomy, and the like.

Proponents of the system maintained that by making these adjustments explicit, the system highlighted the cost of distortions, helping the government to make conscious policy choices. Furthermore, even if policy reforms did not ensue, the system motivated managers to operate at greater efficiency within the degrees of freedom they had. Lack of autonomy was not accepted as a blanket excuse for inefficiency. Critics of the system argued that by adjusting for these problems, the signaling system actually made it easier for government to ignore them. Instead of promoting reform, the system hindered or delayed it. They leveled the same criticism at price adjustments: by adjusting targets for price distortions the system reduced the pressure to remove the distortion. But this was only true insofar as a move to efficiency prices would have worked in favor of the manager, a situation that did not appear to hold in Pakistan. In the past, SOE managers had not been held to efficiency targets; nor had they been lobbyists for reform.

The main constraints on the SOEs mentioned earlier all entailed a cost. Since these costs were typically not directly felt by the government—they either took the form of foregone taxes or dividends or higher prices to consumers—there was a tendency for the tradeoffs never to be considered.

The EAC had not yet used its information base much to promote regulatory reform. One exception was a study of labor costs that may have led to pressures for wage restraint. The EAC adjusted targets to take into account the constraints on enterprises during the negotiations, but it did not formally calculate the costs implied by these adjustments. For example, the cost to an SOE of the government not permitting it to make a necessary replacement investment in a timely fashion would be explicitly calculated while setting targets, but would not be analyzed elsewhere. The costs of other constraints, such as not being able to lay off redundant workers, were treated as normal costs of doing business and no adjustments were made to the target. The costs of meeting government imposed social objectives were not calculated unless these changed considerably from year to year. Thus, the cost of training more people every year than an SOE could possibly employ would not be explicitly estimated because such costs did not significantly affect the trend in operating efficiency. The EAC did produce a diagnostic report at the end of the year that assessed each unit's real performance and that could form the basis for follow-up studies. The EAC did not use the system to illustrate the financial impact of pricing or other policy changes, either at the enterprise level or the aggregate level.

Running simulation exercises to estimate the impact of changes in wages, foreign exchange, electricity prices, and so on on each public enterprise and on the entire SOE sector would have been fairly simple.

However, the EAC was set up for, and was more effective at, influencing management rather than government. Furthermore, the decisions about many of these policies were not in the Ministry of Production's hands. The Ministry of Industry, the Ministry of Finance, and often the very top levels of government played a role in matters such as industrial policy, foreign exchange allocation, or the public sector's stance on layoffs. Nonetheless, the EAC could probably have done more to influence the regulatory environment by making the costs of regulation explicit. It could have done studies of the costs of social objectives, of transporting goods from remote locations, of delays caused by overcentralized decisionmaking, and so on. It could have estimated without too much difficulty the degree to which SOE output prices were distorted: the EAC had calculated the shares of different products in an SOE's output, and international prices were available for most of these (tradeable) products.

Determining the subsidy element in input prices may have been more difficult, but was also possible. Again, the weights were known and studies of efficiency prices for some major nontradeables (water and electricity) had been done, and the EAC could have analyzed the impact of policy changes on individual SOEs as well as on the entire SOE sector. In this regard, it is noteworthy that in late 1988 the EAC was developing a social accounting matrix that would show SOE performance and linkages with the rest of the economy and was expected to be an input into the policy formulation process.

Impact on Decisions to Close or Sell Industrial Public Enterprises

The performance evaluation system calculated the operating efficiency, or X-efficiency, of the enterprises; it was not designed to calculate allocative efficiency. The economic costs of keeping an enterprise operating—even at peak efficiency—can exceed the economic benefits. The SOE may tie up resources in an activity with low, or even negative, economic returns that could be put to far more productive use elsewhere. In some extreme cases where an enterprise has negative value added at international prices, improving its operations may make matters worse. Society may be worse off economically as the enterprise steps up production because the economic value of its output is less than the economic value of the inputs it consumes.

In addition, some SOEs may outlive their original objective or may not be able to adapt to the new rules of a more open market. In some cases, the system might ask managers to improve the efficiency of an outmoded plant or one that is either too small or too large to be efficient. Yet, rehabilitating the enterprise may yield far lower returns than alternative investments.

While these are not problems of the signaling system as such, they cannot be separated from it entirely. In Pakistan, by focusing on the operations of the SOEs and not considering the fundamental question of whether enterprises should be kept alive, the signaling system may have been making matters worse in some cases. Furthermore, the EAC seemed well placed to assess the net economic benefits of SOEs: it was staffed with economists and the computer system was set up to accept shadow prices. Without much additional data the EAC could have calculated the economic costs and benefits (taking into account indirect benefits and externalities) of SOEs that might have been candidates for closure. However, the EAC's work on corporate planning and the social accounting matrix were expected to be tools for assessing restructuring requirements within the sector.

Applying the System in Other Countries

The Pakistani signaling system, despite some flaws discussed here, represents a major advance in holding managers accountable for performance. Many developing countries make no attempt to develop targets and do not require meaningful reporting on public enterprises' results. Good managers go unrewarded and bad managers go unsanctioned. As a result, the interest in the Pakistani signaling system is strong and in 1988 a number of countries were considering introducing something similar, including the Philippines, Egypt, and Venezuela. The Republic of Korea already had a similar system in place. We turn in this concluding section to lessons from Pakistan for other developing countries contemplating reforms in the way SOEs are evaluated.

Potential Costs

The initial cost of the Pakistani system was US$350,000 to US$400,000. This included development costs and a mainframe computer system with remote terminals and a tape unit. Assuming an average salary of US$300 per month for 17 top level professional staff, the system's basic operating cost was approximately US$70,000 a year, or US$1,060 per SOE.

The financial cost of installing and operating the signaling system in another country may be less than the cost in Pakistan for two reasons.

First, the Pakistani system was the first of its kind and considerable learning was embodied in the installation costs. Second, the system could now be operated entirely on personal computers, using easily available commercial software, which obviates the need for computer personnel and reduces equipment costs. The installation cost is more likely to be some US$75,000 (in 1988) and the principal maintenance cost would be the salary of one analyst for approximately every ten companies participating in the system. In addition, since there are no economies of scale—evaluating a small company is just as much work as evaluating a large one—other countries might be able to reduce costs by focusing on fewer, more important companies. This was attempted in Pakistan, but because of the bonus system, managers objected to being excluded.

Several factors could, however, raise the cost of installing such a system in another country. First, the Pakistani system was designed to apply to companies under the Ministry of Production: a maximum of 70 companies. Other countries might aim to include more SOEs; Egypt, for example, is considering extending a similar system to some 200 industrial public enterprises. This will raise the initial cost of data gathering and systemization and require additional staff to operate.

Second, the Pakistani system was applied only to industrial public enterprises. Although the SOEs were diverse, they included a number of similar firms (for example, ten cement companies, six fertilizer plants, seven vehicle manufacturers) and many were relatively simple process industries with narrow product lines (cement, petroleum refining, soda ash). Extending the system to the entire SOE sector and including such diverse enterprises as utilities, transport companies, agricultural marketing boards, or banks would require additional time and staff.

Third, and most important, the data on SOEs in Pakistan were good even before the system began. An effort to develop a uniform information system for the enterprises had begun in 1975/76. By the time the evaluation system was implemented, the SOEs had well-developed internal information systems; private auditors were already auditing information systems according to generally accepted standards; and the EAC was systematically receiving a lot of information. Even in this context, a good deal of time and effort under the signaling system project went into assuring that accounts were accurate, comparable, and received by the EAC on time.

Other countries may need to do a lot more groundwork to improve their internal accounting and auditing systems and ensure a timely flow of information. The accounting improvements required for performance evaluation are also necessary for effective management and should be pursued in their own right. Of course, countries may also choose to begin with a simpler, less data-intensive system than that installed in Pakistan. This could reduce the start up time for the information system, but it will not obviate the need for reliable internal accounting.

Finally, Pakistan boasts experienced, skilled managers in the SOEs and well-educated, competent economists in the EAC. In the 1980s, managerial compensation in Pakistani SOEs was competitive with the private sector and the rate of turnover of skilled staff had been reduced considerably. The necessary skills were also available in the three countries contemplating installing the system. But other, less developed countries will need to budget more for training and technical assistance. A notable feature of the Pakistani system was that the EAC staff were not part of the civil service and their salaries were paid by a levy on the SOEs. This was important in enabling the cell to attract the necessary skills and might usefully be replicated in other countries.

Potential Benefits

The most important potential benefits from the system are improvement in the operating efficiency of state-owned enterprises and improvement in the sector's general contribution to the economy. How realizable are these benefits? Not surprisingly, this study has not been able to provide a definitive answer to that important question. Judging from the short experience in Pakistan, an improvement in operating efficiency may result, especially if the performance evaluation system is combined with other reforms.

By 1988, the Pakistani system had not led to the sort of policy reforms that would promote efficiency, for example, pricing changes, liquidations, deregulation, and so on. Thus, this case does not allow us to conclude that the signaling system can contribute to broad policy reforms. Nevertheless, the system developed all the necessary information and analytical tools for such use, and there were indications that it was beginning to be put to this use in Pakistan. In the long run, this may well prove to be its most valuable contribution.

Prospects for Realizing the Potential Benefits

Pakistan's experience offers some guidance on ways to improve the likelihood that the system's potential benefits will be realized. Among the factors that influence the prospects for efficiency gains are the potential role of competitive forces, the supervisory structure for SOEs and the degree of managerial autonomy, and the role of the labor force.

THE ROLE OF COMPETITIVE FORCES. Ample evidence shows that competition is an important force in promoting efficiency in any enterprise, public or private. Competition may not exist in a developing country for many reasons; absence of competition is often a reason for creating public enterprises. But in Pakistan there were instances where the opportunities for competition had not yet been fully explored, for example, among public fertilizer or cement plants or through further trade liberalization.

The signaling system is in a sense, a market proxy; it creates pressures for efficiency that in other circumstances the market might supply. Of course markets can have many failings, but bureaucracies may do even worse. For this reason, governments will want to consider using competitive pressures to promote efficiency wherever possible through trade liberalization, removal of barriers to private entry, and discrimination between public and private enterprise. In particular, import liberalization is an important way to increase competition in large-scale industries where public enterprises tend to dominate the domestic market. This will greatly simplify the task of evaluating SOEs in competitive markets, since they can be held to a simple profit target at current prices. The performance evaluation agencies could then focus more of their energies on controlling natural monopolies such as utilities and railways.[5] The latter are usually the most important in terms of the government budget and linkages with the rest of the economy; certainly in Pakistan, inefficiencies in the power authority could have had far more damaging effects on economic growth than any industrial SOE.

---

5. Of course competition will still be imperfect and a case could be made for using constant prices even for fully competitive enterprises. For example, should a manager of an oil company have been rewarded for windfall profits in the early 1980s? But in terms of priorities, adjusting the prices of noncompetitive firms is more important.

One likely consequence of freeing market forces is that some SOEs will not be able to compete. In some cases, this may be corrected by changing management and giving managers the authority to cut costs and seek new markets or by restructuring the company's finances and operations. But in other cases the company may be the wrong size or producing the wrong product for present markets. In such cases, liquidation may be the best economic option. Liquidation would also greatly simplify the government's task of monitoring and evaluation.

SUPERVISION OF THE SECTOR AND MANAGERIAL AUTONOMY. If governments choose to focus the system more on SOEs in noncompetitive markets, then a central performance evaluation system might make sense. For one thing, noncompetitive SOEs are found along with competitive ones under the same ministries. For another, many governments lack the skills or funds to create evaluation units in every oversight ministry. Furthermore, Pakistan's Ministry of Production is not a typical ministry. Its role is to supervise the SOEs under it; a separate Ministry of Industry is responsible for formulating industrial policy. In most countries a typical sector ministry combines these roles and often does an inadequate job of supervision, since sector ministries tend to see themselves more as advocates of SOEs than as their evaluators. Finally, having a central evaluation unit would help resolve some of the problems the EAC has in assuming a wider role when that role brings it into issues that are the domain of other ministries. Thus a central unit might be better placed to influence the ministry of finance to grant competitive SOEs greater autonomy. A central unit could also have a broader view of trends in the SOE.

A central unit would not necessarily manage the evaluation system alone; it could draw on the sector ministries' expertise to do the evaluation. In some large countries it might be appropriate for the central unit to delegate most of the operation of the system to the sector ministries or to holding companies (if they exist), and to focus on aggregating information, doing comparisons, maintaining the system, assuring the quality of the evaluations and conducting periodic checks, designing improvements, and doing macroanalyses. Smaller, resource-scarce countries are unlikely to have sufficient qualified personnel to staff more than one or two supervisory units.

An important feature of the Pakistani system was that the performance evaluation system was not introduced in isolation. The "hardening" of the managerial environment was an important influence on the efficiency gains. This implies that the system should be combined with a sharp cutback in access to funds for investment (at least at the outset), reductions in subsidies and easy access to credit, decentralization of authority for personnel decisions and other cost-cutting measures, and most important, a demonstrated readiness to fire managers who do not perform. Strong commitment on the part of top decisionmakers was an important part of both the Pakistani and Korean reforms and is a prerequisite for getting the system off the ground.

The Pakistani experience also shows that the system's impact will be constrained by the managers' degrees of freedom. Autonomy will need to increase in parallel with accountability for the exercise to be meaningful. Thus, in Pakistan, the system's benefits would have been increased if SOE managers could have been given greater flexibility to cut costs by laying off workers, closing uneconomic lines, and seeking lowest-cost suppliers. Managers could also have used greater autonomy in compensation decisions and greater government support for exercising wage restraint to keep costs down. Likewise, procurement could have been streamlined to increase flexibility. Experience elsewhere has shown that a vigorous *ex post* evaluation and auditing system is more efficient in controlling abuses than *ex ante* controls over procurement. The administration of credit was another constraint on public and private efficiency. As Pakistan removes distortions and increases the pressures for business efficiency, a more competitive and flexible multibanking system will become more necessary.

Governments will also want to take a hard look at the social welfare objectives imposed on SOEs. Experience has shown that SOEs are often a costly and ineffective tool for achieving such goals. Furthermore, evaluating the costs, much less the success or failure, of such welfare programs is impossible when they are buried in an enterprise's accounts instead of funded through the government's budget.

ROLE OF THE LABOR FORCE. A critical factor in the operation of the system in Pakistan was SOEs' inability to lay off workers or effectively keep wage increases in line with productivity improvements. The cost to the economy is not just the cost of inflated wages or redundant workers; the wage bill in such capital intensive activities tends to be a relatively small part of their costs. More important is the cost of keeping inefficient public enterprises or unproductive product lines working to provide employment, and the demoralization that brings down productivity in an overstaffed enterprise. Programs to raise public and worker understanding of the need for reform, including in some cases plant closures and layoffs, combined with redeployment and severance pay arrangements, will make implementing a meaningful performance evaluation system easier.

Adapting the System to Other Circumstances

The Pakistani experience suggests that other countries might want to adapt the signaling system in a few areas before applying it in their own environments.

CHOICE OF CRITERION. Other countries may wish to adjust private profits along the lines of the original proposal in Pakistan. This would entail excluding depreciation to eliminate the system's bias in favor of older companies and the possibility that a manager might be rewarded for purely accounting changes. Nonoperating income should be excluded to avoid rewarding managers for windfall gains that have no relation to operating efficiency. The use of pretax profits avoids motivating managers to reduce taxes, evade taxes, or lobby for changes in tax legislation. Excluding interest charges ensures that the system does not judge managers on a cost they could not control; including the cost of working capital judges them on one they can control. Moreover, noneconomists, including SOE management, should easily grasp these redefinitions of profit, following fairly straightforward accounting practices.

One could argue that using a different profit concept for SOEs (public profits) might make comparing the performance of SOEs with private firms harder, and hence impede rather than enhance competitive pressures for improvement. Yet, rather than hindering comparison, these sorts of adjustments are often essential to allow realistic public/private comparisons. Thus, excluding taxes from the analysis would take into account the fact that SOEs are often exempt from many taxes, while they cannot evade them as easily as private firms when they do pay taxes. Similarly, excluding interest charges from the analysis would correct for the possibility that SOEs have access to subsidized capital or pay lower rates of interest because of government guarantees. Depreciation charges would also need to be excluded from the analysis to adjust for differences in SOEs' ages. Finally, nonoperating income is subject to windfall gains that have more to do with an SOE's privileged position rather than its operational efficiency.

In Pakistan's case, the EAC argued with some justification that the introduction of a new indicator could confuse management. However, the EAC had introduced and fairly frequently changed the partial indicators used in addition to profits. The benefits of changing to public profits may well have exceeded the cost of some initial confusion. Using unadjusted profits distorted the results and allowed inefficient firms to earn passing grades.

The EAC made a concerted effort to make up for the deficiencies of standard profitability by making adjustments in the course of its evaluation. However, managers protested against these "arbitrary" corrections and frequently succeeded in forcing the EAC to award them their grade on the basis of the original, unadjusted indicators. A more realistic indicator would have avoided this problem and given a clearer signal to management.

Furthermore, partial indicators of physical efficiency could have unintended and perhaps even perverse effects. Using these indicators in combination with profitability double counted certain items and not others. In some cases, this may have been intentional (for example, to count energy costs twice as a way to reinforce the need for conservation). But in other cases the results seemed contrary to the intention, for example, using both the volume of production and profitability as performance criteria counted outputs twice and inputs only once, and thus deemphasized cost control. EAC was aware of this problem. When the cell was instructed at one point to give explicit targets for four costs (raw materials, energy, labor, and financial expenses), it chose rightly not to give these an additional weight, but to make them constraints on the profit target. This, however, raised a related problem. Each additional indicator reduced management's degrees of freedom; the virtue of profitability is that it leaves management free to judge how best to minimize costs and maximize benefits. Moreover, systems that instruct managers how to minimize costs require a good deal more information on the inner workings of the firm.

SIMPLER SYSTEMS. The signaling system's design was based on some basic and sensible principles (Jones 1985). One of these is that targets should be few, comprehensible, and weighted. The reason for this is that the targets are meant to signal to managers what government considers desirable behavior and to allow government to control enterprises on the basis of results, not their conformity to bureaucratic processes. The targets should therefore give a clear indication of government's objectives and priorities, but not second-guess management on how to reach those goals. For example, setting targets for profits and for working capital, inventory levels, and the like, tells managers not only what to achieve, but how to achieve it. It becomes impossible to then hold management responsible for success or failure.

A second principle of the system is to use indicators that count all costs and all benefits once and only once. This avoids double counting and asymmetric counting. Profit has the advantage of being a weighted indicator of benefits minus costs that meets these principles. But in countries where financial data are unreliable, where profits would have to be calculated in constant or shadow prices to be meaningful, and where skills are scarce, some simple engineering indicators coupled with cost per unit of output targets may be a useful starting point. These indicators tend to distort managerial behavior by focusing on only one aspect of performance (for example, by counting costs and not revenues you may encourage managers to forego expenditures with high returns), but the Pakistani case provides some evidence that efficiency could be improved with a far simpler system. If, as hypothesized, SOE managers responded to an imperfect target (private profits) with efficiency gains because they had (or thought they had) no other way to achieve the bonus, then other imperfect indicators (such as cost per unit of output) might have the same effect, at least in the initial years.

Another way to simplify the system and still give correct signals to managers is to use shadow prices for only a few critical items, such as electricity, wages, or foreign exchange. This would simplify the calculations and make it easier to pinpoint and estimate the costs of price distortions and to identify enterprises that are not viable from an economic standpoint. It would also give managers greater incentive to react to fluctuations in world market prices.

Finally, the system could focus on fewer public enterprises. The largest enterprises causing the biggest fiscal drain or with the most linkages with the rest of the economy would be the logical place to begin. In most countries no more than 10 to 15 enterprises need be covered. However, Pakistan's experience shows restricting the system to a few SOEs may prove hard, especially if bonuses are given.

THE INCENTIVE SYSTEM. Other countries should consider rewarding the managers of firms that reduce losses by improving efficiency. The government could treat the bonus payments as a *quid pro quo* for any burdens it imposed on the SOEs, and the cost of bonus payments should be offset by the increment in operating efficiency. Experts have estimated that if Pakistan's SOEs achieved on average a 5 percent improvement in their productivity, only about 3 percent of the increase in profits would be needed to pay all nonunionized staff a one-month bonus. In 1988, the Ministry of Production was even considering ways to award bonuses to loss-making firms.

Furthermore, if possible bonuses should not be allocated uniformly across all employees in an SOE. Other countries may wish to give more emphasis to the public recognition of top performers than did Pakistan. Depending on the cultural context, the public announcement of grades and the award of medals or other nonmaterial honors may be more important to top management than the bonus. Discussions of the achievement of the targets in meetings with permanent secretaries, ministers, and (as in Korea) the head of state have proven very effective in motivating managers.

THE INFORMATION SYSTEM. Besides performance evaluation, a government needs information on its SOEs to develop informed macroeconomic policies. If the system is centralized and its scope is broad, then using it to frame macro policies would be easy. The Pakistani system provided information on SOE production, value added and investment in current and constant prices; it generated all standard financial ratios and debt information; it gave data on production and sales volumes, number of employees, energy consumption, labor productivity, and the like; and it provided detailed price indices for items of public production and consumption. Since all of this information was computerized and standardized, it could be easily aggregated to provide trends for macroeconomic planning and decisionmaking.

References

Jones, Leroy. 1985. *Performance Evaluation for Public Enterprises.* Boston, Massachusetts. Processed.

Jones, Leroy, and Istaqbal Mehdi. 1985a. *Pakistan Signaling Project.* Draft.

Shirley, Mary. 1989. *Evaluating the Performance of Public Enterprises in Pakistan.* PPR Staff Working Paper 160. Washington, D.C.: World Bank.

11

CONTRACT PLANS: A REVIEW OF INTERNATIONAL EXPERIENCE

John Nellis

Worldwide, many governments are attempting to improve their ability to control and guide state-owned enterprises. Among the various reform efforts is the contract plan (CP) approach. This chapter reviews the experience in the use of contract plans in France, Senegal, Morocco, and a few other developing countries. The contract plan approach emerges as an innovation that holds promise, but is beset by a number of practical problems. Developing countries considering using this mechanism can learn much from countries that have preceded them along the same path.

The Issue

Contract plans are negotiated agreements between governments, acting as owners of a state-owned enterprise, and the enterprise itself.[1] The essential idea of a contract plan is that it spells out the rights and duties of both parties. The concept was devised to attack the problems of vague or shifting objectives, insufficient autonomy of managers, and excessively constraining control systems; problems perceived as major hindrances to SOE efficiency and productivity.

---

1. Terminology varies from country to country or from period to period within the same country. These agreements are also known as enterprise contracts, program contracts, performance agreements, or action plans. The underlying principle—mutual specification of rights and responsibilities by government and state-owned enterprise—is the same in all cases.

Based on negotiations between government representatives and enterprise managers, a contract plan sets out the intentions, obligations, and responsibilities of the two parties. Its period of activity extends beyond the budgeting cycle, covering three to five years. A typical CP specifies enterprise objectives in terms of the desired overall socioeconomic impact, production goals, and/or quantities and quality of service to be provided. It defines policies and parameters with regard to such items as numbers employed, size and growth of the enterprise's wage bill, and social or noncommercial activities. Many CPs stipulate the physical and financial indicators that will measure enterprise performance. What distinguishes the CP from a set of directives imposed by a firm's owners or from a corporate plan produced by the firm on its own, is that it also spells out the government's obligations and limitations. Many CPs establish the principle that the government will compensate the enterprise for costs incurred in fulfilling noncommercial objectives, and specify the means and mechanisms by which the compensation will be made. A typical CP lays out the enterprise's financing and investment program, noting the amount the enterprise must generate internally, the amount to come from government subsidy or equity injections, and the amount to be raised by credit, with or without a government guarantee.

Historically, CPs first came to prominence and fruition in France in the late 1960s and early 1970s. From 1970 to 1988, eight of that country's largest and most important state-owned enterprises were submitted to varying forms of what the French call "the contractualization process." The test cases, in the energy, transport, and utility subsectors, were all monopolies or oligopolies with heavy social service responsibilities. In 1983, following a socialist electoral victory, the government concluded 13 more CPs with industrial public enterprises, a few of which had long been in the public sector, but most of which the Mitterand government had nationalized in 1981-82. French experts judged the results of both these experiences as moderately positive, though the criteria used to make this assessment have been more institutional/managerial and qualitative rather than economic and quantitative in nature. Finally, French analysts are at pains to point out the difficulties of determining the exact relation between shifts in enterprises' economic and financial results and the presence or absence of a contract plan.

Given the mechanism's provenance, it is not surprising that the developing countries that attempted to borrow or adopt the CP were mostly francophone. The first recorded attempt to export the process was in 1973, when negotiations produced a CP for a Tunisian public textile firm. For unknown reasons, the agreement was never signed or implemented. However, starting in Senegal in 1980, and spreading through most of francophone Africa up to 1988, CPs were adopted or being prepared in roughly 75 state-owned enterprises in ten different francophone Sub-Saharan countries. The process was advanced in Morocco, where six CPs were being installed in 1988 in several of the most important SOEs. The device was again being applied in Tunisia. In many of these instances, World Bank structural adjustment or public enterprise reform programs supported, and increasingly required, the installation of CPs.

Variations on the CP theme were also in preparation or in place in four anglophone African countries: The Gambia, Ghana, Kenya, and Sudan. Outside the African continent, the need to improve the performance of state-owned enterprises combined with the hope that the CP or something like it would effect desperately needed improvements where so many other procedures and reforms had failed. This led to the adoption or consideration of a CP process in Argentina ("program agreements" in negotiation and preparation in the transport sector), in Mexico, Bangladesh, and India ("memoranda of understanding" in major enterprises in the energy, industrial, and engineering sectors), and inquiries into the prospect of using the CP in a number of other countries. Worldwide, as of the end of 1988, over 100 contract plans were in operation or advanced preparation, and 100 or more were under active consideration.

The purpose of this chapter is to examine what CPs were designed to achieve, how they were constructed, where they have been applied, with what results—economic, financial, and institutional—and what lessons have been learned. The concern is the utility of the device as a way to improve performance in developing country SOEs. Most of the available information on that subject comes from Sub-Saharan Africa, much of it from Senegal, the country most experienced in CP use. The study thus examines in detail the Senegalese experience, and reviews more briefly the CP process in other African countries, Morocco, and India. However, the seminal nature of the French experience necessitates that we first review the CP process in that country.

The French Experience

Before 1981, French SOEs employed 12 percent of salaried workers outside agriculture, contributed 13 percent of value added, and accounted for 30 percent of gross fixed capital formation. All three ratios rose substantially after the nationalizations of 1981-82; all three declined, perhaps to less than 1981 values, following the 1986-87 privatization of 30 SOEs. Nonetheless, in 1988, the French SOE sector accounted for a higher percentage of GDP than in most industrialized countries.

The French state-owned enterprise sector came into existence following World War I, and underwent surges of expansion in 1936 (the period of the Popular Front), 1945-46 (the reaction to World War II), and 1981-82 (the nationalizations following the election of the socialist government). No dramatic shift of policy occurred during 1947-67, yet the sector expanded steadily in that period as many state-owned enterprises created a large number of subsidiary or affiliated companies. In 1966, the Gaullist government, increasingly concerned with the poor financial performance, and particularly the large deficits, of the monopoly public service enterprises, commissioned a high-level panel to review the situation. The result was the Nora Report of 1967, which first suggested the concept of the contract plan, known at that juncture as the program contract (Nora Report, 1967).

The Nora Report

The Nora Report deplored the poor state of SOEs' accounts and budgeting systems; the enterprises' inability to finance their own investments; the ineffective, time consuming systems of government control and supervision; the lack of clarity of objectives; the government's failure to award enterprises sufficient or timely tariff increases; and the resulting general transfer of the costs of running these enterprises from the users of the goods or services to taxpayers at large.

The dual prescription for reform the report offered was to clarify objectives and set commercial profitability as a fundamental aim. Principal subobjectives were to increase management's autonomy and improve state/enterprise supervisory arrangements. The state was no longer to supervise by means of direct "commands, by *a priori* authorization, or by taking day-to-day decisions best left to managers, but rather by the clear setting of criteria and of the rules of the game." The report recommended that the costs imposed by social service obligations be determined, and compensation mechanisms created. The report distinguished between SOEs operating in competitive markets and monopolies; the former were to be lightly supervised, while the latter were subject to stricter controls. Only the latter were to be subjected to the CP process. However, the report argued that all enterprises, including monopolies, could benefit from increased autonomy.

The report devised the concept of *engagements réciproques* (mutual commitments or obligations), which lies at the heart of the CP process. The report suggested that through negotiations the two parties would reach a binding agreement stating what the enterprise would accomplish and what the state would do—and not do—to guide, support, and evaluate the accomplishments. Contracts were to be used to set appropriate levels of enterprise inputs and outputs, the amounts of capital subventions, borrowing limits, tariff parameters, and wage bills and determine the margin of latitude of enterprise managers and directors.

The reasoning was that if goals were clearly set, government could lighten its *a priori* controls. The social costs of the operation would become more transparent, and this would make evaluating the firm easier. The expectation was that as public awareness about the enterprise's real costs grew, then pressure to reduce these costs would also grow. A higher percentage of the operating costs might then be shifted to users. This, in turn, would create pressure to increase competition between public and private enterprises. The report thus envisaged the evolution of a drastically changed public sector "mentality," where costs—especially personnel costs—would be reduced, technology would be modernized, and management methods would change. The contract process was to serve a key role in bringing about this set of improvements.

Implementation: First Phase

Preparatory negotiations for CPs started in 1969. The first two CPs were signed in 1969-71 with the national electricity company (Electricité de France or EDF) and the national railway (the Société Nationale des Chemins de Fer or SNCF). Each was supposed to remain in force for five years. The 1970 contract plan for EDF was considered as the model CP. It spelled out a system of lighter, more flexible government supervision that reduced the powers of the government's permanent representatives within the firm and the ministries of Finance and Energy. The CP supported expansion by EDF into nuclear power generation. An early draft called for large rate increases that would allow EDF to cover the heavy investment costs and still turn a profit. Analysts note that it was the Ministry of Finance that insisted that the final agreement hold price increases to less than increases in the consumer price index. Nonetheless, from 1970 to 1973, the selling price of electricity was sufficient to cover the variable costs of EDF's production and to meet two-thirds of the cost of new investments.

The oil shock of 1973 led to vastly increased costs of major inputs, economywide inflation, and a snap political decision to increase sharply the capacity to generate electricity by nuclear reactors, which in turn meant a spate of loans and subsidies to EDF not called for in the CP. In the altered circumstances, it became apparent that many of the elaborately prepared numbers and ratios in the CP were suddenly dated and irrelevant.

In the first SNCF CP, signed in 1971, the goals were to reduce the railway system's deficit by cutting staff by 15 percent, and by giving the enterprise considerable latitude on rate setting. The full achievement of all the CP's objectives would have substantially diminished the rate of loss, but would not have turned the SNCF into a profitable company, but SNCF did not attain even the modest financial goals set in the first CP. Again this was partly due to unanticipated increases in the costs of major inputs. An important second factor was a lack of political willingness to tolerate the service and staff reductions and price hikes necessary to cover costs. Finally, the railway's inability to compete with truckers in transporting goods reduced the demand for rail service below projected levels.[2] The SNCF CP was nonetheless extended for two years, running through to 1977. The rail system's financial difficulties were not resolved as the government repeatedly cited regional development policies or possible social tensions as reasons for failing to increase prices or reduce costs, even though these had been accepted in the CP.

---

2. This section on the French experience utilizes the following sources: Durupty (1986); de Chalander (1984a); Anastassopoulos and Nioche (1982, especially chapter 1).

Despite the bleak picture with regard to financial results, assessments of the first CP experience were positive. Enterprise managers and government supervisors alike agreed that the CP negotiating process did lead to clarified objectives and increased understanding of the constraints operating on both sides. Budgetary aid to EDF and SNCF declined by 20 percent during 1969-72, though it then shot up to historically high levels following the first oil shock. This was important, for the budgetary burden issue was the one that most interested the French government (and was the key issue for most developing country governments using the process in the 1980s).

Transparency was somewhat increased, and government controllers recognized that "management autonomy did not inevitably mean waste" (Durupty 1986, p. 368). These were substantial achievements. Still, much of the optimism, with regard to forward budgeting and financial projections had faded in the light of the unforeseen changes in the world economy starting in 1973. Some observers outside the government thus called the process into question on the basis that any CP was only as good as one's ability to predict the economic future accurately. Clearly that ability was poorly developed. Others felt that the first experience, especially in the SNCF case, showed that the government's power inevitably overwhelmed the enterprise; when a dispute or crisis arose, the government's position prevailed. This led some to believe that the concept was misnamed and perhaps unworkable. None of the observers discussed the time or resources devoted to the preparation of the CPs, which must have been considerable. Note that neither of the two first-phase CPs was immediately renewed, though the SNCF CP was first prolonged and subjected to a second phase of negotiations.

Implementation: Second Phase

The period 1973 to 1977 was one of acute economic crisis and uncertainty during which the CP process was not expanded; but as a modicum of stability returned the French government again turned its attention to contracts. Two follow-up committees to the Nora body were formed. They issued reports that modified the CP process in light of lessons learned. The first change was to scale down the timeframe of CPs from 60 to 36 months, with greater provision for annual revision as and when circumstances altered. The second change was to tighten the CPs' focus, and they were henceforth to be based on three principles: (a) transparency of social transfers, that is, letting the public know who is paying for what; (b) transparency of results of SOEs, by publishing and publicizing performance statistics; and (c) transparency of investments, which henceforth had to be justified in cost-benefit terms. Heightened emphasis was placed on costing out and compensating for socially imposed operations. To emphasize the shift in focus, these agreements were called "enterprise contracts."

Four of the new style CPs were negotiated and signed during 1977-79. The companies involved were the national coal company, Air France, the General Maritime Corporation, and the only repeater from phase one, the SNCF.

The coal company, Charbonnages de France, was given a freer hand in pricing. This was combined with a strong demand for coal as oil prices stayed high. These factors led to the company breaking even in 1980, after adding in the government subsidy; a significant advance because the accounts had not previously been in balance even with the subsidy. Company managers hoped that the CP would "put an end to the arbitrary regime" under which they had labored. However, with the election of the socialists in 1981, the company's top management was changed. The new managers simply ignored the conditions of the CP negotiated by the previous regime, and the new government reversed previous decisions to close several old, unproductive, costly mines. In the last year of the CP, government subsidies to the coal company grew rapidly.

The second CP negotiated with the SNCF gave limited price setting power to the enterprise's management. The major innovation of this particular document was its use of quantified indicators of physical and financial performance for evaluating results and rewarding management. This feature was widely adopted in subsequent CPs in France and elsewhere. But management's latitude in price setting was marginal, and in a very important cost area, that of personnel, management was powerless.[3] In the first two years of the CP, several uneconomic passenger lines were closed, which improved the financial picture.

---

3. French CPs did not normally tackle numbers or pay rates of personnel head on. Except in the case discussed in the following paragraph, national conventions handled these matters. The failure to deal directly with personnel issues was a deficiency of the program.

However, here as well, the socialists' victory led to a government order to freeze fares and to reopen most of the closed lines. Subsidies grew and the financial situation worsened.

The shipping company CP was more of a restructuring plan than a contract. It was a statement of directives, along with a warning of what would happen if performance did not improve. In 1979, the government viewed the company as having too many advantages and workers, and the CP's goal was to suppress the former and, in a rare move, reduce the number of workers. A capital subsidy was specified and the compensation policy for the money-losing Corsican service was established. The main components of the CP were the directives to reduce the workforce by 25 percent and the number of ships from 98 to 36. The CP stipulated that if the enterprise did not meet these goals in three years, the government could sell or liquidate the firm. Yet again, the 1981 election changed government policy; the CP was abandoned and the company was allowed to survive without reducing its workforce.

The CP process in Air France was a much more positive experience. This was the first CP in an enterprise operating in a competitive market. Largely because of this factor, the negotiated CP gave the airline a greater degree of managerial autonomy than was accorded other firms. Since commercial profitability was a fairly accurate measure of Air France's performance, the CP's goals could be specified with greater precision. The deviations from commercial operation were also easily demarcated, such as the need to use inefficient Caravelles and the Concorde, the splitting of Parisian service between Orly and Charles de Gaulle airports, and the continued operation of certain uneconomic flights. The compensation for these noncommercial activities imposed on Air France could be and were calculated precisely.

The targets set in the Air France CP for growth in operations, financial objectives, and key physical indicators, such as the number of flight hours per year by aircraft type, were met or exceeded in 1978 and 1979, and were just short in 1980. The firm turned a profit in 1980, making it one of the very few European airlines to present positive financial results in that difficult year. It is not clear from available documents how the government's "capital endowment" to Air France figured in the calculation of profitability. Nor can one gauge the role of factors outside management's control, such as the reduction in the price of fuel.

Nonetheless, what is clear is that Air France met or exceeded financial targets set in the CP in each of the three years covered in the period. This was enough to term the process a success. Air France's CP was renewed every three years thereafter.

Third Phase: 1981-88

After 1981, CPs of a more or less traditional type continued to be installed in several of the monopoly or oligopoly public enterprises with heavy social service obligations: Gaz de France, EDF, Air France, and for the third time, following lengthy and difficult negotiations, the SNCF. But in the first half of 1983, the socialist government also installed what it insisted was a quite different type of CP in 13 industrial and manufacturing public enterprises, several of which had been nationalized in 1981-82.[4] To show that the new contracts in the industries differed from past activities in the utilities, the agreements were finally given the name by which they have since come to be known, contract plans. In these CPs, enterprises were to be given only guidance and policy orientation of a long-term, strategic nature; operational tactics were, in principle, left to managers and boards (but similar promises had been made concerning the earlier processes). The documents drafted placed much less emphasis on productivity and financial targets and stressed instead the creation of new product lines, research and development, and market share. They also tried to harmonize the efforts of these state enterprises, working in competitive markets, with the national goals of technological modernization and enhanced international competitiveness of French industry.

The government negotiated CPs with parent corporations and subsidiaries and did not deal with affiliates directly. The CPs were designed to be all-encompassing, that is, to replace all other forms and procedures of control. They were also supposed to be supervised by a single agency, the appropriate ministry of technical supervision. In addition, for the first time, workers' representatives were involved in the CP negotiations.

---

4. The 13 were CGE, Thomson, Bull, Renault, Usinor-Sacilor, CDF Chimie, EMC, St. Gobain, Pechiney, Aérospatiale, SNECMA, Matra, and SNPE. The last two firms produced armaments and were under the control of the Ministry of Defense. The first 11 were supervised by the Ministry of Industry and Research.

For several reasons, the impact of this last group of CPs is particularly difficult to judge. First, the details of these CPs were, at the enterprises' insistence, kept confidential. Thus, one cannot systematically compare post-CP performance to the projections in the agreement. Second, even if the CPs had been available, they would have been of limited value as mechanisms to evaluate performance because they concentrated on long-term objectives, not quantified short-term targets. As before, after the CPs had been finalized the circumstances changed: first, a center-right government gained power in parliament, and second, in 1988, Mitterand was reelected and a socialist cabinet was reinstated.

Following the first socialist victory, the wave of nationalizations, and the drafting of the new CPs, the government took general stock of the state-owned enterprise situation in the utility sector. The conclusions of its review were disquieting. Although the CP process had been brought into being to combat SOEs' poor financial performance, especially their persistent tendency to drain budgetary resources, net transfers from the government to state-owned enterprises had increased from F12.8 billion in 1975 to F49.5 billion in 1982. These increases took place despite, not because of, the CPs. Some argued that unforeseen shifts in economic and political circumstances had brought about the higher level of funding, but this excuse only seemed to illustrate the marginal nature of the CP. The implication was that CPs could do little to predict, much less offset, market conditions. This raised the question of whether the CP process was worth the administrative and supervisory investment made by the French.

It was to combat the problem of uncertainty that the second- and third-phase CPs had been reduced in length from 60 to 36, or at most 48, months. Further, the socialist government, in line with the philosophy shown by its industrial sector CPs, had altered the objectives of the process. In essence, the government increased the social as opposed to the technical content. The modified objectives of the CP process became:

- to assure coordination between the enterprise's medium-term objectives and the state's policy;
- to associate the enterprise in the "realization of objectives of national interest;"
- to mobilize the personnel of the enterprise to support the defined objectives;

- to allow autonomy of management;
- to define and specify the financial relationship between the enterprise and the state.

These goals were more general and less technical in nature, than those put forward by the ambitious Nora Report. As such, they were less likely to be called into question by shifts in economic conditions (the lists of objectives above and lessons below are found in Chalander 1984a).

The goals were redefined in light of the four major lessons that emerged from previous experience.

1. *Keep contract plans short and simple.* Initial attempts were too ambitious, long, and complicated. They attempted to specify too minutely the economic future and the actions and reactions of the enterprise. The preferred CP became shorter, and concentrated on grand aims and principles.

2. *Keep CPs flexible.* Every CP should be treated as a "sliding" or rolling plan, with every aspect subject to renegotiation if the numerous assumptions about future conditions proved inaccurate. The last round of CPs had built-in provisions for review and modification on an annual basis, with even more frequent review if necessary.

3. *The contracting process is more important than the plan's content.* The utility of the CP is less in its quantified performance indicators or goals and more in the formalized periodic exchange of views between government owners/supervisors and managers. It is the very process of being exposed to the other side's point of view while negotiating an agreement that is the contract plan's major accomplishment, even though the specific numbers produced in the exercise are sometimes misleading or incorrect. Thus, the contracting activity is seen as beneficial in and of itself.

4. *The weaker an enterprise's performance, the greater the difficulty of negotiating and implementing a contract plan.* Negotiations with the SNCF for its third CP took close to two years, and produced one of the thicker and more complicated documents (31 pages of

text, 44 articles, 7 annexes). Negotiations with the national steel company took place over several years starting in 1979, but never led to the signing of a CP. Both were cases of generally weak past performance, combined with particularly high levels of uncertainty about future demand. Apparently a modicum level of both economic stability and optimism concerning the firm's future is required before enterprise officials can envisage committing themselves to a concrete set of short-term goals and obligations.

Finally, the reviewers recognized a fundamental problem with CPs, a problem that proved even more intractable in the developing countries that attempted to use the device: CPs were not really contracts because the state could not be subjected to legal proceedings by the enterprise in the event that it failed to honor its obligations. Thus, fare increases tended to be reduced or postponed, several uneconomic factories or lines slated for closure were kept open, and the workforce in various firms was maintained at excessively high levels. The CP was only as good as the degree of government commitment to it.

French analysts have tended to judge the utility of the CP process on the basis of whether the set targets—physical, financial, and social—were met, and whether the actors involved in the process assessed the CP as being worthwhile. These are important issues, but they do not adequately address two fundamental questions: what was the comparative performance of state-owned enterprises before and after the introduction of CPs, and what was the comparative performance of enterprises with and without the CP? On both of these critical counts, information is, at best, sketchy.

With regard to the first question, we noted that the financial performance of a number of the French public enterprises subject to CPs registered improvement. However, in all but Air France, the improvement was short-lived, either because of macroeconomic shocks or government failure to take or sustain cost-cutting or revenue enhancing measures, or both. Thus, the CP seems to have been capable of influencing, but not determining, enterprise performance.

As for the comparison of SOEs with and without CPs, the analysis is even more problematic. Consider the case of Air France, which presents one of the easier cases for analysis because its goals were largely commercial in nature and it operated in competitive markets. Air France consistently produced positive financial results in line with the goals set in its CPs. (An economic assessment would be much more difficult.) However, the decline in energy prices had nothing to do with the airline's management. Yet, other airlines also benefited from falling oil prices, and most failed to translate this gain into a demonstrably improved financial position. In brief, Air France did fairly well when most European airlines, operating in roughly the same economic environment, did not. During the period of good performance Air France was operating with a CP when the other airlines were not. The CP was thus associated with comparatively good performance, but to what extent did it cause that performance? Available data do not allow one to say. About all that French observers could do was examine whether physical and financial targets were met, and assess subjectively whether participants approved of the CP process.

Conclusions on the French Experience

The conservative government in power in France from 1986 to 1988 concentrated its energies on privatizing state-owned enterprises; reform of SOEs retained in state hands and concerns about the CP process slipped to secondary importance (see Balladur 1987, minister of finance at the time). However, all 30 of the privatized firms were in competitive sectors. Unlike Great Britain, the French did not divest natural monopolies in the utility sector. This suggests that CPs, in some shape or form will continue to be used in the future, a possibility increased by the socialists' success in the 1988 elections.

The French have invested a fair amount of administrative and intellectual resources in the CP process. In most instances, performance did not improve dramatically, but whether this was because of or despite CPs was not clear. At no point in the process did the French attempt to link management or worker incentives with fulfillment of a CP's objectives. In France, this issue appeared to have been generally ignored. Still, managers and government supervisors alike supported CPs because they enhanced the clarity of goals, the transparency of operations and achievements, and the ease of evaluation. These were advances, but partly because the costs of creating the CP were not calculated, one cannot tell if the benefits justified the costs.

The Senegalese Experience

The first concerted effort to replicate the CP process in a developing country took place in 1980-82 in Senegal.

Ambiguous or contradictory goals, political interference, and rigid and excessive bureaucratic controls plague SOEs in both rich and poor countries, however, some of these problems are particularly intense in developing countries. For example, rarely would one find a European public enterprise completely failing to produce accounts, being incapable of submitting accounts to auditors for several years running, having no internal financial control systems, or not receiving payments for its goods or services from the government itself to the tune of millions of dollars of arrears. Yet these difficulties are common in poor countries. It was to attack grave deficiencies of this nature that in 1976, the World Bank and the Government of Senegal launched an effort that led to a technical assistance project to the Senegalese SOE sector. It was the first of its kind in Africa, and in the Bank.

A 1977 Bank review of the Senegalese SOE sector had stated:

> Supervision needs to be carried out on a contractual basis for enterprises to be able to manage themselves. Management by objectives could thus meaningfully be introduced under which each enterprise would negotiate with government annually the targets to be set for it and would then be judged according to the results it achieved.

This idea was not pursued in the early stages of the ensuing project, which became effective in 1978. It was not until 1980, and partly in response to the project-assisted improvement in the flow and accuracy of information on the poor performance of state-owned enterprises, that the government decided to adopt CPs, create a CP "cell" in the Prime Minister's Office, and ask the Bank for assistance with this aspect of SOE reform. The objectives were the same as those that had inspired the French CP process.

Between March 1981 and May 1988, contract plans were signed in nine different state-owned enterprises. Since three of the nine were in their second CP in 1988, a total of 12 sets of negotiations had been concluded. The first three Senegalese CPs were prepared between March 1981 and January 1982 in SOTRAC (transport), SAED (agriculture), and

SODEFITEX (rural/regional development). In 1984, the government decided to renew the process in these three SOEs, and to apply CPs to other major enterprises in telecommunications, water, electricity, agriculture, and rural development. In 1988, CPs were negotiated with SOEs in housing, post and savings, railway, and ports. Thus, in 1988, in terms of the number and types of SOEs affected, Senegal had the largest CP program in the world.

The 1977 diagnosis of the SOE sector had revealed fundamental problems in a number of important enterprises. In some cases, including SOTRAC and SAED, the government thought that the main improvement and restructuring method should be the installation of a CP. In other cases, most notably that of the telecommunications/post office (the OPT), the government decided that the problems were so severe that reorganization should precede the application of the CP. In the case of the OPT, the result was to split the firm into two enterprises, both of which (SONATEL and OPCE) were then subjected to the CP process. This raised a question that as of the end of 1988 had not yet been resolved: should CPs be used on the most severely troubled enterprises, or should their use be reserved for healthy or mildly troubled companies? Developing countries tend to use CPs as rescue devices for poorly performing firms, with questionable results. The Air France experience indicates that their utility as improvement devices in basically sound, quasi-competitive firms has been insufficiently examined.

The first set of Senegalese CPs closely followed the French model. In line with the lessons learned in France in the 1970s, they were fixed for three-year periods. Good examples of the first group of CPs that illustrate the range of bodies to which the process was applied and of subsequent implementation and modification problems were the cases of SOTRAC (the Dakar region bus company) and SAED (the Senegal River and Delta Development Authority). Note that of the first three, only the SOTRAC CP was carried through to conclusion. The SAED agreement came close to conclusion since it was signed, but it was never fully implemented. The third CP, in SODEFITEX, was dependent on resources to be made available through the first structural adjustment credit negotiated with the World Bank in 1981 to fund its investment program. Due to a dispute over agricultural prices, the expected funds did not materialize and the preparation of the SODEFITEX CP was delayed.

The First Phase

The SOTRAC CP was a short document of eight articles that set out the enterprise's purpose, the assets to be deployed during the period of the CP, its projected performance, the government's obligations, and the means to implement and modify the CP. SOTRAC's future position, the agreement stated, could only be secured by dealing with three critical issues: renewed investment in vehicles, payment to SOTRAC of the substantial arrears (CFAF1.1 billion) in government subsidies, and government permission to increase prices. The agreement specified SOTRAC's three-year investment program, and projected a stabilization of losses, as opposed to the substantially increased losses that might have been expected during a period of massive investment. Improvements were projected in the cash flow position.

The government's obligations were clearly spelled out. The government agreed to a precise timetable to pay off the arrears on previously promised subsidies, and to pay future subsidies according to a set schedule. SOTRAC was declared exempt from normal duties and taxes on the materials it imported. The government promised to do its utmost to persuade the communal government of Dakar to bear some of SOTRAC's subsidy, maintain the regional road network, and to help construct and maintain SOTRAC's terminals.

A technical innovation of the SOTRAC CP was the use of three different pricing hypotheses. During negotiations the government committed itself to allowing SOTRAC a price increase during the CP period, but government representatives were unable to specify the amount by which prices would be authorized to rise. The CP posited three different scenarios that traced out differing financial results according to the amount of tariff increase allowed.

The CP covered the main issues of enterprise purpose, prices, investment capital, financial results, and CP monitoring. It did not cover performance indicators other than net financial results. This was an inadequacy; commercial profitability is an imperfect indicator of the performance of a heavily subsidized public monopoly, especially one receiving indirect subsidies as well. This shortcoming was corrected in the second SOTRAC CP.

In contrast to SOTRAC, the statement of objectives with SAED (the Senegal River and Delta Development Authority) was a long document produced after complicated negotiations. Covering the period 1981-84, the agreement was more a restructuring device than a contract: its purpose was to resolve the fundamental operational difficulties of an extremely expensive and inefficient rural development agency. This was the first time that the contract process had ever been applied to an enterprise of this type (though whether the targets were negotiated, as they would and should be in a CP, or whether the goals were simply imposed by government directives is not clear).

The document laid out a variety of quantified production goals for SAED: number of undeveloped hectares to be turned into farmland, number of existing farms to be expanded, and production and marketing targets for paddy, tomatoes, and maize. The agreement dwelt on the reorganization of SAED. It emphasized the need for management information and budgetary control systems, rational personnel management, and improved accounting and expenditure control, the details of which were spelled out. Government obligations were stated more vaguely, for example, the CP noted that the state "would be required to provide (SAED) with adequate working capital." The document admitted that only half of the essential investment funds were available, and that the "government now has to find the remaining 50 percent, i.e., CFAF 5.435 billion." On the crucial matter of farmgate pricing, the agreement was less than legally precise: "Government will maintain producer prices at levels sufficiently remunerative not to interfere with debt servicing and sufficiently attractive to stimulate production."

The CP set out the schedule for the government's quarterly subsidy to the enterprise, necessitated by "the difference between the billing rate set by the Government and the actual cost of production and services rendered," and to cover those operations imposed on SAED "for which there is no billing provision." A second table presented the estimated payment dates for the clearing up of previously promised subsidies, then substantially in arrears. The document concluded with a statement that it was "binding on the two parties." It was signed by the director general of SAED, the chairman of SAED's board, and—for the government—the prime minister, the minister of finance, and the minister of rural development. The letter of understanding had been conceived, prepared, negotiated, and signed in seven months. (This appeared long at the time; subsequent CPs have generally taken much longer to prepare.) The overall result was a document of some 30 pages, not including annexes, but with most of the specificity on the side of the enterprise's goals, while the government's obligations remained vague.

Fundamental Problems

The initial experience with CPs was judged as only moderately positive. Management autonomy did not increase to the anticipated degree. The lack of physical performance indicators in the SOTRAC CP proved to be a problem, as did the shortfall in specificity of government obligations and undertakings in the SAED agreement. However, from the outset the two most important problems with the CP concept in Senegal were the government's inability to keep its financial promises, and the inability of the enterprises or their supervising ministries to force, pressure, or cajole the government into honoring those commitments. In SOTRAC and SAED, and later on in almost every enterprise submitted to the CP process, the government committed itself in the CP and then either failed to settle its arrears to the firm, honor an agreement to pay off subsidy sums promised in the past, meet timetables on current subsidy payments, inject promised amounts of equity, give final approval to previously agreed upon investments, or allow price or rate increases that would have improved the enterprises' self-financing capacity. In most cases, a combination of these defaults was present.

Neither the government's lack of resources nor its lack of financial discipline was caused by the CPs; rather, the CPs rendered transparent and quantified the government's shortcomings (and we can argue that these were necessary and progressive steps). The government itself recognized the problem. In a 1988 review of the reforms underway in the SOE sector the agency responsible for supervising SOEs in the Office of the President stated: "Nonrespect of the state's financial commitments remains the central problem with letters of mission and certain contract plans. The result is that the credibility of the CPs is weakened."

The problem's general aspects would have been familiar to the French, but in the Senegalese case the difficulty was of a greater magnitude and intensity in terms of the number of enterprises participating in the process, and the size of the gap between what government had said it would do, and what it actually did. Several factors contributed to this problem. First, the Senegalese planning tradition and experience led to the production of extensive, ambitious lists of desirable activities, without sufficient specificity on where the money to pay for them would come from (Guislain 1987). CPs proved to be but another example of this problem. A second factor was that the CPs were all produced, in first draft form at least, by consultants who attempted to maximize the interests of their main client, the SOE involved. Moreover, these drafts were produced in isolation one from the other; no drafter of one CP knew the budgetary implications of any other CP. Thus, the draft CPs tended to specify ideal financial conditions that would allow the firm to carry out what management and the drafting consultants saw as the enterprise's mandate. The question of what the state could afford was secondary, if taken into consideration at all.

The first level of review for the draft CPs was, theoretically, in the technical ministries. Officials and managers interviewed stated that the supervising ministries almost always approved whatever proposals were put forward by the consultants/enterprises without questioning or changing them. No sectoral consideration of what the government could afford took place at this level. Indeed, one could argue that expecting the technical ministries to restrain the growth or operations of "their" enterprises was unrealistic. This meant that responsibility for the aggregate financial impact of the CPs rested with the central agencies, the Delegation for the Reform of the Parapublic Sector in the Office of the President, and the Parapublic Sector Cell in the Ministry of Finance.

These bodies did not do their jobs; they tended to accept the draft CPs uncritically. At first, they often failed to appreciate the financial implications of the agreements. The resource implications surfaced later, and either delayed the signature or implementation of the CP, or only became apparent after signature, leading to problems discussed below. With experience, reviewers of CPs in the Ministry of Finance recognized that financial commitments called for in some CPs were unrealistic or excessive. They informed higher officials about their concerns, however, they were told that they had to approve and sign the CPs, even though they knew the promised resources were unlikely to become available. The justification was that the political situation required the signature of the obviously unrealistic document, and that the resources might become available during the course of the CP.

In short, central officials regularly approved expenditure forecasts that, in total, far exceeded the government's resources. They then applied what one might call traditional budgeting techniques, namely: use whatever resources are on hand to deal with the most acute crisis as determined by the political process or leadership; ignore previously determined budgets, agreements, commitments, contract plans, and so on; and give the squeakiest wheels the smallest amount of oil that will quiet them for the moment. The CPs were supposed to solve precisely this kind of problem, but given the situation, they did not.

Revisions to the Process

Despite the overall financial problems, can one perceive differences in microperformance between enterprises with CPs and those without? One study undertaken to answer this question compared the performance of the first six SOEs with contract plans with the performance of 18 other state-owned enterprises during 1980-83. Both groups ran losses in these three years, and both groups reduced their rate of loss by about the same percentage at the end of the period. Perceptible differences occurred in only two areas: in the contracted public enterprises sales grew by 93 percent, as opposed to 66 percent in the other firms; and personnel costs rose 13 percent in the contracted firms, versus 45 percent in the other enterprises. Levels of debt reduction were about the same in both groups.

For several reasons, these moderately positive results should be interpreted cautiously. First, the indicators showing variance are of secondary importance. The major performance indicators—profitability, self-financing ratios, and return on capital invested—were the same (poor) for both sets of firms. Second, the differences were modest in size and significance. Third, the period reviewed was relatively short. Fourth, the enterprises compared differed greatly in structure, purpose, market position, and so on. Like was not compared to like. Nonetheless, despite the study's drawbacks, it deserves praise as the only attempt to assess quantitatively the impact of the CP. More and better studies of this nature are required.

Regardless of the lack of major improvements in performance, like their French counterparts, Senegalese managers and government supervisors working with CPs almost universally concluded that they were beneficial devices that should be continued. Interviews with 18 Senegalese officials and managers concluded in January 1986 indicated strong support for the CP process. Managers approved of the heightened clarity of goals, the specification of the government's financial responsibilities, and the concept of government compensation for noncommercial activities imposed on enterprises. Officials saw the major advantage as the increase in the autonomy and responsibility of management. One could argue that both groups liked those features that highlighted the responsibilities of the other party. Indeed, all involved parties, including project officers from the World Bank, found the CP irresistibly appealing. In theory, it clarified objectives, determined priorities, allocated resources, guided and stimulated productive behavior, and eased evaluation.

The Second Phase

Problems continued with the second group of CPs. The SONEES (water company) example, while perhaps something of an extreme case, reveals the workings of the process. The main features of the agreement were increases in the tariff structure, and a rehabilitation/investment program to be funded through settlement of the government's outstanding debts to the company. The functioning of the CP was subjected to a review at the end of 1985, when major difficulties became apparent. The review revealed that, despite the price increase, SONEES' revenues were 16 percent lower than anticipated, while costs were 5 percent higher. But the critical problem was that neither the state nor the local governments respected their commitments to settle outstanding accounts. The result was a deficit five times greater than anticipated, and a reduction by half in the essential rehabilitation/investment program.

As of June 1985, the total public agency debt to SONEES was CFAF5.5 billion. The company's financial situation was desperate. It was financing its operating costs by short-term bank overdrafts at high interest rates. Suppliers were demanding higher and higher advance payments, adding substantial "waiting premiums" to their bids, or—most commonly—simply refusing to do business with the company. SONEES stopped paying its bills, with one result being a threat of stoppage of electricity services. "These financial difficulties have led us to juggle our creditors, and put them off as long as possible," noted one company report. The company cancelled all training programs, ignored scheduled maintenance procedures, and froze employment in an attempt to cut costs. The negative implications of at least the first two of these measures are obvious.

In accord with the provisions of the CP, SONEES approached the Ministry of Finance to request that the government honor its commitments. Despite repeated resubmissions of their case, they received no reply during the whole of 1985. The simple fact was that "...despite the provisions of the contract plan, no deposit has been made to our account since 1 January 1985." The suggested solutions were obvious: the government and the other public agencies must pay their bills at once, and steps must be taken to see that the arrears do not simply start again. SONEES officials suggested that at the start of each fiscal year the government should deposit in SONEES' account 65 percent of the previous year's budgeted payments. At the very least, pleaded the enterprise, the government should pay its outstanding debts.

Despite the difficulties with enforcing the provisions of the SONEES' and other CPs, "contractualization" was made a key feature of the government's "New Policy Toward the Parapublic Sector," announced in mid-1985. CPs were cited as one of the principal means by which enterprise performance would be improved. The policy stated that each year five enterprises would be subjected to the process (the schedule was not met). Money-losing enterprises with a heavy social service obligation were to be given first priority.

A Detailed Example: The SONATEL CP

A positive example of the more recent crop of Senegalese CPs, showing how they were modified in an attempt to deal with the prevailing high level of budgetary and economic uncertainty, can be found in the contract negotiated with SONATEL, the telecommunications parastatal that was created after the break-up of the posts and telecommunications enterprise. The CP with SONATEL was signed in 1986 after almost two years of negotiations. The following features were added to the standard elements of other Senegalese CPs: a detailed set of physical, financial, and quality of service performance indicators; several means to pressure the government in case it failed to honor its obligations; and a section on how the plan could be modified quickly in case its financial and operational assumptions proved inaccurate. A review of the sections of this carefully prepared CP is revealing.

The preamble noted the high level of unsatisfied demand for telephone services in Senegal. It recalled the government's decision to create a new, commercially run and autonomous body to deal exclusively with this service. The first section of the CP summarized the laws and decrees creating and regulating the company, emphasizing that the supervising ministries should "not interfere, in either their advice or their actions, in the daily management of the enterprise." SONATEL's objectives, according to the CP, were to improve the quality of service, complete major investment and supply projects on schedule, use the firm's human resources better, attempt to provide every citizen easy access to a telephone, and improve the image of the national telephone service.

PERFORMANCE INDICATORS FOR SONATEL. SONATEL committed itself in the contract period to hold constant the number of employees and to limit the annual rate of growth of its wage bill to 10 percent. The main measures of physical production were number of requests filled for new principal telephone and telex lines and growth of the total number of telephones in use. Quantified subtargets were fixed for each activity for each of the three years of the CP. The enterprise contracted to improve service quality, as measured by reducing the length of repair time, reducing the delay in obtaining a dial tone, and reducing the number of misdirected and incorrect calls due to faulty equipment or switching. Again, precise numerical measures of each of these indicators was stated in the CP (for example, repair of a telephone within eight days of request would rise from 66 percent of cases in 1985 to 80 percent at the end of the CP period).

SONATEL contracted to improve the productivity of its personnel. The measurement was that personnel costs, as a percentage of operating revenues, would fall from 5.0 to 4.4 percent. With regard to the important issue of customer rates, the CP noted that a study on SONATEL's tariffs was scheduled to be completed in January 1988. In the interim, rates would be frozen at their 1985 levels as long as the company maintained a minimum self-financing level of 40 percent. If the ratio fell below that figure, SONATEL could request an emergency rate hike.

Financial forecasts and performance indicators were equally detailed. Revenues, cash flow, profits, and operating coefficients were projected for each year of the CP period. The same was done for investment matters: the contract estimated annual investment costs, and the amounts to be generated internally and raised externally to cover the investments. SONATEL agreed to devote a small, precisely defined portion of its investments to creating telephone service in rural and remote localities. This was labeled an "investment of a social character."

The CP paid considerable attention to the issue of cost recovery. First, the company agreed to speed the issuance of bills to customers: the delay between meter reading and bill issuance was projected to fall from 51 days (1985) to 20 days in 1989. Second, SONATEL undertook to improve the position of its accounts receivable. The CP projected a complete cleaning up of the public overdue accounts by 1988, but only a modest diminution of outstanding private arrears. An annex laid out a precise schedule for the payment of public arrears and dealt with SONATEL's repayment of a large outstanding loan to the state.

GOVERNMENT OBLIGATIONS TO SONATEL. The government agreed "not to impose on SONATEL investment charges for expanding service to remote localities" over and above those previously agreed to. It gave a commitment to pay overdue accounts according to a set schedule. Of course, most earlier CPs had such provisions and, as noted, the government had failed to honor them. To counter this problem, article 23 of the SONATEL CP introduced a new idea:

> In order to avoid the recurrence of unpaid bills, the state commits itself to clearly set out in its budget, as well as in the budgets of the local governments and public enterprises it supervises, the sums necessary to settle the accounts and credits of SONATEL.

This linking of the CP directly to the budget process, not simply of the national government, but of local governments and other public enterprises, had not previously been seen (though it had been called for in the SONEES review.) It was a simple and clever idea that promised to attack the root financial problem of many state-owned enterprises in Africa.

The state agreed to abide by the recommendations of the tariff study. This was tantamount to agreeing to substantial increases, since a recommendation for increases was very likely. It also contracted to treat seriously and sympathetically any price increase SONATEL requested under the emergency provisions mentioned above. With regard to the enterprise's ambitious investment program, the government agreed "to take all measures to facilitate SONATEL's access to necessary external financing," within the limits of the public sector debt ceiling agreed with the IMF.

MONITORING ARRANGEMENTS. In what became a standard Senegalese practice, and in sharp distinction to French procedure (where the supervisory ministry handled government monitoring of the CP), the CP created a monitoring committee to supervise and modify (as necessary) SONATEL's CP. This committee was composed of the director general of SONATEL and "his principal collaborators," and for the government, an eight-person team consisting of officials from the Office of the President, SONATEL's financial controller (the representative in SONATEL of the Ministry of Finance), and other representatives of the ministries of Finance, Planning, and Communications.

The CP stated that this committee would meet at least twice a year, once to examine the firm's performance during the past year and to review the annual report submitted by management, and a second time to review the firm's progress in light of the CP's provisions. The agreement stated that if the firm was not attaining its objectives as contracted, or if the government was not honoring its commitments, the committee would examine the reasons for the problems and "propose appropriate measures to remedy them," including, if necessary, a thorough revision of the CP. Finally, the committee bore the responsibility for reconciling disputes between the enterprise and government, but in case a matter could not be resolved at committee level "the arbitration of the President of the Republic will be solicited."

The SONATEL contract contained a number of worthwhile innovations: very detailed performance criteria, including quality of service criteria; a detailed timetable to resolve outstanding financial problems; direct linkage to the budget process; and a potentially powerful supervisory committee to oversee implementation and help resolve problems. Information obtained from SONATEL management and the supervising agency in May 1988 revealed that the firm was indeed achieving satisfactory performance on many of the indicators contained in the CP, specifically those referring to quality of service, productivity of personnel, internal financial projections, and investment expenditures. However, problems were surfacing because nothing had been done about the key issue of settling the state"s arrears, for which a precise timetable had been laid out in the CP. In sum, the CP provisions that were within SONATEL's control were being met and were having a positive effect, but these were offset by the state's continuing failure to pay its bills.

A Senegalese Assessment of the CP Process

A government seminar on the CP process held in December 1986 concluded that despite shortcomings, the CP device had brought about several benefits. The seminar's final report concluded, without offering much in the way of supporting data, that enterprises with CPs showed better personnel management; a superior capacity to estimate their investment needs; more success in gaining approval for rate increases; and improved relations with suppliers of inputs, resulting, in several cases, in lower prices ("Rapport de Synthèse du Séminaire de Décembre 1986 sur les Contrats Plans"). These were significant improvements, although they may have occurred in a few enterprises rather than in the majority of cases.

The seminar also confirmed the expected: the main problem was the government's failure to meet its financial obligations, although other issues were raised. Among the latter, managers complained that in practice, managerial latitude remained quite limited. They also expressed concern over the quantity and quality of performance indicators, arguing that the CP should distinguish between the enterprise's formal commitments and projected desirable outcomes. They felt that the former should be as few and as clear as possible and be included in the body of the CP. Managers also wanted to see some link between enterprise performance and rewards, and felt this could be built into the CP process.

On the question of government finances, managers asked for treasury officials to be involved in the negotiations and monitoring of CPs. They requested that each CP include a formal payment timetable, agreed to by the Ministry of Finance, and that the ministry at least inform SOEs when payments were likely to be late and explore ways to simplify the paperwork required to verify charges and payments. They also made a number of suggestions about linking SOE payments to the budgeting cycle. Finally, they called for two new committees, one specifically to follow the arrears issue, and the other to restructure financial matters as a whole. The CP process was adopted precisely to help resolve such problems. One could argue that the CPs were indeed achieving the first step towards resolution: quantifying the extent of the difficulties.

When the state's failure to pay became widespread, the World Bank made the settlement of state obligations a condition of releasing the second tranche of the third structural adjustment loan (1987-88). The government managed to meet the condition at the very last moment by unilaterally decreeing that the sums given in the CPs and *lettres de mission* had all been revised downwards, thus allowing the state to claim that it had met the conditions. On the one hand, this was a welcome admission that the sums contained in the CPs were unrealistic, and that they had to be reduced. On the other hand, the unilateral change of figures negated the principle of open negotiations of mutual obligations. Most managers interviewed in May 1988 said that many aspects of the CP process were worthwhile, and cited the positive points referred to earlier, but others complained that the meager results coming out of the CP process were not worth the time and effort involved.

Conclusions on Senegal

In Senegal, most of the problems encountered in the CP process resulted from the government's shortcomings. To be sure, SOE managers were insufficiently trained and experienced, and some of the blame for poor performance could be assigned to management and workers. However, the CP exercise highlighted the government's failures. For example, it clearly revealed that one problem in Senegal was the relative weakness of the officials heading the Contract Plan Supervisory Unit in the Office of the President. As late as 1988, this (admittedly overworked and understaffed) review body failed to exert sufficient pressure on budget and disbursement offices to persuade them to make promised payments on time and in the proper amounts. The unit did not even hold a meeting to discuss SONEES' disturbing December 1985 report until June 1986. Everyone involved hoped that changes made to the leadership and operating terms of reference of this important body in 1988 would lead to greater fulfillment of the stipulations of the CPs.

The Senegalese experience shows that it is not simply the technical quality of a CP's provisions that are important, but also the institutional setting in which the exercise is carried out. In the absence of definitive evidence that the provisions of a CP, even one as carefully constructed as SONATEL's, can overcome the difficulties prevailing in Senegal, the interim conclusion must be that the experience has not yet produced the desired results. The CP process was characterized by delays, missed deadlines, disagreements, and misunderstandings. One CP went through nine drafts over a two-year period before it could be signed. In another case, a manager stated that he had been instructed to sign his CP even though he did not agree with its major provisions. He indicated informally that he had no intention of implementing its measures.

A May 1986 supervision report noted that the scheduled preparation of four statements of objectives and 12 CPs were all delayed, some indefinitely. The problem appeared to be that as drafters dealt with the fundamental financial issues, as in the SONATEL approach, the government grew reluctant to commit itself. If these issues were ignored, however, managers refused to sign. Other cases were awaiting the results of studies, passage of legislation, coordination with the plans of other SOEs, and so on. Some of the fault for the slow pace lay with the ineffective supervision unit, but the negotiation and coordination workload was itself vast and overwhelming. Nevertheless, none of the CPs scheduled for signature in 1986 were signed on time, and many remained unsigned and dormant as late as September 1988. For those that were signed, many key provisions were not kept. Dramatic, short-run improvements in performance have not occurred.

The primary lesson is clear: contract plans cannot by themselves overcome the serious, deeply rooted problems of the Senegalese parapublic sector in particular, much less the related but grander scale problems of the economy as a whole. The fundamental starting point is the country's sheer and intense poverty, the effects of which are compounded by weak budgeting systems (which translate into a lack of reliable information on either the availability or liquidity of funds), weak agencies of review in the technical and financial supervising ministries, and weak political commitment to the concept of financial discipline. The CP process highlights these deficiencies, and shows that not all problems are the fault of management, but it does not eliminate them. Moreover, the contract plan is meant to be both binding and a plan. Yet, the Senegalese experience reveals the difficulty of binding the government, and the difficulty of constructing a plan that is both realistic and implementable. The CP process reproduces, on a small scale, the informational shortcomings of comprehensive planning.

The French tried to solve the problems of complexity and uncertainty by moving away from comprehensive CPs toward shorter, more general statements of intent and broad policy. The idea was to maximize the benefits of mutual goal setting and formalized dialogue, which the CP process provided, without becoming bogged down in specific numbers and quantities. However, like other African users of CPs, Senegal has been obliged to retain a greater degree of both specificity and complexity in its contracts. This was unavoidable given the extent of market imperfections, distortions, and government interference in the Senegalese economy, plus the acute financial weaknesses and poor performance of the firms subjected to the CP process, the rapid and unpredictable shifts in international markets important to Senegal, and weak analytical and institutional frameworks.

The first Senegalese reaction to uncertainty and difficulty in obtaining government commitment to the CP provisions was to use shorter intervals—often now every six months—of review and modification, if necessary. A second move was to strengthen the supervisory committees and agencies, to increase their capacity to understand what was happening at the firm level, and to approach financial authorities directly and push them to honor their obligations. The first initiative led some involved in the process to ask if a document subject to change twice a year could really be called either a contract or a plan; the second proved ineffective.

Irrespective of the problems, the World Bank's involvement with the CP process has continued. The parapublic sector has been an important element of the three structural adjustment operations the Bank concluded with Senegal after 1984 (a fourth adjustment operation was being prepared at the time of writing).

Although complaints about the amount of time and effort required to devise, negotiate, and supervise a CP were common, one could still argue that this was a relatively low-cost tool that was setting the scene for reform. Nonetheless, by 1988 enthusiasm for the CP concept was declining. An October 1987 review reiterated that the "major problem in the sector is the whole area of financial relations between the state and the public enterprises," and noted that privatization and liquidation of SOEs were now the more burning issues.

Theoretically, one way to improve the situation would be substantial downscaling of the SOE sector, which would, presumably, allow the government to concentrate scarce resources on the management of priority enterprises. In October 1987, the government announced the first implementation phase of its privatization program, but as of the end of 1988, no sales had actually taken place. Most of the activity proposed was devoted to reducing the percentage of government holdings in joint ventures; only two wholly owned companies—and certainly none of the large, monopoly, money losers that provided social services—were to be touched.

In the end, the CP cannot substitute for government commitment to managing its resources rationally; but it can provide rationalist reformers with the informational ammunition to structure and implement reform.

Other Developing Countries

Although no other developing country, African or otherwise, has had experience with CPs comparable to that of Senegal, many have started down that path. Table 11.1 summarizes the CP situation in 14 developing countries, 11 of them francophone, 12 of them in Sub-Saharan Africa. The table is neither exhaustive, nor does it include countries with plans to use CPs (for example, Madagascar, Gabon, and Central African Republic). Further, devices similar to the CP that are in use or under preparation in Latin America—in Mexico, Argentina, and Brazil—are neither covered in the table nor reviewed in this chapter. Table 11.2 provides some information on where the World Bank is supporting installation of the CP process. The remainder of this section briefly reviews the information available on CP use in a sample of other developing countries.

The Republic of the Congo

In the early 1980s, the Republic of the Congo, independent of World Bank advice or assistance, produced "program contracts" for ten major public enterprises. The primary purpose of the contracts was to increase managements' autonomy. None ever proceeded to the implementation stage; indeed, none was even signed. The problem appears to have been that the drafting of the agreements degenerated into an open political conflict, with the firms using their versions of the draft CPs to air complaints about government policy. The effort was soon abandoned. In

Table 11.1 Contract Plans in Selected Developing Countries, 1988

Country	Total number of contract plans	Status of plans in 1988				
		Number abandoned	Number completed	Number signed and in progress	Number in preparation	Number envisioned
Benin	7	0	0	2	3	2
Burundi	5	0	0	0	5	0
Congo	18	10	0	0	0	8
Côte d'Ivoire	5	2	0	3	0	0
The Gambia	6	0	0	3	3	0
Guinea	1	0	0	0	0	1
Kenya	1	0	0	0	0	1
Madagascar	1	0	0	0	1	0
Mali	1	0	0	0	0	1
Morocco	8	0	1	1	6	0
Niger	2	0	0	1	0	1
Nigeria	2	0	3	9	10	8
Senegal	30	0	3	9	10	8
Tunisia	6	1	0	0	3	2
Total	93	13	7	28	41	32

Source: World Bank files.

Table 11.2 Contract Plans in World Bank Projects, 1988

Country	Total number of contract plans	Industry and mining	Transport	Utilities	Agriculture	Others
Benin	5	4	1	0	0	0
Burundi	5	1	2	0	0	2
Congo	8	4	1	2	0	1
Côte d'Ivoire	4	1	1	1	0	1
The Gambia	3	0	1	1	1	0
Madagascar	1	0	0	1	0	0
Mali	1	0	0	0	0	1
Morocco	6	2	1	1	1	1
Niger	1	0	0	1	0	0
Tunisia	3	0	0	0	3	0
Total	37	12	7	7	5	6

Source: World Bank files.

1985, the Congolese government announced a restart of the CP program with a new kind of program contract to be applied to the electricity company, the post and telecommunications agency, and three other important SOEs, but no progress was made on this front until a Public Enterprise Sector Adjustment Project came up for negotiation with the World Bank in 1988. A major feature of the proposed project was the restructuring of the six most important SOEs and the negotiation of CPs. At the time of writing the government of Congo, like many other governments, was groping for a way to apply the CP approach.

Morocco

The CP concept was introduced in Morocco in 1980 in a report on SOEs issued by the Prime Minister's Office. The report recommended that the mechanism be applied in large SOEs operating in noncompetitive markets. The goals were to lighten government control and strengthen managerial autonomy. The firm selected for the first CP was the national airline, Royal Air Maroc (RAM).

ROYAL AIR MAROC. In 1982, the Moroccans installed a three-year CP in RAM. It expired in 1984, and despite pleas for renewal from the company and the Ministry of Transport, a second CP has not yet been negotiated. The RAM CP defined the firm's objectives and laid out the airline's required noncommercial operations. It determined the formula for the state's compensation to the airline for losses incurred from public service operations and price restraints. Annual targets were established for volume of sales, manpower productivity, equipment use rates, total productivity, the wage bill, and the company's investment and financing plans. An official of the Ministry of Finance, appointed to oversee the proper implementation of the CP, was supposed to replace, but actually joined the traditional *contrôleur financier* (financial supervisor) who represented the Ministry of Finance in every Moroccan SOE. Finally, the CP established procedures for determining what the government and other SOEs owed RAM, and set payment schedules for clearing up those arrears.

Internal and external observers agreed that some significant improvements came about in RAM due to the CP. Management autonomy was said to have improved, government interference to have declined. A modest but significant start was made on the long process of shifting away from a reliance on *a priori* controls to a less rigid system of *a posteriori* evaluation of performance. Positive results were claimed in RAM's system of internal control and medium-term planning, and, according to the World Bank, the "relationship of dependence of RAM on the government has been replaced by a contractual relationship based on cooperation, constructive dialogue, and clearer definition of responsibilities."

As in Senegal, the CP's physical and financial projections of firm performance proved inaccurate and the government "paid only a fraction of the contributions to which it was committed." With overestimates of sales and revenues and a large accounts receivable burden, RAM was forced to survive on overdrafts, whose interest costs weighed down the balance sheet. One of the benefits of the CP was to quantify the extent to which RAM's losses were a function of its poor capital structure, which in turn was a function of the government's failure to pay. Other problems were more technical: weak cost accounting, failure to revalue assets, productivity targets expressed in current as opposed to constant prices, and inability of the firm's financial officers to deal with exchange rate fluctuations. These were not problems of the CP as such, but their presence severely weakened the impact and utility of the process.

The Moroccans drew several conclusions from this first application of the CP process. They saw the desirability of making the CPs rolling, that is, subject to periodic review and modification; they recognized that the state must honor its obligations or the process will eventually founder; they saw the need to link CP results with sanctions and rewards; and they recognized that for CPs to work, the contracted enterprise had to have an adequate level of accounting, cost accounting, and financial information systems. These lessons were taken into account in the expansion of the CP process.

THE PUBLIC ENTERPRISE RESTRUCTURING LOAN. A public enterprise restructuring loan (PERL), supported by the World Bank, was negotiated in 1987 and became effective in December of that year. One of the main components of the PERL was that CPs would be negotiated and signed in six important enterprises: the national electricity company, the national water company, the railway, two refining firms, and a holding company controlling private sector distributors of petroleum products. At the end of December 1987, the CPs for the water authority and the holding company were signed and approved by the government, and by the end of 1988 CPs had been signed in three other firms. (At the time of writing the CP with the railway had not been signed.)

While too early to judge the effect of this reform on performance, certain elements of the approach merit mention. First, the Moroccans have treated the exercise in an experimental and incremental manner. With the RAM experience in mind, neither government staff nor enterprise officials regarded CPs as ultimate solutions or rigid agreements, but rather as the first step in a lengthy learning process. Second, Moroccan CPs were drawn up by government officers and enterprise staff with minimal consultant involvement, foreign or domestic. The reasoning appeared to be that having imperfect documents constructed by Moroccan civil servants and enterprise managers was better than having technically perfect CPs prepared by outsiders. Of course, this approach had some costs. Drafts produced by the dynamic but inexperienced contract plan section of the Ministry of Finance tended to rely heavily on French examples and models. The draft CP produced by the railway SOE, for instance, was more a statement of enterprise claims on the government than a balanced presentation of mutual obligations and responsibilities. The Ministry of Transport approved the draft, drawn up in September 1985, but ran into prolonged, unproductive negotiations with the Ministry of Finance during the next four years. As in the French cases, this example showed that the more difficult an enterprise's financial position, the greater the difficulty of negotiating a CP.

THE OFFICE NATIONAL D'ELECTRICITÉ. The national electricity company, ONE, had a more positive experience. A rough draft of a CP was produced as early as 1981. Although the idea was raised several times in the next five years, it was only in 1987, within the framework of the World Bank-supported PERL project, that more elaborate drafts were prepared and negotiations conducted. These resulted in a CP in December 1988.

The ONE CP had two main objectives: first, to shift government supervision away from *a priori* controls to *a posteriori* evaluation of performance; and second, to promote the enterprise's financial health by rationalizing its tariff regime, by clearing up arrears and cross-debts (government with ONE and ONE with other SOEs), and by ensuring that arrears did not recur. For the period 1989-91, ONE committed itself to least-cost provision of national energy needs, an investment program to meet forecasted demand, and improvements in internal management. The government, for its part, agreed to modify control mechanisms, produce a new rate system, clear its arrears, and participate in investment financing (or guarantee debts) (for a thorough review of the ONE experience see Saulniers 1989, especially pp. 10-15).

ONE had hoped to eliminate the financial controllers and accounting agents appointed by the Ministry of Finance. Instead, their powers were reduced, and management's direct control over several parameters enlarged. Over the years, the Moroccan Ministry of Finance had consistently opposed suggestions to reduce *a priori* controls. That these were substantially lightened in the ONE CP indicated substantial progress. Equally impressive, on paper at least, was that the government agreed to a rate structure based on marginal cost pricing, that all arrears and cross-debts would be retired, and that ONE would be compensated for noncommercial objectives. The notion that imposed sociopolitical objectives require transparency and compensation is positive; less positive is that the government decided to finance the imposed objectives by allowing ONE to charge higher rates to other portions of its clientele. Saulniers (1989) notes that in early 1989, the government decreed lower electricity rates for agricultural users and allowed ONE to raise rates for other sectors. This cross-subsidization is not the optimal solution to ONE's financial problems, but it reflects a recognition of the relationship between social objectives and foregone revenues.

The CP contained 12 indicators of physical and financial performance.[5] Overall, through 1989, the Moroccan experience was quite promising. A long-term, learning perspective was adopted, and reliance on external consultants was minimal. Moroccan SOE managers were sufficiently experienced and self-assured to recognize the potential benefits of CPs. Ministry of Finance officials, perhaps with some reluctance, learned to be

---

5. These are level of productivity of personnel, level of productivity of equipment, yield level of the network, consumption of inputs, debt-equity ratio, debt service ratio, ratio of the contribution of self-financing to investments, sales by type of user, accounts receivable, accounts payable, ratio of inventory to sales, average cost per kilowatt hour. The method of calculating all the indicators is given in an annex to the CP.

more flexible about *a priori* controls. In line with experience elsewhere, negotiating the contracts took much longer than expected.

Benin

Benin implemented two instruments related to CPs in the water/electricity state-owned enterprise and in the national brewery. No information is available on their impact on the firms' performance. Four other "action plans," which were not CPs, but imposed restructuring programs, were prepared for five major money-losing companies: two cement plants, a textile firm, the port authority, and a shipping line. These agreements were prepared at the insistence, and with the support, of the World Bank.

Burundi

Burundi was preparing "performance contracts" in five key SOEs in 1988: a pharmaceuticals company, a glass factory, a savings association, a trucking company, and an urban transport provider.

Côte d'Ivoire

Côte d'Ivoire, on its own, initiated a CP process in two public enterprises, but abandoned them before implementation. Under its third structural adjustment agreement with the World Bank, the country committed itself to extend the CP process to four major firms: Palmindustrie, the national telecommunications agency, the port authority of Abidjan, and the electricity company. As of 1988, Palmindustrie was implementing its signed contract, apparently with considerable difficulty. The others appeared to be indefinitely delayed.

The Gambia

The Gambia was one of the first anglophone African countries to adopt the process. In late 1986, three "performance agreements"—basically, restructuring plans to put the enterprises on a sound footing—were drawn up for the peanut marketing enterprise, the water and electricity firm, and the port services company. The principal architects of the approach were external consultants, paid for by a World Bank loan. These agreements reviewed, in the traditional form of a management consultant's diagnosis, the past performance, problems, and prospects of the enterprises. Measures to improve performance were spelled out. The agreements were then followed by "performance contracts," which operationalized the suggested set of improvements and set out an overall strategy for the firm. They also described, in more or less standard CP form, the mutual obligations and responsibilities of the contracting parties.

The resulting documents are an interesting "Anglo Saxon" variation on the CP theme. Particularly intriguing is the attempt to use the CP as a restructuring mechanism at a time when most French analysts had concluded that the process of performance improvement should be separate from the CP procedure. Another pragmatic innovation was the "pilot plan strategy," by which mini-versions of the full CP were signed and closely monitored for a three-month period. When these trial runs produced positive results, the next performance contracts ran for twelve months. At the time of writing, all three firms had passed through the three-month agreements and had amassed over a year's experience with the annual performance contracts. Sketchy and preliminary assessments of the Gambian experience indicated that the CPs had a positive impact on performance. Clear objectives were negotiated, transparency of operations increased, and targets supposedly within the control of management were set. The government took the exercise seriously, as demonstrated by the dismissal of the general managers in the two SOEs with disappointing results. Subsequently, information submission deadlines were met and financial performance improved in all three firms.

Other African Countries

Madagascar, Mali, Niger, and Togo attempted to install CPs in at least one of their public enterprises. In Togo's case, efforts were made in 1982 to draft two CPs, one in an industrial firm, and one in the national water company. Neither proceeded past the first draft stage. The other three countries were negotiating CPs for one major firm each in 1988. In these countries, as elsewhere in the region, CPs were most commonly applied to electricity producers and suppliers. A number of other Sub-Saharan countries were in various stages of CP preparation: a CP was signed in the Ghana Cocoa Marketing Board in 1988 and Kenya Railways concluded a CP in 1989.

India

Indian interest in the contract approach was sparked by a seminar on the CP process presented by officials of the French government. In December 1986, the Sengupta Committee recommended the CP approach for widespread application. In March 1986, well before the release of the Sengupta Committee's document, a trial "memorandum of understanding" (MOU), the Indian term for CP, was created and applied to the Oil and Natural Gas Corporation. This agreement ran for a one-year period. In March 1987, officials of the corporation signed a second MOU for a two-year period. In September 1987, the Steel Authority of India, signed a one-year MOU. Negotiations were well advanced for MOUs in Bharat Heavy Electrical and the National Textile Corporation. MOUs were also under preparation for two public holding companies in the engineering goods sector. These MOUs proved promising, and the process was expanded in 1988.

An October 1987 World Bank mission to review the Indian public enterprise sector included a specialist on CPs. His task was to assess the MOU process. The resulting report noted that the MOU was seen in India as a way to increase managerial autonomy. Though modeled after the French CP process, the Indian version had major differences. Indian MOUs ran for one or two years at most; they defined the enterprise's physical and financial goals in great detail, but did not deal with investments; the sections on the state's obligations dealt only with lightening government controls and not with strategic issues or matters of capital structure; and the autonomy granted to the enterprises was quite modest.

Detailed reporting and monitoring systems were strictly applied by central authorities. Managers complained that MOU monitoring procedures were added on to rather than substituted for older reporting requirements. Managers were not able to obtain autonomy on several critical matters: pricing, schemes linking pay to productivity, and financial restructuring. The report argued that the MOU process had a long way to go in India, as government supervisors so far appeared unwilling to shed their *dirigiste* attitudes and practices.

The report viewed the first batch of MOUs as incomplete. For example, none of the MOUs dealt with the noncommercial objectives of enterprises or financial compensation for those activities. The MOUs were primarily statements of enterprise objectives. Commitments by the state on equity injections, subsidies, loan guarantees, pricing policy, investments, and labor policy were not spelled out. Nonetheless, the report concluded that the MOU was a progressive and potentially beneficial idea. Indian authorities apparently agreed; the process was being applied to most large SOEs in 1991.

Conclusions and Recommendations

In 1967, the Nora Report recommended contractualization as a process to improve the productivity and efficiency of state-owned enterprises. Twenty years later, French proponents of contract plans stressed their utility as devices that could:

> ...establish the "rules of the game" between the state and the enterprise...to define clear objectives and precise and limited mutual obligations...and above all to develop a climate of confidence between the representatives of the state and the managers of an enterprise (Testard 1987 paraphrasing Chalendar 1984b).

The view of what one can expect from CPs has thus evolved. First claims or hopes were quite ambitious, but expectations were moderated in the light of experience.

In both France and the developing countries, individual CPs were carefully crafted by skilled, experienced teams of civil servants and enterprise managers. In Senegal and several other African countries, consultants drawn from well-known European and North American firms helped these national teams. Thus, the technical adequacy of CPs was never a serious issue (with the exception of a few hastily prepared documents in Togo and Congo). Rather, the problems lay in the implementation of those CPs. In France, this manifested itself in the overly ambitious, excessively specific CPs drawn up in the 1970s; but the process was, without too much difficulty, modified, simplified, and rendered more general. With time, CPs' targets became broader.

In the developing world, the situation was different. In Sub-Saharan Africa, the core institutions of macroeconomic management, the ministry of finance, the budget department, the treasury, the planning agencies—all tend to be very weak. The result is that governments commit themselves to expend funds far in excess of what they have available. As the Senegalese experience demonstrated, this tended to undermine the CP process.

In Morocco, the state's financial obligations were met under the PERL program. This was due to the existence of modest and technically thorough CPs, combined with a powerful and determined central body supervising the CP process that was able to persuade and pressure budget and treasury authorities to meet commitments. There was no guarantee that the honoring of commitments would continue indefinitely. Indeed, one could argue that the greater the number of enterprises with contracts, and the greater the sums of money in question, the greater the temptation for treasury officials to delay or withhold payments (but other aspects of the SOE reform program are supposedly alleviating this problem; for example, tariff increases raising the levels of self-financing of enterprises and reducing the need for government subsidies).

The Moroccan case suggests that the process requires a strong, well-placed supervisory agency to assist in CP preparation, review implementation, and push for the proper fulfillment of the agreements. Certainly the absence of a dynamic oversight body created difficulties in Senegal. A change of structure and personnel in the relevant agency in 1987 resulted in some progress. A difficult and delicate task for reformers is finding the proper balance between empowering the managers through the CPs, and endowing an oversight agency with sufficient clout to enforce the agreements.

The comparatively good state of development of Moroccan administrative agencies, and the basically sound management in the Moroccan enterprises chosen to lead the reform program, meant that the CPs could be negotiated without external assistance. The process was thus largely seen as an indigenous Moroccan endeavor, which was a substantial benefit.

Several countries have attempted to use the CP mechanism to restructure or resurrect desperately sick enterprises: France in the case of the CGM, Senegal for the rural development agencies, all three undertakings in The Gambia, and two instances (not discussed in this chapter) in Bangladesh. Except for the Gambian case—where at first glance, performance seemed to be improving markedly in the SOEs using CPs in this manner—this usage has produced disappointing results. Thus, the CP may be best suited to regularize and improve the framework within which a firm operates rather than to turn around a sick company. Results have been more encouraging when the CP was applied to enterprises with competent management, sound financial and reporting procedures, and a basically commercial orientation, for example, Air France, SONATEL in Senegal, ONEP (the water company) in Morocco, and Bharat Heavy Electrical in India.

The fact that the agreements were not legally enforceable contracts is particularly important. Governments could not be legally bound to honor their commitments in the CP. Sometimes, shrill and persistent haranguing—by a government oversight agency, an association of public enterprise managers, or staff of international agencies—increased a government's compliance with a CP's provisions. At any rate, the term "contract" should be eliminated from the name. A more accurate name would be "performance agreement," which is the term used in anglophone Africa and Latin America.

The way in which control structures have differed before and after the introduction of CPs is an insufficiently examined question. In Morocco and India, and probably elsewhere, the main attraction of CPs for enterprise managers was the hope that the supervision process would be simplified and lightened. Yet in most instances, governments proved reluctant to give up control. Thus, the CP process added to, rather than replaced, traditional methods of control. To maximize the beneficial effect of the CP, these instruments should replace existing control mechanisms.

In light of this review, government planners and international agencies contemplating the introduction of a CP should exercise caution. The CP is of value, but its benefits have been oversold. Application of a CP can produce positive results, but it does not guarantee that performance will improve. The existence of a CP—though signed in good faith by both parties—will not, in and of itself, overcome the obstacles of poor policy, fiscal indiscipline, and incompetent management. CPs must be part of a complex and concerted program of reform. Government officials and international agencies should not expect the technique to change long-standing attitudes and behavior patterns, especially when those patterns result in, and are reinforced by, material rewards. CPs thus suffer from a problem common to many other reforms in developing countries: for them to have the anticipated beneficial impact, a complex host of other interrelated factors must be functioning to a modicum standard. If they are not, the impact is minimal.

The complexity of the SOE reform process indicates that goals should be modest at the outset. CPs should be applied in one or two test cases— preferably monopolies providing social services on a trial basis. CPs should be clear, concise, and as simple as the circumstances permit. Lengthy and detailed specification of objectives and operating procedures is usually a sign that the process has been misinterpreted. The process of negotiation is as important as the document produced. Primary objectives for trial CPs might be limited to goal clarification, expansion of managerial autonomy, and the creation of a formal negotiating process. Expansion of the process to more complex goals and larger numbers of SOEs would come about when—or if—the device is shown to be of practical, measurable value. If this cautious approach is adopted, the implication is that the creation and implementation of CPs should probably not be matters for conditionality in agreements negotiated by international agencies, at least until the process has been tested and shown to be workable and beneficial.

Finally, this study raises a number of questions that cannot be resolved with available information. Further analysis should focus on the revised role of enterprises' board of directors under a CP regime; more systematic assessment of the impact of CPs on SOE performance; whether and how CPs change the way governments supervise SOEs; and, in the longer run, a comparison of countries using different forms of the CP mechanism, and another comparison between countries using CPs and those using other types of performance evaluation devices, for example, the systems in use in Pakistan and Korea. (For the Pakistani system see Hartmann and Nawab 1985 and chapter 10 in this volume, and for the Korean system see Park 1986.)

References

Anastassopoulos, J. P., and J. P. Nioche. 1982. *Entreprises Publiques: Expériences Comparées.* Paris: FNEGE.

Balladur, Edouard. 1987. *Je Crois en l' Homme plus qu' en l' Etat.* Paris: Flammarion.

Chalander, J. de. 1984a. "Les Relations entre l'Etat et les Entreprises Publiques en France." Paris: Ministry of Economics, Finance, and Privatizations. Processed.

_____. 1984b. "L'Etat et les Entreprises Publiques dans les Pays en Développement." *Revue Française d'Administration Publique* (October-December):595-610.

Durupty, Michael. 1986. *Les Entreprises Publiques,* Vol. 2, *Gestion/Controle.* Paris: Presses Universitaires de France.

Guislain, Pierre. 1987. "Les Contrats Plans dans les Pays en Développement: Un Modèle d'Organiser les Relations entre le Gouvernement et les Entreprises Publiques en Vue d'Améliorer les Performances des Dites Entreprises." Washington, D.C.: World Bank.

Hartmann, Amtraud, and Syed Ali Nawab. 1985. "Evaluating Public Manufacturing Enterprises in Pakistan: An Experimental Monitoring System." *Finance and Development* 22(3):27-30.

LeRoy, Thierry. 1987. *Etude des Memoranda of Understanding.* Washington, D.C.: World Bank.

Nora Report. 1967. *Rapport sur les Entreprises Publiques.* Paris: La Documentation Française.

Park, Young C. 1986. *A System for Evaluating the Performance of Government-Invested Enterprises in the Republic of Korea.* Discussion Paper No. 3. Washington, D.C.: World Bank.

Saulniers, Alfred H. 1989. "Contract-Program Background and Negotiations: A Case Study of Morocco's National Electricity Company." Rabat, Morocco. Unpublished paper.

Testard, Michel. 1987. *Le Contrat Plan.* Paris: SEMA-METRA Conseil.

INDEX

(Page numbers in italics indicate material in tables or figures.)